ISRAEL

GOVERNMENT AND POLITICS
IN A MATURING STATE

*

GREGORY S. MAHLER

UNIVERSITY OF VERMONT

HBJ

HARCOURT BRACE JOVANOVICH, PUBLISHERS
San Diego   New York   Chicago   Austin   Washington, D.C.
London   Sydney   Tokyo   Toronto

For Marjorie, Alden, and Darcy
and
In the Memory of Irwin Mahler

PREFACE

Although the modern state of Israel is just over four decades old, it has, since its establishment, played a role on the world's political stage far greater than its size alone would suggest. This has led to a significant increase in the number of students interested in studying both the domestic and international environment in which the Israeli political system operates. Despite a corresponding proliferation of scholarship, however, there are only a few textbooks designed to introduce the world of Israeli politics, and those which exist have become dated and are to some extent limited in scope.

In order to study Israeli politics one has to do three things. First, one simply must appreciate the historical background and social context within which the state came into existence. Second, one must master the intricacies of the most important structures and patterns of behavior which exist in the political system. Finally, one must understand the external environment within which the political system operates. This book attempts to help the student to do all three of these; others do not.

Although the study of relevant history is important for appreciating the political environment of any nation, it is *especially* so in the case of Israel, if for no other reason than the fact that the very legitimacy of the state continues to be challenged by some. Since the student is in no position to understand or evaluate the validity of those challenges without an appreciation of the historical record, it is important that any study of Israel devote some attention to historical background, to understanding the general claims of the Israelis (and others) to the territory of the state in question, to understanding *what* was promised *to whom* by the British, and what happened during and after the Second World War. Beyond this, there are a number of other "background" topics that are especially important to Israeli politics that should be discussed, including social characteristics, ethnicity, economic history, the structure and role of religious institutions, and the character and importance of Zionism. After being introduced, however briefly, to the questions and problems raised by these subjects, the student is ready to undertake a direct examination of the overtly "political" characteristics of the Israeli polity.

Accordingly, one must next study the more "traditional" aspects of the political system—constitutionalism, the general structure of parliamentary government, the character and behavior of political parties and interest groups, the electoral system and voting behavior, the traditional political structures of the Knesset (the national legislature), the prime minister and cabinet, the bureaucracy, and the judiciary. An appreciation of the political structures and behavior found in a regime makes up the core of any "area studies" course, and this is no less true for Israel than it is for any other state.

Lastly, one must recognize the foreign policy dimension of the political arena. This is arguably more important in the study of Israel than it would be for other nations, since foreign policy issues and the general questions of war and peace—and the future of peace—are much more contentious in the Israeli setting than they are elsewhere. Included here are such topics as the general foreign policy setting and how policy is made. Beyond this, however, is the broader examination of specific objects of foreign policy, first and foremost those issues dealing with the West Bank and the Palestinians, the city of Jerusalem, and the peace process with Egypt.

I absolutely do *not* mean to suggest that a student who has worked his or her way through the pages of this volume will know everything there is to know about contemporary Israeli politics. Even the most cursory glance at the bibliography included at the end of this text will indicate how truly massive the relevant literature is. The purpose of this volume is not to develop expertise, but to raise consciousness, not to provide all of the answers, but to introduce many of the questions, not to decide which side is "right" and which side "wrong," but to show that sincere and reasonable individuals may, in fact, disagree over what the "facts" are and may, correspondingly, draw different conclusions from the same presentation.

It is probably inevitable that some will be unhappy with a particular aspect of this book, either critical that I have omitted or included certain facts or critical that I have drawn some of the conclusions presented here. Unfortunately, I think that any volume dealing with a large number of essentially controversial subjects, as this one does, faces this dilemma; but I simply do not see any way around the problem. If we are to discuss controversial material—and indeed a fundamental commitment to this type of discussion and inquiry is central to our academic mission—then we regularly face this risk. All I can say here is that I have endeavored to present a *balanced* picture, and I have not sought to offend anyone.

As I indicated in Chapter 1, "we seek to present enough information so that the concerned student can appreciate how truly complex the issues are. . . . Beyond this, the student must turn to special and more detailed resources in his or her quest for a richer understanding of modern Israel." Indeed, the important lesson that I hope is transmitted to the reader of this text is that there *are* different sets of facts, and that it is possible, indeed desirable, to evaluate both sides of the debate before taking a position.

The completion of a book manuscript gives an author the opportunity to acknowledge publicly the assistance and encouragement received in the course of his endeavors. Jerrold Green read an early version of this manuscript and made a number of comments that were very helpful in completing the text. Gina Sample and Sarah Randall at Harcourt Brace Jovanovich designed the book and oversaw the production of the manuscript, respectively. And I especially want to thank Drake Bush and Paul Raymond at Harcourt Brace Jovanovich. Drake was instrumental in the genesis of this project, and it is through his vision and encouragement—and patience—that it has reached this point. To my good fortune Paul was the editor assigned to this project. His perspective and skill were of tremendous value in the process of revising and finishing the manuscript, and his insightful suggestions have contributed a good deal to what is in this book. None of these people, of course, is responsible for any shortcomings that may be found in these pages; and I alone am accountable for any errors of content or omission in this manuscript, as well as its conclusions.

Finally, I want to acknowledge the role of my wife Marjorie, who first introduced me to the study of Israel, first led me through the streets of the Old City of Jerusalem, and who has continued to encourage and support me through this project and so many others.

TABLE OF CONTENTS

MAPS

Chapter 1

HISTORY AND THE CREATION OF ISRAEL

Introduction

The study of the history of any country is often an important prerequisite for a complete understanding of how and why its political system has come to be the way it currently is. This statement is nowhere more true than in the case of Israel. While it might be argued that one could understand the operation of the American political system without a complete exposure to the history and thought of pre–independence America, this simply is not true for the study of the Israeli political system. Modern Israel is a nation conceived in an era of crisis, a nation whose idea evolved during times of struggle and hardship, and a nation born during an epoch of horror, tragedy, and violence. Israel's very existence was challenged from the moment its independence was declared, and this challenge has been continued by most of its neighbors to this very day.

How has modern Israel come to be where it is? What were the factors which led to the movement commonly referred to as Zionism? What did the supporters of this movement do to achieve their political ends? These are each short and straightforward questions, but their answers can be neither short nor straightforward. The issues involved are quite complex and, to make matters worse for the interested and conscientious student, not all of the "facts" are agreed upon by those studying these, and related, considerations.

Our purpose in this chapter is to raise some of the major issues necessary for a general understanding of the historical context from which modern Israel emerged. We cannot, of course, present in a single chapter a comprehensive discussion of all, or even most, of the issues involved. Rather, we seek to present enough information so that the concerned student can appreciate how truly complex the issues are and in so doing can comprehend the linkage which exists between modern Israel and its past. Beyond this, the student must turn to special and more detailed resources in his or her quest for a richer understanding of modern Israel.

In this chapter we shall discuss several different periods of Jewish and Israeli history, beginning with a brief and necessarily superficial discussion of some of the ancient and historically distant roots. The development of the concept of Zionism is, of course, crucial in this process, and we shall briefly trace its origins and evolution from a political current which began in 19th century Europe to the much more fully developed movement which led to the establishment of the State of Israel in 1948. Following World War I Britain was entrusted with a Mandate over Palestine and throughout the interwar period exercised a significant influence on the region as a whole. We will therefore endeavor to show how the most important political activities of this period contributed to the establishment of the State of Israel, as well as the manner in which the Second World War and the Holocaust were significant in emphasizing the immediacy of that end. Finally, we will document the actual transition from mandatory Palestine to independent Israel in the years after World War II.

Historical Roots of Contemporary Israel

We shall not begin our discussion of modern Israel by referring back to Biblical or religious sources, although it should be pointed out that such a start would be possible and even considered necessary by some. There would, however, be several substantive problems for any contemporary social scientist who wanted to base his or her analysis upon such sources, including the fact that the information itself is fragmentary, incomplete, and not always consistent. For example, in the Bible the number of years that the Hebrews "sojourned in Egypt" is given in one accounting as 400, in another as 430, and elsewhere as simply four generations.[1] Territorial descriptions are likewise approximate and inadequate in providing bases for current political claims. The size of *Eretz Israel*[2] is described at one point as running "from the river of Egypt [the Nile] into the great river, the river Euphrates."[3] Elsewhere those dimensions are different,[4] leaving the student in a quandary about what the "real" boundaries of the territory were. In a sense, of course, it is not fair to expect that Biblical passages should meet the standards of detail and exactness required of contemporary historical sources. That was not the purpose for their creation, nor is that the reason they have stayed as visible and significant as they have over the centuries.

It is only with the appearance of the Romans that we begin to find more accurate and detailed histories being recorded. We know, for example, that Alexander the Great conquered *Eretz Israel* in 332 B.C.,[5] and that after his death it was merely one part of the empire caught up in the wars of his successors. We also know from a variety of sources that over a long period of time there was virtually constant instability in this part of the world. Around 167 B.C. a significant Jewish uprising against the Romans took place.[6] After the assassination of Caesar in 44 B.C. *Judea*—the name given to *Eretz Israel* by the Romans—was caught up in the tensions of its civil war. What became known as the Great Revolt against the Romans in 66 A.D. led to a massive retaliation against the Jews. The historian Josephus stated that during the battle of Jerusalem more than a million Jews were killed by the Romans; his contemporary Tacitus placed the number killed at 600,000.[7] Whatever the precise figure, it is at this point that we first witness the disappearance of the Jews from this part of the world and the development of the *diaspora*, the creation of Jewish communities outside of *Eretz Israel*. Indeed, following the Great Revolt the Romans began a concerted series of anti–Jewish acts, ranging from physical expulsion to prohibitions against the existence of synagogues. In 135 A.D. the Roman Emperor Hadrian officially changed the name of *Judea* to *Syria Palestina* so that maps would not contain official references to Jews.[8]

From the end of the Roman period (approximately 600 A.D.) to the advent of the Great Crusades (beginning in 1095) a period of Arab domination of *Syria Palestina* took place. During this five–hundred year interval there was apparently little European interest in the Holy Lands. There continued to exist a very small Jewish community in what would come to be known as Israel, but it was apparently both politically and economically insignificant. The Crusades themselves extended from approximately 1095 through 1291.[9] Beginning with Pope Urban II in 1095, a series of efforts was made by the Roman Catholic Church to rescue the Holy Land from "the infidels" and recover it for Christendom. Several individual Crusades took place, while some groups of Christian pilgrims from Europe actually reached the Holy Land. But by the end of the thirteenth century the Crusaders disappeared from the area, and it once again fell under the total rule of Islamic states.

During the 14th and 15th centuries, many Jews whose ancestors had sought refuge in Europe from Roman persecution began returning to what had by now become known as simply *Palestine*. Their continued sense of cultural isolation, as well as their feelings of vulnerability as a result of the Crusades, prompted them to move back to their "traditional" home. To some extent it also reflected the fact that relations between Palestine's Jewish minority and the Arab majority were for the most part amicable.[10] From approximately 1517 until 1917 Palestine itself was controlled by a number of different Turkish dynasties.[11] What ultimately upset this image of secluded serenity and religious coexistence were forces at work among the European powers and their own Jewish minorities.

The Emergence of Zionism (1830–1917)

The concept of *Zionism* emerged in the 19th century as the rationale for the creation of a Jewish state.[12] The term derives from the word "Zion," which early in Jewish history was taken to be synonymous with

Jerusalem.[13] According to estimates at the time, the total population of *Eretz Israel* by the year 1800 was less than 300,000. The Jewish population itself was a small minority, probably not exceeding 5,000, along with a somewhat larger Christian population of approximately 25,000.[14] Prior to the 19th century, then, the overwhelming bulk of Jews had no contact at all with Palestine.

By the mid–1800's a number of missionary organizations had increased their presence in Jerusalem. To some extent this expanded activity was encouraged by political considerations of the major European powers. Governments declared themselves "protectors" of specific religious groups in the Holy Land and used this as their basis for establishing a significant presence in Jerusalem. For example, Russia sought to protect the Greek and Russian Orthodox believers, France the Roman Catholics, Britain the Protestants, and so on.[15] Because Jews lacked a government patron, individuals would come to play more prominent roles. Sir Moses Montefiore, a British Zionist, was among the first to intervene in support of the establishment of a Jewish state in Palestine. In 1838 Montefiore negotiated with Muhammed Ali, the Viceroy of Egypt (who at that time also ruled modern-day Syria and Palestine), over a charter for land in *Eretz Israel* where Jews might live without interference. But he was unsuccessful in his endeavors, primarily because of the overthrow of Ali in 1841.[16]

Another of the early roots of Zionism can be traced to Rabbi Judah Alkalai, author of an 1839 work entitled *Derchai Noam* ("Pleasant Paths"). In it he suggested that Jewish colonies needed to be established in the Holy Land as a condition for the return of the Messiah. By the time of his death in 1878, Alkalai had organized groups of followers and had moved to Palestine himself to work for increased Jewish settlement there.[17] One of Alkalai's followers was Simon Herzl, the grandfather of Theodor Herzl (of whom we shall hear much more shortly). Indeed, by the mid–1860's an active Jewish community in Palestine known as the *Yishuv* had developed.[18] In 1860 the first Jewish community outside the walls of the Old City of Jerusalem was built. By 1870 they had established an agricultural college adjacent to the Arab city of Jaffa (on the outskirts of modern Tel Aviv) called Mikveh Israel. And in 1878 the *Yishuv* established Petah Tikva, today a town of over 100,000. The reasons for this renewed, even urgent, interest in Palestine were not difficult to detect.

During this period historical events were occurring in Europe which accelerated Jewish migration. In the early 1880s Tsar Alexander III of Russia issued a series of anti–Jewish decrees which drove literally hundreds of thousands of Jews out of their villages. Between 1881 and 1914 an estimated 2,600,000 Jews left Russia and surrounding territories.[19]

Among them was Leo Pinsker. After emigrating from Russia in 1881 he published the following year his *Autoemancipation*. In it he asserted that world Jewry needed a national homeland if it was ever to receive any respect from other nations. Pinsker's general thesis was that Jews were vulnerable without a territory of their own. As he put it: "There is something unnatural about a people without a territory . . ."[20] In 1884 he became the leader of *Hovevi Zion* ("Lovers of Zion"), a group which actively encouraged Russian emigration to Palestine. Between 1882 and 1903 about 25,000 Jews immigrated to Palestine, many motivated by the *Hovevi Zion* movement in Russia, and a number of *Hovevi Zion* organizations were created there.[21]

Another powerful and wealthy backer of Jewish settlement in Palestine was the French Baron Edmond de Rothschild. Although Rothschild was not directly linked with other movements such as the *Hovevi Zion* organization, he was aware of their existence and shared many of their goals. Between 1884 and 1900 Rothschild invested enormous sums in Palestine acquiring property and assisting communities of Jews there.[22]

But certainly the single most significant figure in the growth of Zionism during the 19th century was Theodor Herzl.[23] Born in Budapest in 1860 and reared in a Liberal (Reform) Jewish tradition, Herzl studied law at the University of Vienna, where he developed an interest in culture and literature, writing a number of plays and essays himself. While at the university he also became especially sensitive to "The Jewish Question" and the increasing frequency of anti–Semitic incidents in Europe. In 1896 he published his book *Der Judenstaat* (translated as "The Jewish State"), with the subtitle "An Attempt at a Modern Solution to the Jewish Question."[24] As Herzl put it:

> The idea which I have developed in this pamphlet is an ancient one. It is the restoration of the Jewish state . . . I shall do no more than suggest what cogs and wheels comprise the machinery I propose, trusting that better mechanics than myself will be found to carry the work out . . . The world needs the Jewish state; therefore it will arise.[25]

His central contention was that Europe's hatred for its Jewish population was unavoidable and that Jews were going to be victimized and persecuted as long as they remained a vulnerable and unassimilated minority: "We have sincerely tried to merge with the national communities in which we live, seeking only to preserve the faith of our fathers. It is not permitted us."[26] The only solution to the problems faced by Jews of the day, Herzl wrote, was the establishment of a Jewish homeland.

During this time the "institutionalization" of Zionism became increasingly visible. In August, 1897, the First Zionist Congress met in

Basle, Switzerland. Zionism by now clearly responded to several needs. First, more and more Jews were becoming disillusioned with those events in "modern" and "sophisticated" Europe which demonstrated that discrimination against Jews as Jews was not a thing of the past. One prominent and infamous example of this was the Dreyfus Affair in France.[27] Second was the continuing pattern of anti–Jewish persecution in Russia and Eastern Europe, convincing many that there was no future for them there as well.

Zionism as a national movement, therefore, had two distinct yet interrelated goals. First, it sought to carry out the return of Jews to the land, to a resurgence of agricultural activities, and to a revival of Jewish national life—socially, culturally, economically, and politically. Second, it sought to acquire a publicly recognized, legally secure home for the Jews, where they would be free from European–style persecution.[28] Indeed, the official articulation of the "Basle Program" stated that "the aim of Zionism is to create for the Jewish people a home in Palestine secured by public law."[29] And it was in Basle that Herzl himself had opened his speech with the phrase: "We are here to lay the foundation stone of the house which is to shelter the Jewish nation." In his diary[30] he later wrote: "If I were to sum up the Basle Congress in one word— which I shall not do openly—it would be this: 'At Basle I created the Jewish State.'"[31]

In 1898, at the meeting of the Second Zionist Congress, a resolution was passed sanctioning efforts to obtain a legal charter for Jewish settlement in Palestine. Herzl initially tried to work through Kaiser Wilhelm II, since Germany had influence with the Ottoman Empire, which at the time controlled the region. But the Ottoman Sultan opposed the idea and the Kaiser would not support Zionism over the objections of his ally.

Herzl's attention shifted in 1903 when British Colonial Secretary Neville Chamberlain (the future architect of Britain's "appeasement" policy) indicated that there might be a possibility for the Zionists to receive a land grant in British East Africa in what today encompasses Uganda and Kenya. Herzl preferred land in Palestine, but was a pragmatist and felt that any territory was preferable to no territory. When the Sixth Zionist Congress met in 1903, therefore, a map of East Africa was hung on the dais rather than one of Palestine. After a heated debate Herzl managed to push through a proposal to consider British East Africa as a possible Jewish homeland, although the vote was 295 to 177, with 100 abstentions.[32] While the Zionists fought among themselves over the acceptability of the idea, the British decided against it, and by early 1904 the "East Africa option" was dead. Ironically, so too was Herzl, who died that same year at the age of 44.[33]

By this point two main camps can be identified within the Zionist movement: the "cultural" and the "political" Zionists. The "cultural Zionists" were more concerned with the issues of Jewish and Hebrew culture, language, arts, religion, and identity in general than they were with the establishment of a political state. "Political Zionists," on the other hand, saw the need for a physical territory for the Jews as paramount. Herzl's attitude toward British East Africa was an excellent example of this position, advocating as it did the need for a Jewish state as the number one priority, wherever it might be geographically.

Growth of The Yishuv: 1880–1939

As the Zionist movement grew, more and more Jews migrated to Palestine, expanding existing Jewish communities and developing new ones. In 1909 the first Kibbutz, Degania, was founded on the south shore of Lake Kinneret, the Sea of Galilee. In 1909 Tel Aviv was founded outside the Arab city of Jaffa. Jewish presence in Palestine, in fact, had continually grown from about 5,000 early in the 19th century to 85,000 by 1914.[34] During World War I the Jewish population would temporarily decline to 55,000, largely as a result of Turkish actions taken against citizens of states at war with the Porte.[35] Zionist organizations were banned, their leaders sometimes arrested, and many settlers chose to leave. Only with Turkey's defeat would Jewish immigration resume.

This immigration did not happen in a random pattern, however.[36] There was a discernible sequence of "waves" of immigration, referred to as *aliya* (plural, aliyot, literally meaning "ascent" or "going up") that took place over several decades. The first *aliya* was made up primarily of Russians who arrived between 1882 and 1903. From 20–30,000 Jews are reported to have landed in Palestine during this period, to a large degree as a reaction to and a consequence of growing anti–Semitism in Russia.[37]

The second *aliya* took place during the first years of the 1900's, largely as a result of the failure of the 1905 Russian Revolution.[38] These immigrants were more ideological, espousing "socialist Zionism," and were especially interested in the theme of Jewish labor for Jewish land. It was this wave of immigrants that established the first *kibbutzim*, then, as now, seen as symbols of socialism and Zionism. By 1914 there were 85,000 Jews in Palestine.[39]

The third wave of immigration is considered to have occurred between 1919 and 1923. This group came from Eastern Europe, again primarily from Russia, and is said to have migrated to a substantial degree because of economic conditions in their homelands. Like the second wave of immigrants, they were ideologically committed to Zionism and Palestine. Roughly 35,000 new immigrants arrived during this period.

The fourth *aliya* (1925–1929) found an increased proportion of immigrants from Poland, again as a result of economic conditions in Eastern Europe. As one author later put it: "If the third *aliya* was Russian and ideological, the fourth was Polish and middle class."[40] By 1929 the Jewish population of Palestine had now reached nearly 160,000.[41]

The fifth *aliya* is usually considered to have taken place between 1933 and 1936, this time largely as a response to Hitler's rise to power in Germany. During this period nearly 164,000 Jews migrated to Palestine, and the rate of immigration was increasing. In fact, in the year 1935 alone over 66,000 immigrated.[42] By the spring of 1936, the *Yishuv* totalled nearly 400,000, or almost 30 percent of the total population.[43]

By the time of independence in 1948, the *Yishuv* had changed its character significantly from that which one would have found in 1880. The Jewish population was significantly larger than it was in earlier years, and its makeup had been altered as well: Western European Jews were now a majority of the Jewish population. By the time the Mandate was terminated in 1948, the Jewish population in Palestine had increased substantially from about 55,000 in 1917 to nearly 650,000.[44]

The Balfour Declaration and the British Mandate Period (1917–1947)

Austrian Archduke Franz Ferdinand was assassinated on June 28, 1914, thereby precipitating World War I, which would last until 1918. The War made the Suez Canal—built from 1859 to 1869 by France, and acquired by Britain in 1875—and its adjacent territory strategically important to the British. By extension, the regions near the Canal became strategically important as well. This was especially true because Turkey was a part of the German–Austro–Hungarian Alliance, and the British were very concerned about any allies of the Germans getting too close to the Canal.

In October, 1915, the British High Commissioner in Egypt, Sir Henry McMahon, wrote to Emir Abdullah, the eldest son of Hussein, the Hashemite sherif (governor) of Mecca (and the grandfather of

modern—day King Hussein of Jordan) indicating that Britain was prepared "to recognize and support the independence of the Arabs in all
the regions within the limits demanded by the Sherif (Syria, Arabia,
Mesopotamia) with the exception of those portions of Syria lying to the
west of Damascus" if the Hashemite Arabs would join the allied war
effort against the Ottoman Empire.[45] Spurred on by this invitation, the
Arabs began a revolt against the Ottomans in 1916, led by Emir Faisal
(Hussein's second son) and aided by legendary British officer T. E. Lawrence ("Lawrence of Arabia").

While the Arabs were fighting against the Turks, representatives of
the British and French governments met to negotiate their respective
postwar "spheres of influence" in the Arab world, in essence "dividing
up" the spoils of war in advance of the war's end. The British representative, Sir Mark Sykes, and the French representative, Charles François
Georges-Picot, met in January, 1916. Although the war was by no
means over, they decided, without consulting any Arab ruler, on the
shape of the post—war map of the Middle East: Most of Syria and
Lebanon would be under French influence; Jordan and Iraq would be
under British influence; while most of current day Israel would be ruled
by a "joint allied condominium" for religious and political reasons.[46]
As Britain's wartime position strengthened while France's weakened,
however, London changed its mind about the "joint condominium"
plan. In 1917 Prime Minister David Lloyd George instructed his ambassador in Paris to notify the French that they would simply have to accept a British protectorate over all of Palestine after the War, since Palestine was a "strategic buffer to Egypt."[47]

Indeed, the entire history of the period between the Sykes-Picot
agreement and the Balfour Declaration illustrates that British actions
were continually steered by its perception of the strategic value of Palestine. The record during this period is a consistent one of the British
"playing off" the Zionist forces against the Arab forces, and correspondingly Arabs against the Zionists, using the demands of one to offset
the demands of the other. While it is very clear that the basic responsibility for the conflict in Palestine belonged to the Arabs and the Zionists, it is also true that there were a number of occasions when Britain
found this conflict convenient for its Middle East strategy. This is a
theme which we can see continuing as long as the British were a presence in Palestine.

In 1917, with the outcome of the war still in doubt, America not yet
a belligerent, the Russian monarchy overthrown, and the Eastern Front
collapsing, the British hoped that the support of Jews throughout the

world would aid in their war efforts. There was also more than a little concern that if they failed to attract world Jewry to their side, the Kaiser would. He was, apparently, considering an expression of his own of support for Zionist aspirations. The British Government accordingly issued its own portentious proclamation echoing Herzl's original objective.[48] On November 2, 1917, in a letter to Lord Rothschild, President of the British Zionist Federation, British Foreign Secretary Arthur James Balfour wrote:

> Dear Lord Rothschild: I have much pleasure in conveying to you, on behalf of His Majesty's Government, the following declaration of sympathy with Jewish Zionist aspirations which has been submitted to, and approved by, the Cabinet: "His Majesty's Government view with favour the establishment in Palestine of a national home for the Jewish people, and will use their best endeavours to facilitate the achievement of this object, it being clearly understood that nothing shall be done which may prejudice the civil and religious rights of existing non–Jewish communities in Palestine, or the rights and political status enjoyed by Jews in any other country. I should be grateful if you would bring this declaration to the knowledge of the Zionist federation."[49]

It is interesting to note that the original draft of the document (July, 1917) had suggested the "reconstitution of Palestine as the National Home of the Jewish People." The final version of the plan, however, merely suggested establishing *in* Palestine "a national home" for the Jewish people, something which might be geographically much smaller. The alteration was made after the British Cabinet as a whole would not agree to the broad mandate as originally proposed. The Balfour Declaration, as it has since become known, was thus left as a more vague and general declaration of support.[50]

   Almost a year later, following a great deal of internal negotiation and debate, the Zionist leadership offered the Lloyd George government its own alternative "interpretation" of the Balfour Declaration. To wit:

> The establishment of a National Home for the Jewish People . . . is understood to mean that the country of Palestine should be placed under such political, economic, and moral conditions as will favour the increase of the Jewish population, so that in accordance with the principle of democracy it may ultimately develop into a Jewish Commonwealth.[51]

This was a stronger position than the British were willing to take, however, and London refused to commit itself to this counter–proposal.

Because of their concern about British intentions and general interpretation of the admittedly ambiguous Balfour Declaration, some Zionist leaders sought to establish direct links and work cooperatively with Arab leaders in Palestine. In January, 1919, Chaim Weizmann, a Zionist leader, and Emir Feisal, leader of the previously–cited 1916 Arab revolt against the Turks, signed a formal pact in London. As noted in its preamble:

> His royal highness the Emir Feisal, representing and acting on behalf of the Arab Kingdom of Hejaz, and Dr. Chaim Weizmann, representing and acting on behalf of the Zionist Organization, mindful of the racial kinship and ancient bonds existing between the Arabs and the Jewish people, and realising that the surest means of working out the consummation of their national aspirations is through the closest possible collaboration in the development of the Arab State and Palestine, and being desirous further of confirming the good understanding which exists between them, have agreed upon the following articles . . .[52]

The most important articles for our purposes here were those guaranteeing Jews the right to free immigration into Palestine and legal settlement on the land. It was accompanied by a reciprocal assurance that Arab tenant farmers would be safeguarded on their own plots of land and assisted in economic development. Arab nationalists, however, subsequently repudiated this agreement. This disagreement among the Arabs certainly contributed to Britain's ability to manipulate its Palestine policy to its own ends, rather than the ends of those living there.

Although Britain assumed "de facto" Mandatory control over Palestine with the Ottoman Empire's defeat in 1918, it was not until April, 1920, that the Supreme Council of the Paris Peace Conference awarded Britain a "de jure" Mandate.[53] During the 1920–1922 years tensions in Palestine increased between the Arab and Jewish populations, with both sides resenting the British presence. A case in point for the latter surfaced in 1922 when Colonial Secretary Winston Churchill issued an official "White Paper" offering a more restrictive interpretation of the Balfour Declaration:

> Phrases have been used such as that Palestine is to become 'as Jewish as England is English.' His Majesty's Government regard any such expectation as impracticable and have no such aim in view . . . when it is asked what is meant by the development of a Jewish National Home in Palestine, it may be answered that it is not the imposition of a Jewish nationality upon the inhabitants of Palestine as a whole, but the further development of the existing Jewish community . . . in order that it may become

a center in which the Jewish people as a whole may take . . . an interest and a pride . . . But in order that this community should have the best prospects of free development . . . it is essential that it should know that it is in Palestine as of right, and not on suffrance.[54]

Churchill's "White Paper" concluded that Palestine as a whole would not become the Jewish national home and introduced the concept of "economic absorptive capacity" into regulations governing Jewish immigration. Unlimited Jewish immigration would no longer be permitted and Jewish immigrants henceforth would have to demonstrate that their presence in Palestine would be of an economic benefit to the land.

As mentioned earlier, in July, 1922, the fledgling League of Nations formally awarded Britain the mandatory power over Palestine which it had in effect possessed since the end of the war. The Mandate contained the text of the Balfour Declaration regarding the establishment in Palestine of a national home for the Jewish people that would extend to both sides of the Jordan River. Immediately upon receiving mandatory power, however, Britain proceeded to partition "Palestine" into two territories: one called "Palestine," and the other "Transjordan." Divided by the Jordan River, Jews were prohibited from settling to the east of it. The Mandate for Palestine[55] was nonetheless important for several reasons, among them the fact that it formally recognized both Zionist claims and the Zionist movement itself.[56] It was, however, sufficiently vague in its wording to serve as the basis of much debate and disagreement. (See Map 1.1)

During the 1920's and early 1930's Palestine was "run like a British crown colony."[57] The British High Commissioner during this period, a Jew by the name of Sir Herbert Samuel,[58] sought to do what he could to calm the anger of the Arab residents over continued and substantial Jewish immigration. Despite his efforts, significant civil unrest continually plagued relations between the Jewish and Arab communities. In November of 1936 a Royal Commission of Inquiry, known as the Peel Commission after its Chairman (William Robert Wellesley Peel, Earl of Peel) was sent on a fact–finding mission to Palestine by the British Government. Its subsequent Report of July, 1937, concluded that the competing claims of Arabs and Jews were essentially "irreconcilable," and that since the situation was a "fundamental conflict of right with right" the only solution was to partition Palestine. The partition plan suggested creation of a Jewish State in one part of Palestine, and an Arab State made up of Transjordan and the rest of Palestine, with a British zone of control around the city of Jerusalem. (See Map 1.2)

MAP 1.1
The First Partition of Palestine

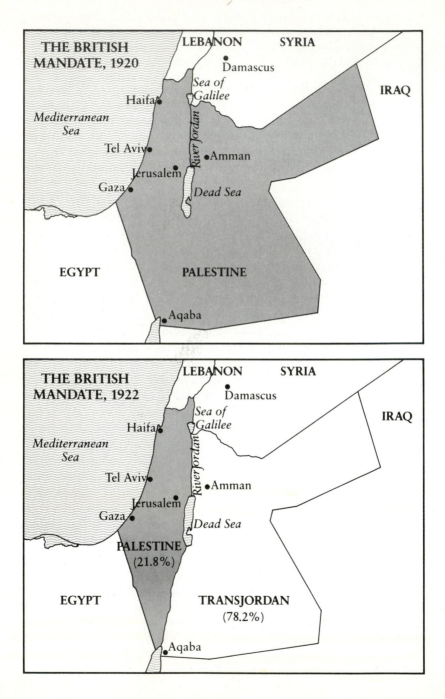

MAP 1.2
The Peel Commission Partition Recommendation

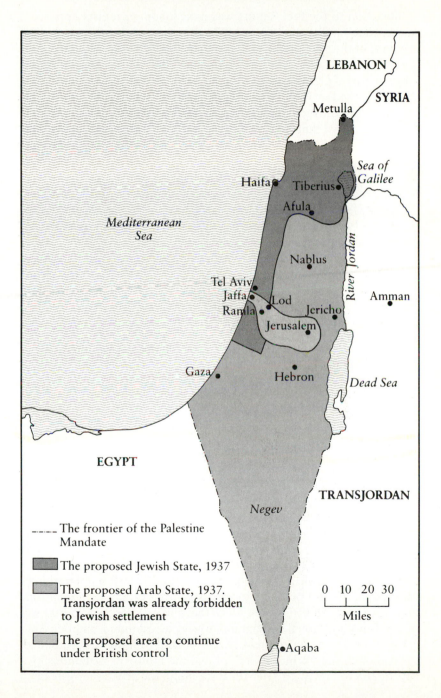

LEBANON

SYRIA

Metulla

Sea of
Galilee

Haifa

Tiberius

Afula

*Mediterranean
Sea*

Nablus

River Jordan

Tel Aviv

Jaffa

Lod

Amman

Ramla

Jericho

Jerusalem

Gaza

Hebron

Dead Sea

EGYPT

TRANSJORDAN

Negev

- - - - The frontier of the Palestine
Mandate

The proposed Jewish State, 1937

The proposed Arab State, 1937.
Transjordan was already forbidden
to Jewish settlement

0   10   20   30

Miles

The proposed area to continue
under British control

Aqaba

Reaction to the Peel Report was mixed. Some Zionists opposed a Jewish state smaller than that of 1922 Palestine, while others urged acceptance of the plan on the grounds that at least it was a concrete proposal for a real state. After more violence (this time primarily Arab), another Royal Commission—the Palestine Partition Commission—was dispatched in 1938. When the Woodhead Report (named after Sir John Woodhead, the Commission chair) was issued on November 9, 1938, it declared that the Peel Report had been unrealistic and its proposed partition lines unreasonable. A new partition plan, creating a much larger Arab state and a much smaller Jewish state, was proposed. This time the Zionists objected most strongly, noting that the Jewish State to be created under the Woodhead Report would be less than 1/20th of West Palestine, and less than 1/100th of the original Mandate territory.[59] Arab nationalists, for their part, opposed *any* plan that would establish *any* Jewish state. (See Map 1.3)

By February, 1939, the imminence of another war with Germany once again raised concerns in Britain about the political status of the Middle East. Colonial Secretary Malcolm MacDonald met with both Zionist and Arab leaders and asserted that the British government had no choice but to look at the Middle East from a strategic perspective.

> His Majesty's Government was left with no choice but to ensure that the Arab governments were not tempted to accept support from hostile powers. If it came to a choice between Arab and Jewish support, MacDonald explained, Jewish help, however valuable, represented no compensation to Britain for the loss of Arab and Moslem goodwill.[60]

In brief, the Arabs were strategically important to Britain, and needed to be placated. The Jews were not.
The outgrowth of this sentiment came in May with yet another "White Paper." This time it declared that the authors of the original Mandate "could not have intended that Palestine should be converted into a Jewish state against the will of the Arab population of the country,"[61] and announced that within ten years it would organize an independent Palestinian State—*in addition to* the Jordanian state already created—and would then gradually transfer political power to it. The British also established a new quota for future Jewish immigration to Palestine at 10,000 per year for the next five years, plus a one–time allotment of 25,000 refugees. Once this five year total of 75,000 was reached, no additional immigrants would be admitted without Arab consent. Effective immediately, all sale of land to Jews was prohibited.

Although the "White Paper" passed the House of Commons by a vote of 268 to 179 (with 110 MPs abstaining), the new policy generated

MAP 1.3
The Woodhead Commission Partition Recommendation

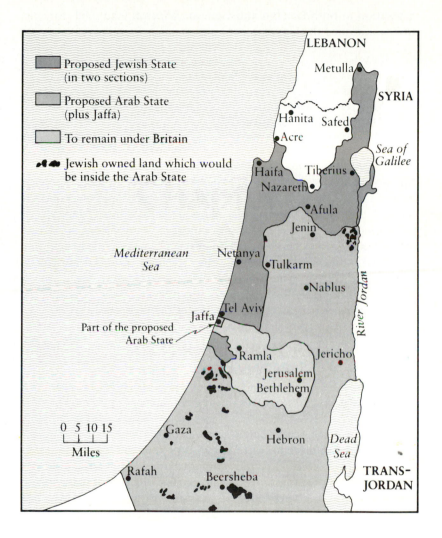

opposition in both London and Geneva. Winston Churchill, for one, now condemned the Government's action:

> This pledge of a home of refugees, of an asylum, was not made to the Jews of Palestine . . . but to the Jews outside Palestine, to that vast, unhappy mass of scattered persecuted wandering Jews whose intense, unchanging, unconquerable desire has been for a national Home . . . That is the pledge which was given, and that is the pledge which we are now asked to break . . ."[62]

The League of Nations Mandates Commission likewise declared that "the policy set out in the White Paper was not in accordance with the interpretation which, in agreement with the Mandatory Power and the Council, the Commission had placed upon the Palestinian Mandate."[63] In the opinion of the League, Britain's most recent decisions in relation to its Palestine policy had reneged on its commitment to the League and to the Zionist movement to support the principles of the Balfour Declaration and the needs of the Jewish people. The advent of World War II, however, rendered the Commission's position moot and relegated the question of Palestine to the back burner of Britain's priorities.

World War II and the Holocaust

The Holocaust, certainly the darkest experience in the history of the Jewish people, is a subject which a text of this nature cannot possibly do justice. Indeed, a recent definitive work on the subject takes up three substantial volumes of over 1200 pages![64] The often–quoted figure of six million Jews killed between 1939 and 1945 (and we should not forget that nearly the same number of East Europeans were also killed) represented almost 90 percent of all Jews in those parts of Europe occupied by the Germans and close to one–third of world Jewry.[65] Much attention has also been paid to the issue of whether or not the Western Powers "knew" about the full magnitude of the Holocaust. It is probably true that at the outset of the war there existed a substantial amount of disbelief over rumors circulating about atrocities and exterminations in some of the German camps. Yet there is clear evidence that within a relatively short period of time the Allied nations did, in fact, know what was happening in these camps and opted—for a variety of reasons— not to set their destruction as a top military or political priority.[66]

Certainly one consequence of the Holocaust was its mobilization of many Zionist groups all over the world to intensify their efforts to convince the British to expand Jewish immigration quotas to Palestine and assist Jewish transit there. Another related and important aspect was the fact that it was instrumental in weakening if not eliminating opposition to Zionism in most non–Arab countries. Public sentiment outside of Palestine, both Jewish and non–Jewish alike, had often been pointedly unenthusiastic about Zionism in the period prior to the Second World War. However, once the horror and the enormity of the Holocaust became known, many changed their views and openly supported the idea of a homeland for the Jewish people.

An ironic and even tragic problem for the Jewish refugees, however, was the fact that while many Western powers were appalled at what the Germans had done, they were not prepared to encourage increased Jewish resettlement in their own countries. When the war ended in 1945, it is reported that American President Harry S. Truman asked British Prime Minister Clement Atlee to "open up" immigration to Palestine as a humanitarian gesture. In response Atlee told Truman that if he was so concerned about the plight of Jewish refugees, he should increase quotas for admission to the United States.[67] Their dispute further underscored two essential "lessons" that came out of the Holocaust for Jews, lessons which are still seen as important in Israel today, and lessons which have a direct impact on contemporary Israeli policymaking, both domestic and foreign. These two "lessons" are, first, that nothing is ever "too horrible to happen;" and second, that Israel must never again be in a position in which it must depend upon others for its very survival. A brief comment on each is in order here.

As rumors of the Holocaust started appearing in Germany, across Europe, and around the world, one of the most common reactions was: "That can't be! That is simply too horrible to happen. People just wouldn't do something like that in the modern, civilized world." We know today, of course, that the Holocaust was not just "too horrible" to happen; it *did* happen. Both Jews and subsequently Israelis drew from this event the "lesson" that one simply cannot take as an act of faith that a given act is, indeed, "too horrible" to happen. This belief, obviously, has consistently carried enormous implications for Israeli foreign policy, as we shall later observe.

The other "lesson" frequently invoked by Israelis is that much of the Holocaust happened because the Jews of Europe were dependent upon someone else—Britain, the United States, and others—to protect them. The inference is that Jews must always be prepared to protect themselves; they cannot permit a situation in which they are dependent upon another actor to defend them, because when the time comes that other party may be unable or actually decline to do so. This too has produced direct foreign policy implications for the Israeli political system, implications which we shall return to in the third section of this book.

Transition to Statehood: 1945–1948

As World War II drew to a close, more and more pressure was brought to bear on Britain to amend its earlier policies and reinstate permission for Jewish refugees to emigrate to Palestine. Nevertheless, the British government continued to follow the policies outlined in its 1939 "White Paper." Despite trying their best to prevent other governments from selling boats or generally assisting Jewish refugees, however, the flow towards Palestine continued. The unintended result of Britain's policy of "no more immigration" was that illegal immigration to Palestine actually increased, and within a few years a significant number of new Jewish refugees had successfully settled there.[68]

In Palestine itself the violence escalated, with the British tending to blame the Zionists for most of the problems that arose. The *Haganah* (the Jewish Defense Force), became more active, as did the *Irgun* (the shortened name of the *Irgun Zvi Leumi*—the National Military Organization) and *Lehi* (the name comes from the initials of the words for the "Fighters for the Freedom of Israel") organizations. The latter two were clearly viewed as "terrorist,"[69] and the British made every possible effort to destroy them. In 1944, nonetheless, the Irgun was linked to several bombings in Jerusalem, Haifa, and Tel Aviv. Their targets were usually British governmental offices and officials.[70] This battle between Britain and the indigenous terrorist organizations continued until the British withdrawal in 1948.[71]

In 1946 the violence further increased after the British decided to set up "relocation camps" for Jewish refugees on the Mediterranean island of Cyprus. All illegal Jewish immigrants seized in or en route to Palestine were sent to Cyprus for repatriation. Perhaps the most dramatic illustration of this occurred in 1947 when "The Exodus" arrived in Haifa with a boatload of nearly 4,000 refugees.[72] The British would not permit them to disembark, insisting instead that the ship return to its French port of origin. Eventually, after France would not cooperate with Britain, the British government actually sent the refugees back to their occupation zone in Germany.[73]

Examples like the "Exodus" not surprisingly failed to win the British much sympathy. Rather they resulted in a worldwide increase in support for the plight of Jewish refugees. In 1946 an Anglo–American

Commission of Inquiry was established to investigate the refugee problem, and that May recommended that 100,000 Jews be permitted to immigrate to Palestine immediately. In response to this the British Government proposed the so–called Morrison Plan (named after Herbert Morrison, its chair), which would convert the Mandate for Palestine into a "trusteeship," divide the country into Jewish and Arab provinces, and create separate districts for Jerusalem and the Negev. The British would retain control over police, defense, foreign relations, customs courts, prisons, harbors and railways, aviation, communications, and other essential services.[74]

The Morrison Plan accepted the goal of admitting another 100,000 Jews to Palestine as advocated by the Anglo–American Commission. After this one–time exception, the principle of "economic absorptive capacity" would again be the basis of Palestine's immigration policy. The United States would be responsible for both the logistics and the costs of this undertaking. However, despite the Anglo–American Commission and the Morrison Plan, neither was accepted due to both Arab and Jewish opposition.[75] At this point, the British government decided to transfer the problem to the infant United Nations,[76] and requested a special session for this purpose on April 2, 1947.[77]

In response the United Nations agreed to create a Special Committee on Palestine (UNSCOP)—composed of Australia, Canada, Czechoslovakia, Guatemala, India, Iran, the Netherlands, Peru, Sweden, Uruguay, and Yugoslavia. After many hearings and much debate the Committee recommended termination of Britain's Mandate and partition of Palestine into independent Arab and Jewish states, along much the same lines as the Peel Commission a decade earlier.[78] There was, apparently, some debate as to the exact nature of the partition. Seven of the eleven nations on the Committee recommended partition into two states, with Jerusalem remaining an international trusteeship of the United Nations, while three (India, Iran, and Yugoslavia) favored a federal–type arrangement of separate Jewish and Arab provinces. This minority group argued that outright partition would not be "fair" to the Arab population of Palestine. Australia remained neutral in this discussion.[79] (See Map 1.4)

Debate on the UNSCOP report lasted two months. Britain opposed any kind of partition and the Arab states opposed anything other than a single Arab state in Palestine. However, in November of 1947, the United Nations voted 33–13 to accept the UNSCOP's recommendation, with Britain abstaining. Jews in the *Yishuv* as well as Zionists outside of Palestine generally supported the recommendations of UNSCOP. Arab governments opposed them.

MAP 1.4
The United Nations Partition Recommendation

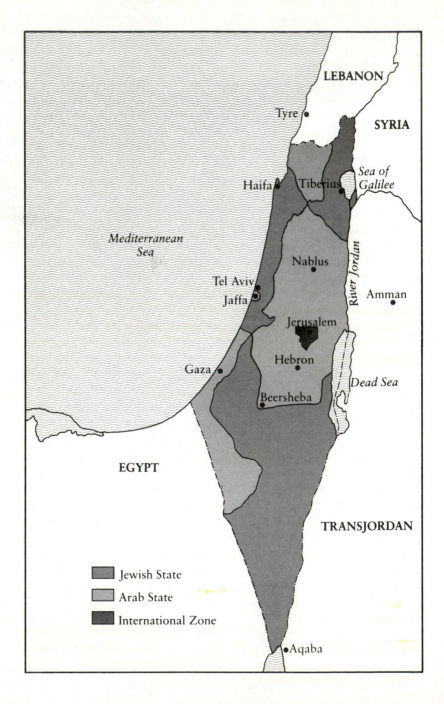

LEBANON

SYRIA

Tyre

Sea of
Galilee

Haifa   Tiberius

*Mediterranean
Sea*

Nablus

Tel Aviv
Jaffa

River Jordan

Amman

Jerusalem

Hebron

Dead Sea

Gaza

Beersheba

EGYPT

TRANSJORDAN

■ Jewish State

□ Arab State

■ International Zone

Aqaba

United Nations General Assembly Resolution 181 had several components, including:

1. Termination of the Mandate and British withdrawal by no later than August 1, 1948;
2. Establishment of a "Jewish State," and "Arab State," and a special region for the City of Jerusalem, administered by the United Nations;
3. Cooperation by the two new states in economic, transportation, currency, customs, and a variety of other respects;
4. Formation of a Palestine Commission of five states to promote peace in the region and the effective operation of the partition plan.[80]

The official termination date of the British Mandate was to be May 15. But, since the 15th was also the Jewish Sabbath, leaders of the newly–created Zionist National Council met on the afternoon of May 14, 1948, and declared the State of Israel's independence. The first three countries to recognize it were the United States (May 14),[81] Guatemala (May 15), and the Soviet Union (May 18).[82] Within eight hours of the declaration of independence, however, Israel was simultaneously attacked by seven Arab armies.

The war of independence was eventually to last more than eight months, with two intervening truce periods (June 11–July 8, and July 18–October 15).[83] On November 16, 1948, the United Nations Security Council ordered the parties concerned to enter into an armistice. A cease–fire was signed by Israel and Transjordan on November 30. On December 13 the parliament of Transjordan annexed almost 2200 square miles of the "Arab State" territory not occupied by Israel and declared its union with Transjordan, despite angry reactions from both Syria and Egypt.[84]

A cease–fire with Egypt was agreed to the following January. By that time all of the fighting had stopped. Israel had gained almost 2500 square miles of territory which under the original UNSCOP partition plan would have gone to Arab states, while Jordan and Egypt divided up the rest. Several different armistices were subsequently signed: with Egypt (February, 1949); Lebanon (March, 1949); Transjordan (April, 1949); and Syria (July 1949).[85] It was only with the signing of the Camp David Treaty thirty years later that for the *first time* an armistice agreement was replaced by an actual peace treaty with Egypt. Israel still remains technically "at war" with all of her other neighbors. During the fighting literally hundreds of thousands of Palestinian Arabs fled from the new State of Israel.[86] These nearly 650,000 refugees will return to our analysis later in this volume.[87] (See Map 1.5)

MAP 1.5
1949 Armistice Lines

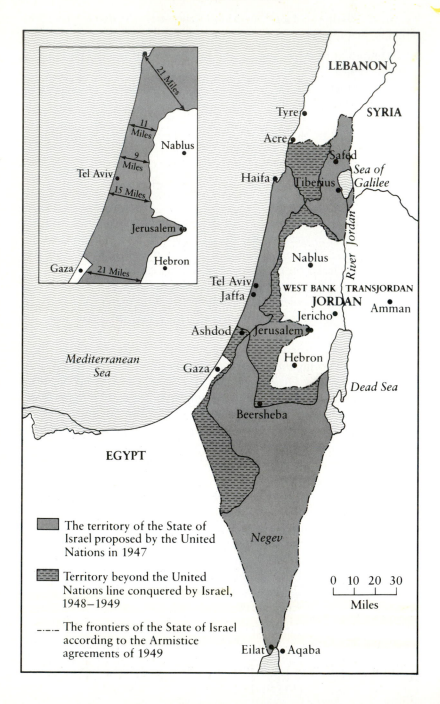

21 Miles

11 Miles

9 Miles

Nablus

Tel Aviv

15 Miles

Jerusalem

Gaza

Hebron

21 Miles

LEBANON

Tyre

SYRIA

Acre

Safed

Sea of Galilee

Haifa

Tiberius

River Jordan

Nablus

Tel Aviv

WEST BANK

TRANSJORDAN

Jaffa

JORDAN

Amman

Jericho

Ashdod

Jerusalem

Mediterranean Sea

Gaza

Hebron

Dead Sea

Beersheba

EGYPT

Negev

The territory of the State of Israel proposed by the United Nations in 1947

Territory beyond the United Nations line conquered by Israel, 1948–1949

0 10 20 30
Miles

The frontiers of the State of Israel according to the Armistice agreements of 1949

Eilat Aqaba

History and the Creation of Israel

We began this chapter with the statement that the history of any society is always an important prerequisite for a complete understanding of its political system. It should now be clear to the new student of Israeli politics why this is so. Not only was Israel born out of disaster, despair, and conflict, but many aspects of the "birth" itself are subject to dispute. It has not been our intention here to authoritatively side with one or the other viewpoint in the debate, for there are various sets of "facts" on both sides which one can invoke. The important lesson for the student is to know that there *are* different sets of "facts," and to know that it is possible, if not desirable, to evaluate both "sides" of the debate before taking a position.

The emergence of Zionism as a political movement was a result of religious, historical, and political variables, and its appearance on the scene in Palestine was one of those factors which shape the history of society. The community of Jews in Palestine, the *Yishuv*, grew dramatically over a period of several decades as a result of economic, political, and religious factors. The presence of the *Yishuv* not only encouraged subsequent waves of immigrants to move to Palestine, but set the scene for an increased level of conflict there between the new immigrants and a native population which did not approve of the greatly increased Jewish presence in the land.

The British were the power charged with the responsibility of overseeing a peaceful outcome of the whole process. From their appearance on the scene during World War I through their ultimate departure in 1948, they attempted to control the political environment in a way that would please all the various segments of the population. Commitments made in the McMahon Letter of 1915 and the Balfour Declaration of 1917 set the stage for a seemingly inevitable and irresolvable conflict. The Peel Commission acknowledged this in 1937 when it declared that a conflict of "right with right" existed. Both groups had legitimate and mutually incompatible claims. Completely satisfying each was impossible, and in the end the British decided that they could *not* give all the parties involved what they demanded. The eventual abdication of the Mandate to the United Nations was the result of this tension which the British alone were not able to resolve.

The horror of the Second World War, combined with the intensity of feeling emerging from the Holocaust, increased Jewish demands for statehood. In the end the United Nations authorized a partition of Palestine as the best conceivable outcome. Ultimately, of course, a peaceful resolution to the problem could not be achieved. A virtual civil war followed before the first round of fighting stopped. We say "first round," of course, because the fighting resumed in 1956, 1967, 1969, and 1973, and there *still* is not a stable peace in this region.

What this chapter has sought to convey is a sense of the major issues central to the birth of the modern State of Israel. It is important to realize that we have only just scratched the surface for much more remains to be presented and discussed. However, because the focus of this text is on Israeli politics, not Israeli history, we must leave those endeavors to others.[88]

NOTES

1. See Genesis 15:13; and Exodus 12:40, respectively. Also, Hanoch Reviv, "Until the Monarchy," in *History Until 1880* (Jerusalem: Keter Publishing, 1973), p. 7.

2. *Eretz Israel*, literally "The State of Israel," will be used to refer to the territory roughly corresponding to what we today call Israel.

3. Reviv, "Until the Monarchy," p. 7; also see Genesis 15:18–21.

4. See Deuteronomy 1:7–8; 11:24; and Joshua 1:14

5. A note should be said about terminology used here in dating. While the traditional Christian—and hence Western—format is to use the initials B.C. and A.D., both refer to historical events which occurred before or after the birth of Christ. It should be obvious to the student who thinks about it that Jewish history would not be recorded in such a way. Indeed, a Jewish Calendar does exist. Thus the year beginning in September, 1989 was the year 5750 in the Jewish Calendar. For convenience, however, because many Jews have realized that they cannot expect non–Jews to be familiar with and use their calendar, they also adhere to the Christian, or Gregorian, calendar. However, rather than adopting initials which mean Before Christ and Anno Domini (year of our Lord), Jewish annotation uses the initials B.C.E. and C.E. (referring to Before the Common Era, and Common Era), respectively. In this book we shall abide by the standard American practice of using B.C. and A.D. where appropriate.

6. The uprising was called the Hasmonean Revolt, involved the Maccabees, and gave rise to the modern Jewish holiday of Hanukkah. See Menachem Stern, "Second Temple: The Hellenistic–Roman Period: 332 B.C.E.–70 C.E. in *History Until 1880*, p. 105.

7. Shmuel Safrai, "Destruction of the Second Temple to the Arab Conquest (70–634 C.E.)," in *History Until 1880*, p. 127.

8. Ibid., pp. 149–50.

9. See Haim Z'ew Hirschberg, "Crusader Period, 1099–1291," in *History Until 1880*, pp. 185–200.

10. See, for instance, "Mamluk Period (1291–1516)," in *History Until 1880*, p. 206.

11. Haim Z'ew Hirschberg, "Ottoman Period (1517–1917)," in *History Until 1880, pp. 212–50.

12. Mordechai Chertoff (ed.), *Zionism: A Basic Reader* (New York: Herzl Press, 1975), and Israel Cohen, *A Short History of Zionism* (London: F. Muller, 1951), are two examples of the huge literature in this area.

13. *Zionism* (Jerusalem: Keter Publishing, 1973), p. 1.

14. Hirschberg, "Ottoman Period," in *History Until 1880*, p. 232. According to him: "By 1880 the total population had grown considerably to 450,000, including 24,000 Jews and 45,000 Christians," p. 237.

15. Ibid., p. 242.

16. Ibid., p. 243.

17. Jacob Katz, "Forerunners," in *Zionism*, p. 5.

18. Dan Horowitz and Moshe Lissak, *Origins of the Israeli Polity: Palestine Under the Mandate* (Chicago: University of Chicago Press, 1978).

19. Katz, "Forerunners," in *Zionism*, p. 21.

20. Howard Sachar, *A History of Israel: From the Rise of Zionism to Our Time* (New York: Alfred A. Knopf, 1981), p. 15.

21. Asher Arian, *Politics in Israel: The Second Generation* (Chatham, N.J.: Chatham House, 1985), p. 13.

22. Yehuda Slutsky, "Under Ottoman Rule (1880–1917)," in *History From 1880*, p. 12.

23. One of the best studies of Herzl is by Amos Elon, *Herzl* (New York: Holt, Rinehart, Winston, 1975).

24. Sachar, *History*, p. 39.

25. Ibid., p. 40. See Herzl, *The Jewish State* (New York: Scopus Publishing Company, 1943).

26. Sachar, *History*, p. 40.

27. Ibid., p. 38.

28. Norman Levin, *The Zionist Movement in Palestine and World Politics, 1880–1918* (Lexington, Ma.: D.C. Heath, 1974).

29. Alfred Katz, *Government and Politics in Contemporary Israel: 1948–Present* (Washington D.C.: University Press of America, 1980), p. 5.

30. Theodor Herzl, *Complete Diaries* (New York: Herzl Press, 1960).

31. Don Peretz, *The Government and Politics of Israel* (Boulder, Co.: Westview Press, 1979), p. 20.

32. Sachar, *History*, pp. 60–61. A related project involved Mesopotamia. See Stuart Cohen, "Israel Zangwill's Plan for Jewish Colonization in Mesopotamia," *Middle Eastern Studies* 16:3 (1980): 200–8.

33. Sachar, *History*, p. 63.

34. Peretz, *Government and Politics*, pp. 25–26. On the subject of the Ottoman Empire and the Zionists, see Mim Kemal Oke, "The Ottoman Empire, Zionism, and the Question of Palestine, 1890–1908," *International Journal of Middle East Studies* 14:3 (1982): 329–42.

35. For a thorough history consult Moshe Burstein, *Self Government of the Jews in Palestine Since 1900* (New Haven: Hyperion Press, 1934).

36. This section is based upon a much longer discussion in Arian, *Politics in Israel*, pp. 13–19.

37. Ruth Kark, "Jewish Frontier Settlement in the Negev, 1880–1948," *Middle Eastern Studies* 17:3 (1981): 334–56.

38. Peretz, *Government and Politics*, p. 37.

39. *Facts About Israel* (Jerusalem: Israel Information Centre, 1977), p. 43.

40. Arian, *Politics in Israel*, p. 16.

41. *Facts About Israel*, p. 49.

42. Sachar, *History*, p. 156.

43. *Facts About Israel*, p. 50.

44. Peretz, *Government and Politics*, p. 36.

45. Sachar, *History*, p. 92. See also Isaiah Briedman, "The McMahon–Hussein Correspondence and the Question of Palestine," *Journal of Contemporary History* 5:2 (1970): 83–122.

46. Sachar, *History*, p. 93.

47. Ibid., p. 96.

48. For background to this see D. Z. Gillon, "The Antecedents of the Balfour Declaration," *Middle Eastern Studies* 5:2 (1969): 225–37.

49. Sachar, *History*, p. 109.

50. Perhaps the "definitive" work on the Balfour Declaration is by Leonard Stein, *The Balfour Declaration* (New York: Simon and Schuster, 1961).

51. Sachar, *History*, p. 118.

52. Ibid., p. 121.

53. See D. Edward Knox, *The Making of a New Eastern Question: British Palestine Policy and the Origins of Israel, 1917–1925* (Washington, D.C.: Catholic University Press, 1981), and John McTague, "The British Military Administration in Palestine, 1917–1920," *Journal of Palestine Studies* 7:3 (1978): 55–76.

54. Sachar, *History*, p. 127.

55. Michael Cohen, *Palestine, Retreat from the Mandate: The Making of British Policy, 1936–1945* (New York: Holmes and Meier, 1978).

56. Peretz, *Government and Politics*, pp. 32–33.

57. Ibid., 34.

58. Elie Kedourie, "Sir Herbert Samuel and the Government of Palestine," *Middle Eastern Studies* 5:1 (1969): 44–68.

59. Sachar, *History*, p. 218.

60. Ibid., p. 220.

61. Ibid., p. 222.

62. Ibid., p. 224.

63. Ibid.

64. Raul Hilberg, *The Destruction of the European Jews: Revised and Definitive Edition* (New York: Holmes and Meier, 1985).

65. Peretz, *Government and Politics*, p. 45.

66. See Gideon Hausner, *Justice in Jerusalem* (New York: Holocaust Library, 1966) for a full discussion of this. His twelfth chapter, "The Great Powers and the Little Man" (pp. 226–64) specifically addresses the subject of the international reaction to Hitlerism.

67. See also the volume by Irving Abella and Harold Troper, *None is Too Many: Canada and the Jews of Europe, 1933–1948* (Toronto: Lester and Orpen Dennys, 1982) which deals with Canadian policy toward Jewish refugees.

68. Abba Eban, *My People: The Story of the Jews* (New York: Random House, 1968), p. 434. There is actually quite a substantial literature describing both this period and the illegal immigration actions. See, for example, Arie Eliav, *The Voyage of the Ulua* (New York: Funk and Wagnalls, 1969).

69. The term "terrorist" clearly is one laden with emotional significance, especially in light of contemporary activities in the Middle East, and perspectives of the Palestinians and Israelis in relation to the problem of terrorism will be discussed in Chapter 10. One anecdote illustrates some of the problems caused by different perspectives associated with the term: In 1975 the author interviewed Mr. Menachem Begin (then leader of the opposition party in the Knesset) and asked the following: "Mr. Begin, some people would say that there is no difference between what the P.L.O. is doing today and what you did to the British as leader of the Irgun. How would you respond to that?" Mr. Begin replied: "Of course there is a difference. Arafat is a terrorist. I was a freedom fighter."

70. J. S. Hurewitz, *The Struggle for Palestine* (New York: Norton, 1950), p. 199. See also J.B. Bell, *Terror Out of Zion: Lehi and the Palestine Underground, 1929–1949*. (New York: St. Martin's Press, 1977).

71. An autobiographical history of this period is to be found in the work of Menachem Begin, *The Revolt* (New York: Nash Publishing, 1977). In this volume, Begin admits to virtually everything he was accused of doing by the British. His justification for his actions, as described in Footnote 69, was that he was acting as a "freedom fighter," not a "terrorist."

72. For an example of this kind of incident, see Eliav, *The Voyage of the Ulua.*

73. See Eban, *My People*, p. 437, and Marie Syrkin, *Golda Meir—Israel's Leader* (New York: Putnam's Sons, 1969), p. 161.

74. For a more detailed discussion of this proposal see Katz, *Government and Politics*, pp. 14–15.

75. Ibid., p. 15.

76. Miriam Haron, "The British Decision to Give the Palestine Question to the United Nations," *Middle Eastern Studies* 17:2 (1981): 241–48.

77. Oscar Kraines, *Government and Politics in Israel* (Boston: Houghton Mifflin, 1961), p. 2.

78. Kraines makes an interesting observation: "Although the [territory] allocated to the 'Jewish State' amounted to about 55 percent of the total area of Palestine, and the 'Arab State' was given nearly 45 percent, more than half of the territory assigned to the 'Jewish State' was to consist of the Negev, an arid, bare, and largely uncultivable desert area in the south bordering Transjordan and Egypt." Kraines, *Government and Politics*, p. 4.

79. Kraines, *Government and Politics*, p. 3. A very interesting analysis of the legal status of partition is to be found in N. Elarby, "Some Legal Implications of the 1947 Partition Resolution and the 1949 Armistice Agreement. *Law and Contemporary Problems* 33:1 (1968): 97–109.

80. Kraines, *Government and Politics*, p. 3.

81. On early American–Israeli relations, see John Snetsinger, *Truman, the Jewish Vote, and the Creation of Israel* (Palo Alto, Ca.: Stanford University Press, 1974).

82. Arnold Krammer, "Soviet Motives in the Partition of Palestine, 1947–1948," *Journal of Palestine Studies* 2:2 (1973): 102–19 on the vote. More generally, see Walter Eytan, *The First Ten Years: A Diplomatic History of Israel* (New York: Simon and Schuster, 1958).

83. Dan Kurzman, *Genesis 1948: The First Arab–Israeli War* (New York: World, 1970).

84. Saul Mishal, *West Bank East Bank: The Palestinians in Jordan, 1949–1967* (New Haven: Yale University Press, 1976).

85. On the armistices, see Muassasat al–Dirasat al–Filastiniyah, *The Arab–Israeli Armistice Agreements, February–July, 1949. U.N. Texts and Annexes* (Beirut: Institute for Palestine Studies, 1967). For an Israeli–authored perspective of this period see David Ben–Gurion, *Israel: A Personal History* (New York: Funk and Wagnalls, 1971), 94–330. Another excellent study is that by Jon and David Kimche, *A Clash of Destinies: The Arab–Jewish War and the Founding of the State of Israel* (New York: Praeger, 1960).

86. The argument over *why* the hundreds of thousands of refugees fled from their homes has been a point of dispute since 1949. Two very good contemporary histories by Israelis which discuss why the Arabs fled from Palestine, or were chased out by the Israelis, can be found in works by Tom Segev, *1949: The First Israelis* (New York: Free Press, 1986), and Benny Morris, *The Birth of the Palestine Refugee Problem, 1947–1949* (New York: Cambridge University Press, 1987). This is a topic to which we shall return later in this volume.

87. A good single–volume study is to be found in David Gilmour's *Dispossessed: The Ordeal of the Palestinians: 1917–1980* (London: Sidgwick and Jackson, 1980).

88. Again, probably the best comprehensive text is that of Howard Sachar, *A History of Israel.*

Chapter 2

THE ISRAELI POLITICAL CULTURE
AND ECONOMY

Introduction

Although this is a study of the Israeli *political* system, it is our view that an understanding—or at least an awareness—of the cultural and economic dimensions of Israeli society, along with its history, are needed for a more complete appreciation of political phenomena. As discussed in this and later chapters, social, cultural, and economic factors can be directly translated into political variables. For example, in this chapter we shall introduce the concepts of ethnicity and immigration. In our subsequent discussion of political parties it will become apparent that many of them have made special efforts to appeal to specific immigrant groups, to claim to be "the party" of the immigrants from certain parts of the world. Thus it is clear that social and cultural factors, such as being a Jewish immigrant from Yemen as distinct from a Jewish immigrant from France, *can* make a difference in the political world.

The fact that Israel's population is as heterogeneous as it is, that not all Israelis are Jewish and that not all Jewish Israelis come from the same ethnic, geographic, or religious background, has significant implications for Israeli society, and consequently for Israeli politics. Although the Israeli–Arab conflict has been of paramount significance over the last four decades as a source of concern and anxiety in the lives of Israeli citizens, it is nevertheless the case that the kinds of issues described in Chapters Two and Three, issues such as ethnic group membership, social class, education and culture, economic policies, and degree of religious orthodoxy, are all regular sources of significant tension in the Israeli political arena.

Israeli Arabs

Although the majority of Israel's population of 4,331,300 is native–born, this situation has taken over three decades to come about.[1] One of the most obvious characteristics of Israel, then, is the remarkable heterogeneity of its population, with substantial communities coming from a wide range of national and ethnic origins.[2] The various communities constituting the country have likewise maintained many of their national characteristics, thereby making Israeli society extremely diverse and stimulating.[3] In the next chapter, to cite one example, we shall discuss the subject of "Religion in Israel," and in particular the role of Judaism in domestic politics. Of relevance here is the fact that not all of Israel's population is Jewish and that not all of the Jewish population in Israel comes from identical backgrounds. In other words, to say that Israel has a Jewish majority is correct, but to assume that all Jews are alike in social and cultural characteristics or their degree of "religiousness" is not. The implications of this for the overall political process can be both invigorating and divisive.

Israel also has a substantial non–Jewish population;[4] nearly 18 percent of the population within the pre–1967 borders, according to recent census data, are non–Jewish, with most being Moslem. Of these 769,900 non–Jews, roughly 13.1 percent are Christian, 77.2 percent Moslem, and 9.6 percent Druze, a religion which is an outgrowth of Islam but which contains elements of Judaism and Christianity.[5] Nearly ten percent of the Arab population is Bedouin, the majority of whom still live in a nomadic style in Israel's southern deserts. This diversity is furthermore the source of much discussion and debate in official policymaking circles. One of the central tenets of Zionism, as noted in Chapter One, was the goal of creating and sustaining a Jewish majority in a Jewish state. Not lost on the political leadership, however, is the inescapable fact that this 18 percent is increasing at a rate greater than the natural rate of increase for the Jewish population, so that in the future the proportion of Israel's non–Jewish population can be expected to increase even more.[6]

Beyond this, of course, is the status of the Palestinians in the Occupied Territories. Should the nearly one–million Palestinians in the West Bank and Gaza Strip—who are not included in the 18 percent non–Jewish figure—ever become Israeli citizens, the religious proportions of the population would change even more dramatically, raising the possibility that Israel would no longer continue to have a Jewish majority. This would be completely unacceptable to a substantial segment of Israel's population. As one scholar has noted:

> After the 1948 war and the flight of most Arab inhabitants, a non–Jewish, mostly Arab minority remained. Largely concentrated along the borders of the adjoining states with which Israel had been at war, the Arab minority was perceived by many as a security problem. The fact that Israeli Arabs have one of the world's highest birth rates has increased their number by 400 percent since 1948, from about 10 percent of the population to over 15. Some demographers estimate that Israeli Arabs will equal the number of Israeli Jews within a century. Socioeconomic, cultural, linguistic, and political differences between Israeli Jews and Israeli Arabs have increasingly politicized the issue and raised serious questions about the future of Israel as a Jewish State.[7]

As to one security consideration, it should be noted in passing that members of the various Arab communities are not required to serve in

TABLE 2.1	
Non–Jewish Populations in Israel	
Moslem	77.2%
Druze	9.6
Christian	13.1

Source: Statistical Abstract of Israel: 1987 *(Jerusalem: Central Bureau of Statistics, 1987), p.30*

the Israel Defense Force (IDF), although they are permitted to volunteer. The only exception has been male members of the Druze community, who have been required to serve in the armed forces since 1950, at the request of their community leaders.[8]

Ashkenazim and Sephardim

Perhaps the central dimension along which Israeli society and culture can be, and often has been, divided involves the ethnic communities of Israel's Jewish population. Simply put, these communities can be categorized into two groups based upon their geographical roots.[9] One group, the Ashkenazic Jews (or "Ashkenazim"), look to Europe for their ancestry. These are Jews who immigrated to Israel (or Palestine) from such countries as Britain, France, Germany, Austria, Hungary, Russia, Poland, and Lithuania, to name but a few. The label "Ashkenazic" also applies to immigrants from North and South America. Many Ashkenazic Jews historically used Yiddish as a second language in the communities in which they resided.

The other group, termed Sephardic Jews (or "Sephardim"), includes those with Mediterranean roots, coming from ethnic communities in the Middle East and even Africa. Sephardic Jews have lived in the Middle East since their expulsion from Spain in 1492.[10] It is important to note that not all non–Western Jews are Sephardic. Many Sephardic Jews had as a common second language a tongue called Ladino. Many non–Western Jews, especially those coming from some Middle Eastern and African areas, have very little in common with either the Ashkenazic or the Sephardic cultures. These Jews are sometimes referred to as "Oriental," and might include immigrants from Persia, India, and even China.

The two major groups are not equal in size: about 85 percent of the over—14 million Jews in the world are Ashkenazic, while only 15 percent are Sephardic. On the other hand, while a mere 10 percent of all Ashkenazic Jews in the world live in Israel, two—thirds of all Sephardic Jews do. Thus, Sephardim today make up a majority of Israel's Jewish population.[11]

The Ashkenazic—Sephardic distinction is an important one because it has been a significant source of tension in Israeli society over the years. The Sephardic and Ashkenazic Jews each have their own Chief Rabbi and separate synagogues. Although they actually differ very little in terms of religious substance and laws, they do differ in cultural and social practices, dress, music, architecture and so on.[12] Nor does one need to look far to find manifestations of this division.

In recent years, one of the most dramatically divisive issues—and one that is illustrative of how relatively insignificant issues can sometimes assume significant proportions—involved grass growing out of the holy Wailing Wall in Jerusalem. The Ashkenazic Chief Rabbi, Shlomo Goren, announced that since grass growing between the huge rocks making up the Wailing Wall would eventually cause the Wall to crumble, all Jews had an obligation to pick it. The Sephardic Chief Rabbi, Ovadia Yosef, announced that the grass symbolized the quest for life, and thus should be permitted to grow and be protected.[13] This, of course, resulted in tension, and even occasionally physical violence, between the two groups. Not wishing to antagonize either, the government ended up taking no position on the issue.

There have also been social barriers between Ashkenazic and Sephardic Jews over the years. Often they have been a function of education, with Western or European—Ashkenazic—Jews having higher levels than their Sephardic counterparts.[14] One result of this gap has been that Ashkenazic Jews have held a disproportionately greater percentage of "good" or high paying jobs in the Israeli economy and government bureaucracy.[15] Until the advent of Menachem Begin in 1977, the political elite in Israel was systematically dominated by the Ashkenazim. One of the most significant political changes in Israeli politics brought about by the Begin government was a recognition of the Sephardim and their political leverage.

Immigration and Emigration

One of the central notions of Zionism is the "ingathering of the exiles," the return of Jews from all over the world to their "traditional" home in Israel. This has meant that immigration has been a significant and meaningful component of the social planning of Israeli governments since independence, despite the considerable budgetary demands this has sometimes created.[16] The Law of Return (1950) asserted the right of all Jews to "return" to Israel and be automatically granted citizenship. Since then, hundreds of thousands of Jews have used this Law as the basis for such a claim. Israel's first Prime Minister, David Ben–Gurion, noted that:

> This law lays down not that the State accords the right of settlement to Jews abroad but that this right is inherent in every Jew by virtue of his being a Jew if it but be his will to take part in settling the land. This right preceded the State of Israel; it is that which built the State.[17]

The policy laid down in the Law of Return has been highly successful. Israel's Jewish population more than doubled between 1948 and 1952 from 650,000 to almost 1.4 million, and today is over 3.5 million. This increase in population has been the result of both natural increase and

TABLE 2.2 Jewish and Arab Population to 1986			
Year	Jewish Population	Arab Population	Total
1882	24,000	426,000	450,000
1922	84,000	668,000	752,000
1940	464,000	1,081,000	1,545,000
1948	650,000	156,000	806,000
1954	1,526,000	192,000	1,718,000
1961	1,932,000	247,000	2,179,000
1967	2,384,000	393,000	2,777,000
1973	2,845,000	493,000	3,338,000
1977	3,077,000	576,000	3,653,000
1981	3,320,000	658,000	3,978,000
1985	3,510,000	740,000	4,250,000
1986	3,539,300	759,500	4,298,800

Source: Adapted from Michael Wolffsohn, Israel: Polity, Society, and Economy, 1882–1986 (Atlantic Highlands, N.J.: Humanities Press International, 1987), p. 121, and Statistical Abstract of Israel, 1987 (Jerusalem: Central Bureau of Statistics, 1987), p. 65.

continued immigration from the free world, Eastern Europe, and, despite restrictions, from Islamic lands and the Soviet Union.[18]

The largest single wave of immigration came immediately after independence. In 1949 alone there were almost 250,000 new immigrants. During this period there were substantial numbers from displaced persons camps in Europe, as well as survivors of the Nazi concentration camps. A significant bloc came from Eastern Europe, especially Poland and the Soviet Union. This left the population in Israel and its political leadership heavily dominated by Ashkenazic Jews.

The great increase in the Sephardic immigrant population followed that of the Ashkenazim. During the 1950s immigrants began arriving from Asia and North Africa, resulting in substantial Moroccan, Iraqi, and Yemeni communities in Israel. In the years 1949 and 1950 alone almost 50,000 Yemeni Jews were flown to Israel in "Operation Magic Carpet." In 1950 over 120,000 Iraqi Jews arrived. By the end of the 1970's nearly 750,000 Jews from the Middle East and Northern Africa had migrated to Israel.[19]

In recent years the rate of immigration has declined sharply, primarily for two reasons. First, perhaps most obvious, the number of Jews outside Israel seeking to resettle there has declined dramatically as a result of the overwhelming rate of past immigration. By the late 1970's, for example, there were only 30,000 Jews remaining in Morocco, 10 percent of those who lived there when Israel declared statehood.[20] Similarly, the rate of immigration from Europe immediately following Israeli independence could not continue since the number of Jews remaining there has decreased just as dramatically.

A second reason for a declining immigration rate has been more of a source for concern for Israeli authorities. With increasing frequency

TABLE 2.3 Sources of Jewish Immigration, 1986		
Jewish	Born in Israel	Born Abroad
Israeli Origin	672,800	—
Asian Origin	461,700	286,000
African Origin	449,900	328,700
European-American Origin	571,700	768,500

Source: Statistical Abstract of Israel, 1987, pp. 76–77.

TABLE 2.4
Jewish Immigration to Israel 1948–1985

Europe		813,867
Romania	260,188	
USSR	199,467	
Poland	168,533	
Bulgaria	39,887	
Hungary	28,175	
Czechoslovakia	23,459	
France	21,702	
United Kingdom	19,798	
Germany	15,649	
Other Europe	37,009	
America, Oceania		115,762
USA, Canada	57,832	
Argentina	32,670	
Other Americas and Oceania	25,260	
Asia		357,230
Iraq	129,497	
Iran	69,755	
Turkey	60,134	
Yemen	46,411	
India/Pakistan	24,789	
Other Asia	26,644	
Africa		430,745
Algeria	184,413	
Morocco	140,365	
Libya	35,778	
Egypt, Sudan	30,002	
Tunisia	14,703	
South Africa	11,918	
Other Africa	13,566	

Source: Facts About Israel *(Jerusalem, 1985), p. 83.*

in the last few years stories have appeared in the press about the "drop-out rate" in the Soviet Jewish emigré population, about how Soviet Jews who succeed in obtaining exit visas to leave the USSR decide when

FIGURE 2.1
Immigration to Israel

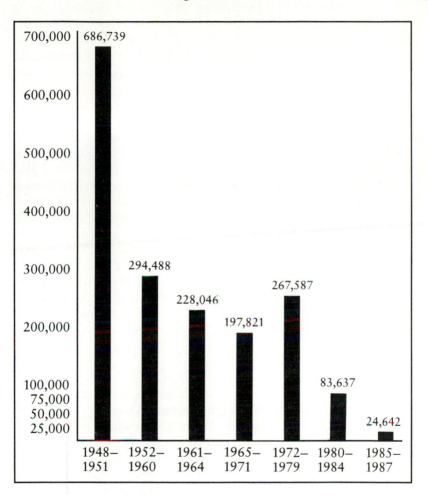

Source: Table 5:4 "Immigrants . . . By Period of Immigration," in Statistical Abstract
of Israel *(Jerusalem: Central Bureau of Statistics), p. 150.*

they arrive in Vienna to choose other Western European or American
destinations rather than Israel. Despite the fact that the Soviet Union
under Gorbachev has been permitting significantly more Jews to emigrate, the "dropout rate" continues to exceed 90 percent. The Israeli
government has therefore sought to channel Soviet émigrées directly to
Israel via Bucharest, Romania, so that they would not have the opportunity to opt for alternative destinations after they leave the Soviet

Union. The United States government, for one, has opposed these proposals, arguing in favor of giving Soviet émigrées freedom of choice. It is entirely possible that the current "disturbance" (*indifada*) on the West Bank has also had an effect on this "dropout rate," although figures are not conclusive in this regard. Officials are also concerned that stories about the Israeli economy have made Israel a less attractive goal for immigrants, and much policy debate in this area has been, and continues to be, undertaken.[21]

A number of agencies and offices in Israel, some official and some "quasi–governmental," are active in the process of immigrant resettlement. A cabinet–level agency, the Ministry of Absorption, is responsible for coordinating assistance. The Ministries of Housing, Labour, Education, and Health all are important in the overall absorption process. Immigrants are eligible for up to five months' temporary housing in an absorption center, financial assistance for locating permanent housing, tax benefits and customs privileges (importing items otherwise subject to duties), job placement, language training, complete health care, and other forms of governmental assistance. Non–governmental agencies likewise participate in the process. The Jewish Agency, the Women's International Zionist Organization (WIZO), United Jewish Appeal, and many other organizations of a similar nature all contribute to the many support services offered to new immigrants.

Social Class

Despite the opinions of some early Zionist thinkers, the "ingathering of the exiles" has proven to be an insufficient common experience to produce an entirely unified society.[22] Notwithstanding a Jewish majority in a Jewish state and a resurgence of Jewish culture, not all Jews are sufficiently alike to attain the degree of social cohesion expected by Zionist thinkers. Not only do we find the social tensions between Israeli Jews and Israeli Arabs, or between Israeli citizens and residents of the Occupied Territories, but we also find social tensions between and among various groups of Israeli Jews.[23] The Ashkenazic-Sephardic distinction introduced earlier in this chapter has given rise to merely one aspect of social tension.

One of the most remarkable characteristics of Israeli society over the last forty years has continued to be its heterogeneity, a direct if presumably temporary, product of the Zionist goal of the "ingathering of the exiles." Jews from Europe, the Soviet Union, Asia, Africa, North America, and South America have come together, and what has become clear is that on occasion the respective "Jewishness" of these many and varied groups is not enough of a common bond to guarantee social unity.[24] Some groups have been more visible than others in Israeli society in their process and problems of assimilation. A group made up primarily of Black Americans claiming Jewish descent caused quite a stir when they arrived to establish their own community.[25] Similarly, the appearance of Ethiopian Falashas (a tribe of Ethiopian nomads claiming to be Jews) was a highly publicised injection of a new and different community into Israeli society. Much was made of the fact that most of these individuals had never even seen electric appliances or lived in "modern" society before arriving at a designated landing strip in Ethiopia and then being airlifted to Israel.[26] They have, since their arrival, settled in and become an established community, although to a large degree they have not been assimilated or become part of the "mainstream" of society.[27]

At one point in recent years the Government decided that in order to accelerate social interaction immigrants from different parts of the world should be settled together. German, Moroccan, American, and Russian immigrants, to take only four examples, would occupy the same multi–story apartment building. This experiment in social homogenization failed when it became clear that their common "Jewishness" was insufficient to make them good neighbors because their individual backgrounds and customs were simply too difficult to change overnight. In some cultures it is socially acceptable to do one's cooking and laundry in open, communal areas. In others this is simply not done. These small-scale experiments in creating "melted pots" were terminated when it became clear that many European Jewish immigrants did not appreciate being given apartments next to immigrants from North Africa who hung laundry from their windows and did their cooking in the stairwells![28]

Ironically, one of the few institutions contributing to social integration has been the army.[29] The fact that the army and military service are the one phenomenon common to virtually *all* in Israeli society means that it is in the army that Ashkenazim meet Sephardim, and it is in the army that they all share a common experience.[30]

Education and Culture

One of the earliest legislative acts of the Government of Israel was the Compulsory Education Law (1949), which provided free and compulsory education to all children between the ages of 5 and 14. Since

1978 education has been mandatory to the age of 16 and free until age 18. Separate school systems exist for the Jewish and Arab communities, with the Jewish schools being taught in Hebrew and the Arab schools, which also serve the Druze community, being taught in Arabic. The Ministry of Education oversees both.

The Jewish schools are of three types: state, state–run religious, and private religious certified by the government. State schools are co-educational and essentially secular,[31] while both the private and the state–run religious schools include a substantial religious component in their curricula in addition to the standard academic content of the "regular" schools. The non–Jewish schools, both for Druze as well as other Arab groups, provide academic and religious content appropriate to those communities. Religious instruction for both the Islamic and Christian populations is offered in Arab schools, while in Druze schools it is controlled by community leaders.[32]

Culture is important in the Israeli social agenda. The Ministry of Education and Culture supports a wide range of activities in this area, as do a number of private and semi–private agencies. Classical music is widely supported and many of the rural *kibbutzim* (agricultural collectives) have their own string quartets and musical groups! There are

		TABLE 2.5 Israeli Universities
Year Open	Number Students	University
1924	9,000	Technion—Israel Institute of Technology (Haifa)
1925	16,000	Hebrew University of Jerusalem
1934	500	Weizmann Institute of Science (Rehovot—postgraduate)
1955	10,000	Bar-Ilan (Ramat Gan, Tel Aviv)
1956	16,900	Tel Aviv University
1963	6,000	Haifa University
1969	5,500	Ben-Gurion University of the Negev (Beersheba)

Source: Facts About Israel *(Jerusalem: Ministry of Foreign Affairs, 1985), p. 101.*

several publishing houses in the country, which print books, magazines, and newspapers in Hebrew, Arabic, French, English, Russian, German, and many other languages. A number of theater and dance companies operate across the country, too. Israel is deservedly famous for its museums of antiquity, but it equally deserves note for many of its other museums.

Israel also has many fine institutions of higher education, which are available to Jewish and non–Jewish students alike. Many universities operate in Israel, with a very high foreign student population. The major Israeli universities are indicated in Table 2.5. There was "a veritable explosion"[33] in Israel's student population in the 1970's. Israel's universities are financed to a significant extent by the government and the Jewish Agency, which together contributed 82.9 percent of the total university budgets in 1973–74, 69 percent in 1977–78, and 75.4 in 1984–85. Tuition and fees have made up the bulk of the remainder.[34]

Health Care and Social Services

Israel has a comprehensive and socialized health care system available to all citizens.[35] The Ministry of Health supervises health care, although many Israelis still prefer to go to private clinics, doctors, and hospitals run by other, many political, organizations. Approximately 25 percent of Israel's 145 hospitals are owned by the government; others are either privately owned, run as non–profit organizations, or supported by private sick–funds (health care organizations).[36] About 95 percent of Israel's population is covered by one of several national health insurance plans.[37]

On a broader scale, Israel is a political system committed to the "welfare state" approach to social services. This means that the state will make sure that certain minimal standards of social goods are available to all citizens. This includes such items as education and health care, which have already been discussed, and several others. Israel has a guaranteed minimum annual income; if someone is unable to earn a certain amount of money each year, the state provides the income to the individual directly. The state runs a variety of services for families, children, and the handicapped, as well as a guaranteed retirement plan. Included among these services are a state–supported network of pre–schools and other support for child care, subsidized meal plans in public schools, reduced fares on public transport for children, socialized medicine (including both visits to doctors and hospitals, and prescription drugs), physical therapy, maternity leave from jobs, unemployment compensation, job–training programs, and assistance in job placement, to name only some of the programs available.

Cities, Villages, Kibbutzim, and Moshavim

Over 85 percent of Israel's population lives in some form of urban setting, whether it is a large city or a small town. The largest cities would include Jerusalem (1985 population 428,700), Tel Aviv–Jaffa (327,300), Haifa (225,800), Beersheba (110,800), and Eilat (18,900), each of which has its own identity and character.

Jerusalem has been the capital of Israel since the time of King David, or roughly 1000 B.C.E. In the post–1860 period there began to develop a substantial Jewish community outside of the walls of its "Old City." Since then Jerusalem has grown steadily and today is the largest city in Israel. Between 1949 and 1967 it was divided between Israel and Jordan, but at the end of the Six Day War the city was reunited, with many Israelis vowing that it would never again be separated. In July, 1980, the Knesset passed a law permanently unifying Jerusalem and annexing the "occupied" portions of the city as Israeli territory. A substantial proportion of Jerusalem's population is religiously devout, and entire neighborhoods are closed to traffic on the Sabbath.

Tel Aviv, originally founded in 1909 as a Jewish suburb of the Arab city of Jaffa, has grown to become the industrial and commercial center of Israel. The greater Tel Aviv area includes a population of over 1,300,000,[38] including suburbs such as Ramat Gan, Bat Yam, Bnei Brak, and many others. Tel Aviv has the image of being a more "secular" city than Jerusalem, and there have been instances of clashes between religious and secular groups over such issues as whether movie theaters and restaurants will be open on the Sabbath.

Haifa is the country's largest port and major urban center of Israel's north. It has a substantial industrial base, a major university, and is significant as a commercial center because of the trade moving through its harbor. Haifa is perceived as even more "secular" than Tel Aviv. Recently a dispute developed there because the city wanted to run a (city–owned) cable–car on the Sabbath, since the Sabbath was the day that the largest number of citizens were not working and might pay to go on the ride. The religious segment of the population protested what they characterized as a government–supported "desecration," but the cable–car continued to run.

In the south, Beersheba is commonly referred to as the "capital of the Negev." Once known as simply a "development town," today it is a rapidly growing city and regional center whose focus is on industrial and residential development. Further to the south lies Eilat, called by many a "gift" to Ben-Gurion during Israel's War of Independence. The significance of this port city on the Gulf of Aqaba (which in turn provides access to the Red Sea) was extremely important to Israel's founding fathers. Today, Eilat has been developed as a major tourist center, with a number of major hotels and direct non–stop air connections to many European cities. Both Beersheba and Eilat are essentially totally secular cities, with virtually nonexistent actively religious Jewish populations.

In addition to nearly forty-five cities and towns, Israel has a substantial number of what are referred to as "development towns"—areas intended to draw industry and population away from the major centers and toward the underpopulated areas of the country. The government has used these development towns as targets for immigrant settlement by offering numerous financial incentives—including low–interest loans and subsidized housing—to encourage both new immigrants and already–established Israelis to relocate there. These "development towns" have proven to be of great social significance for two reasons. First, they have contributed to the Israeli economy by helping to settle the land and create jobs. Second, they have provided the government with a place to send new immigrants to settle and also further the assimilation process.[39] These "development towns," which were created purely for reasons of economic expansion, are *not* the same thing as the new settlements established after 1967 on the West Bank for reasons of military security or religious commitment.

While most of the Israeli population lives in towns and cities, over ten percent still resides in rural areas. Certainly the most well–known Israeli structures in this latter category are the *kibbutz* and the *moshav*, both of which merit a word here. The kibbutz is a collective community in which communal ownership of property is the norm.[40] Members of the kibbutz own no substantial property of their own. Rather, the kibbutz owns the cars, tractors, houses, television sets, and even sailboats. In exchange for not being paid salaries, members of kibbutzim (plural of kibbutz) have all of their expenses taken care of—including housing, clothing, education, medical needs, pocket money, and even vacations. The motto of the kibbutz is "to each according to his need, from each according to his ability." Many might recognize this motto as coming directly from the writings of Karl Marx, for it indicates its socialistic philosophy. The kibbutz is run democratically, with all adult members having a vote in the decisions of the community.[41] Today nearly 3 percent of Israel's population—almost 116,000 people—lives on over 260 kibbutzim.[42]

The *moshav* is a slightly different type of community, one in which individuals and families own their own property, but also one in which major economic ventures are undertaken cooperatively. For instance, the moshav may own major agricultural equipment, although the individual farms upon which the equipment is used will be owned privately. The moshav may serve as an economic cooperative, helping individual farmers to market their products, although individual participants will retain their own profits when the goods have been sold. Nearly 4 percent of Israel's population lives on approximately 450 moshavim today.[43]

One of the most remarkable characteristics of the kibbutz and moshav populations in Israel is how *consistent* they have been and how *consistent* they remain. They have continued to account for approximately the same proportion of Israel's population for the last few decades and show no indication that their collective and socialist orientation is declining in popularity in Israeli society.

The Economy

Israel's economy since 1948 can be characterized as similar to other centralized economies with strong social welfare dimensions.[44] From the time of independence, and in fact even before, the state played a major role in providing for the well-being of its citizens. This was true in a variety of social policy areas, including medical care, housing, employment, education, the provision of food and transportation, and many other social goods. The Israeli economy has, since its inception, been "planned."[45]

Israel's economy grew rapidly between 1948 and 1973, averaging 10 percent per year.[46] This was a consequence of factors which would not have been found in many other nations, including a rapid expansion of the labor force as a result of immigration, and an artificially high rate of investment, substantially provided by Jews living abroad who funnel their contributions to the economy through such agencies as United Jewish Appeal, Hadassah, and other Zionist organizations.

As a result of the 1973 Yom Kippur War and other international factors,[47] Israel's economy slowed considerably, with a growth rate of 5.0 percent in 1978–1979, 3.2 percent in 1980–1981, 1.2 percent in 1982–1983, and 1.8 percent in 1983–1984.[48] This slowdown has re-

TABLE 2.6
Table of Exchange Rates, 1975–1988

One U.S. Dollar Would Buy:

Date:	Israeli Pounds	Israeli Shekels	New Israeli Shekels
7/75	7.50		
7/76	7.97		
7/77	9.39		
7/78	17.90		
7/79	25.24	(triple–digit inflation begins)	
7/80	49.85		
—introduction of new currency: Israeli Shekels[50]			
7/81	[116.10]	11.61	
7/82	[245.40]	24.54	
7/83	[479.00]	47.90	
7/84	[2,417.00]	241.70	
7/85	[10,000.00]	1,000.00	
—introduction of new currency: New Israeli Shekels			
7/86	[14,880.00]	[1,488.00]	1.49
7/87	[15,000.00]	[1,500.00]	1.50
7/88	[15,850.00]	[1,585.00]	1.59

Source: New York Times Business Section on first business day of month indicated.

sulted in serious economic problems, with inflation at one point running at nearly a 1000 percent annual rate.[49]

The major difficulty facing the Israeli economy has been the vast and continuing budgetary increases in the areas of defense and security.[51] These, combined with worldwide inflation and an overwhelming increase in the price of oil, have put severe strains on Israeli economic development. Another has been economic policy–making in the Occupied Territories and, specifically, the appropriate role for Israeli government there.[52] According to many, the Israeli contribution to West Bank development has been much more active and constructive since 1967 than that of Jordan during the preceding two decades, when *it* was the occupying power.[53] But the debate over what the future role of the Israeli government should be continues.

One result of this constant strain on the Israeli economy, especially since the 1973 Yom Kippur War, has been a reexamination and to some extent a retrenchment of the government's social spending. In an effort to make some progress in balancing its budgets, and with military and defense expenditures largely immune from reductions, the government has capped and in many cases cut its spending in a wide range of social programs, including education, medical care, and general welfare. Those who felt the brunt of this budget cutting, of course, were those who could least afford it, the poor and the unemployed. This has not spilled over into the "political" realm as much as it otherwise might have, however, because the party forming the government, the Likud, is also the party that has the poorer Sephardic Jews as a "natural" constituency. Thus they are less likely to protest these cuts than they would be were the Labor party to undertake them. As well, the Likud's political sensitivity has led its leaders to realize that severe cuts in the "social sector" might cause it to lose a significant part of its most important constituency.

Generally speaking, Israel's Gross Domestic Product (GDP) is composed of three parts: (a) general governmental services and private non–profit institutions, (b) dwelling ownership, and (c) the business sector. The governmental services and non–profit institutions make up approximately 20 percent of the GDP, dwelling ownership accounts for about 10 percent, while the business sector accounts for almost 70 percent of the GDP.[54] Almost one quarter of Israel's labor force is employed in industry, and industry accounts for nearly 20 percent of the GDP.[55] In recent years the kibbutzim, long thought of simply in agricultural terms in the national economy, began to develop significant industrial output, with individual kibbutzim selecting specific products for local production. This production made up 5 percent of Israel's total industrial output; with over 330 kibbutz factories currently active in the economy.[56] Complementing this has been the international attention received in the realm of overall agricultural productivity. New techniques in irrigation and hydroponics, new breeding programs for both plants and animals, and remarkable agricultural success rates in a region of the world not traditionally known for its agricultural output have made this aspect of Israel's economy worthy of note.

Foreign Economic Relations

Foreign economic relations have traditionally been one of Israel's greatest concerns, as the data in Tables 2.7–2.9 illustrate. In particular, there have been three significant sources of funding from outside of

TABLE 2.7
Contributions by World Jewry to Israel
(Percent of One–Directional Transfer Payments)

Year	Percent
1950–55	45.4%
1956–60	26.7
1961–70	43.0
1971–73	24.3
1974–81	24.0
1982	18.9

Source: Wolffsohn, Israel: Polity, Society, and Economy, 1882–1986, *p. 264.*

the country for the Israeli government over the years: the world's Jewish population, and the governments of the United States and the Federal Republic of Germany. These sources of funds have provided both grants—not requiring repayments—and loans.

The country's major international financial concern has traditionally been its balance of payments problem. Simply put, spending as much as Israel must on armaments makes it difficult to maintain a trade equilibrium when the nation's major exports include oranges and carnations and a major source of foreign revenue is tourism. In recent years, as Israel has begun to ship more arms abroad and indeed has become one of the largest arms exporters in the world, this situation has improved gradually, but the economy can still use much more foreign capital before the broadly conceived balance of payments problem is gone.

One report on the Israeli balance of payment problem has not been terribly optimistic about the prognosis for the situation, suggesting that Israel has not demonstrated "anything even resembling 'economic independence'" since independence in 1948.

> Israel has been and remains dependent on imports, the costs of which cannot be met by the income from exports. To put it crudely: Israel has constantly lived beyond its means. This purely economic judgement cannot, however, remain the sole consideration. For political and psychological reasons, no Israeli government has been able to apply a stronger brake to private demand for imported goods than that effected by the already high import duties. The government of a nation seeking to attract

TABLE 2.8
Foreign Trade Balance

Year	Imports	Exports	Excess of Imports Over Exports	Exports as % of Imports
1949	251.9	28.5	223.4	11.3
1950	300.3	35.1	265.2	11.7
1955	334.4	89.1	245.3	26.6
1960	495.7	211.3	284.4	42.6
1965	814.5	406.1	408.4	49.5
1970	1,451.8	807.5	644.3	55.6
1975	4,230.3	2,202.2	2,028.1	52.1
1980	8,105.1	5,863.5	2,240.6	72.3
1984	8,334.9	6,256.3	2,078.6	75.1
1985	8,500.9	6,858.4	1,642.5	80.7
1986	9,909.8	7,933.4	1,976.4	80.1

Figures are in $US millions. Figures include the West Bank and Gaza since 1967.
Source: Michael Wolffsohn, Israel: Polity, Society, and Economy, 1882–1986 (Atlantic Highlands, NJ: Humanities Press, International, 1987), p. 258, and Statistical Abstract of Israel (Jerusalem: Central Bureau of Statistics, 1987), pp. 216–217.

immigration, a government which requires its citizens to assume the burden of enormous defence costs, sees itself compelled for reasons both of state and of coalition politics to cultivate the kind of support and popularity obtainable by promoting consumption.[57]

A very important figure for the Israeli economy over time, of course, has been the proportion of aid that Israel receives that is classified as "non–repayable" transfer payments, the percent of its foreign aid that does not need to be repaid. West Germany has been very significant in this regard, because it has provided a significant proportion of grants to Israel over the years. At one point, in fact, West Germany provided 74.4 percent of Israel's total "non–repayable transfer payments."[58]

Israel's foreign debt has increased consistently over the years, as indicated in Table 2.9, and has been a major concern of policymakers. Most of Israel's debt is owed to the United States.

TABLE 2.9
Israel's Foreign Debt (in $ million)

Year	Loans Outstanding at End of Year
1977	13,294
1978	15,947
1979	19,419
1980	22,091
1981	24,621
1982	28,306
1983	29,826
1984	30,366
1985	30,333
1986	31,498

Source: Statistical Abstract of Israel, 1987, *pp. 206–207.*

The Political Culture and the Economy

The goal of this chapter has been to introduce a number of social and economic factors to the "equation" of Israeli politics. If we had to sum all of the material presented here in a single word, that word would be "diversity." The Israeli culture is not a homogeneous one, but includes significant dimensions of both Jewish and Arab *cultures*. In fact, we find not only tension between Jewish and non–Jewish elements of the Israeli population, but also a significant division *within* the Jewish component of the population itself. The tensions between the Jewish and non–Jewish portions of the Israeli population are exacerbated, of course, by the added ingredient of many non–Jewish non–citizens: the Arab inhabitants of the Occupied Territories. We shall have occasion to return to each dimension of the "Arab problem" later in the text.

The focus of our examination here has been the majority Jewish culture of Israeli society. But even the Jewish dimension of Israeli culture is not a homogeneous one, for we have noted both the Ashkenazic and Sephardic components of Israel's population. We have identified the tensions that exist between these groups, and the variety of ways in which these tensions can manifest themselves.

We further introduced a variety of other institutional variables into the discussion, variables which affect the quality of life of Israeli citizens, including education and culture, health and other social services, and the types of communities within which they live. Again, we saw a tremendous diversity in lifestyles and settings. Complementing this was the factor of economics. The economy has been a major source of concern in the Israeli political arena for the past two decades, primarily because of the country's balance of payments deficit and the terrible problems of inflation it has faced. Although recent coalition governments have attempted to directly address the problems—actions which we shall discuss in later chapters of this book—the economy must be considered a major hurdle to be overcome in the day to day operations of Israeli politics.

This, then, is the *setting* within which the operation of Israeli politics takes place. As we progress in our study of the political system, we shall see again and again that many of the social, cultural, and economic variables introduced in this chapter play significant roles in both the generation of problems for the political elite and in the policy responses designed to resolve them.

NOTES

1. *Statistical Abstract of Israel: 1987* (Jerusalem: Central Bureau of Statistics, 1987), p. 30.

2. One of the most impressive studies in this area is that by Dov Friedlander and Calvin Goldscheider, *The Population of Israel* (New York: Columbia University Press, 1978).

3. See Alex Weingrod, "Recent Trends in Israeli Ethnicity," *Ethnic and Racial Studies* 2:1 (1979): 55–65. One of the classic studies in this area is that by Sammy Smooha, *Israel: Pluralism and Conflict* (Berkeley: University of California Press, 1978).

4. Smooha, *Social Research on Arabs in Israel, 1948–1977: Trends and an Annotated Bibliography* (Ramat Gan: Turtledove Publishing, 1978).

5. *Statistical Abstract*, Table 2.1, p. 30.

6. Table 2/20 of the *Statistical Abstract of Israel, 1987* shows projections of population in Israel by different religious groups, and demonstrates the "closing" of the "religion gap."

7. Don Peretz, *The Government and Politics of Israel* (Boulder, Co.: Westview Press, 1979), p. 4.

8. *Facts About Israel* (1985), p. 86.

9. Lee Dulter, "Eastern and Western Jews: Ethnic Divisions in Israeli Society," *Middle East Journal* 31 (1977): 451–68.

10. Asher Arian, *Politics in Israel: The Second Generation* (Chatham, N.J.: Chatham House, 1985), p. 22.

11. Ibid., p. 24.

12. For a discussion of some of these characteristics, see Walter Zenner, "Sephardic Communal Organizations in Israel," *Middle East Journal* 21:2 (1967): 173–86.

13. An article about this by Judy Siegel, "Religion and Politics in Israel," appeared in the *Jerusalem Post Weekly Edition*, Tuesday, September 9, 1975.

14. Arnold Lewis, *Power, Poverty, and Education* (Ramat Gan: Turtledove Publishing, (1979).

15. Nimrod Raphaeli, "The Senior Civil Service in Israel," *Public Administration* 48 (1970): 169–78; and Raphaeli, "The Absorption of Orientals into Israeli Bureaucracy," *Middle Eastern Studies* 8 (1972): 85–92.

16. See Golda Meir's description of her early days in the Ministry of Housing in her book *My Life* (New York: Putnam, 1975).

17. David Ben–Gurion, as quoted in Don Peretz, *The Government and Politics of Israel*, p. 52.

18. *Facts About Israel*, (1985), p 82. See also Colin Shindler, *Exit Visa: Detente, Human Rights, and the Jewish Emigration Movement in the USSR* (London: Bachman, Turner, 1978).

19. Peretz, *The Government and Politics of Israel*, p. 53.

20. Ibid.

21. Georges Tamarin, "Israeli Migratory Processes Today: Does Israel Really Want All Its Immigrants? *Plural Societies* 8:3–4 (1977): 3–32.

22. Eva Etzioni–Halvei, *Political Culture in Israel: Cleavage and Interaction Among Israeli Jews* (New York: Praeger, 1977).

23. Sammy Smooha, "Ethnic Stratification and Allegiance in Israel," *Il Politico* 41:4 (1976): 635–51.

24. Yochanan Peres, "Ethnic Relations in Israel," *American Journal of Sociology* 76:6 (1971): 1021–47.

25. Israel Gerber, *Heritage Seekers: American Blacks in Search of Jewish Identities* (New York: Jonathan David Publishing, 1977).

26. Louis Rapoport, *The Lost Jews: Last of the Ethiopian Falashas* (New York: Stein and Day, 1980).

27. Avraham Shama, *Immigration Without Integration: Third World Jews in Israel* (Cambridge: Schenkman Publishing, 1977).

28. Georges Tamarin, "Three Decades of Ethnic Coexistence in Israel: Recent Developments and Patterns," *Plural Societies* 11:1 (1980): 3–46.

29. Maurice Roumani, (ed.) "From Immigrant to Citizen: The Contribution of the Army in Israel to National Integration: The Case of Oriental Jews," *Plural Societies* 9:2–3 (1978): 1–145.

30. Victor Azarya and Baruch Kimmerling, "New Immigrants in the Israeli Armed Forces," *Armed Forces and Society* 6:3 (1980): 455–82. For some discussion of the process of socialization in the armed forces, see Zvi Gitelman, *Becoming Israelis: Political ReSocialization of Soviet and American Immigrants* (New York: Praeger, 1982).

31. "Essentially" secular because although they do not include a substantial religious component, they do recognize all official Jewish holidays sanctioned by the government.

32. *Facts About Israel* (1985), p. 99.

33. Wolffsohn, *Israel: Polity, Society, and Economy, 1882–1986*, p. 198.

34. Ibid., p. 201.

35 Alan Arian, "Health Care in Israel: Political and Administrative Aspects," *International Political Science Review* 2:1 (1981): 43–56.

36. *Facts About Israel* (1985), pp.104–5.

37. Ibid.

38. Ibid., p. 11.

39. On the subject of "development towns," see A. Kirschenbaum and Yochanan Comay, "Dynamics of Population Attraction to New Towns: The Case of Israel," *Socio–Economic Planning Sciences* 7:6 (1973): 687–96; Myron Aronoff, "Political Change in Israel: The Case of a New Town," *Political Science Quarterly* 89:3 (1974): 613–26; Yochanan Comay and Alan Kirschenbaum, "The Israeli New Town: An Experiment at Population Redistribution," *Economic Development and Cultural Change* 22:1 (1973): 124–34.

40. Eliyahu Kanovsky, *The Economy of the Israeli Kibbutz*, (Cambridge: Harvard University Press, 1966).

41. Lionel Tiger and Joseph Sheper, *Women in the Kibbutz* (New York: Harcourt, Brace, Jovanovich, 1975); and Daniel Katz and Naphtali Golomb, "Integration, Effectiveness, and Adaptation in Social Systems: A Comparative

Analysis of Kibbutzim Communities," *Administration and Society* 6:4 (1975): 389–422.

42. *Facts About Israel*, (1985) p. 13.

43. Ibid.

44. Benjamin Akzin and Y. Dror, *Israel: High Pressure Planning* (Syracuse: Syracuse University Press, 1966).

45. Raphaella Bilski, *Can Planning Replace Politics? The Israeli Experience* (Boston: Martinus Nijhoff, 1980).

46. David Horowitz, *The Enigma of Economic Growth: A Case Study of Israel.* (New York: Praeger, 1972).

47. Edi Karni, "The Israeli Economy, 1973–1976," *Economic Development and Cultural Change* 28:1 (1979): 63–76.

48. *Facts About Israel* (1985), p. 64; Wolffsohn, *Israel: Polity, Society, and Economy, 1882–1986*, p. 223.

49. For an excellent analysis of the economic problems of the first Begin government and the 1977–1984 economic policy of the Israeli government, see Yakir Plessner, "Israel's Economy in the Post–Begin Era," in Gregory Mahler, (ed.), *Israel in the Post-Begin Era* (forthcoming). See also Donald Losman, "Inflation in Israel: The Failure of Wage and Price Controls," *Journal of Social and Political Studies* 3:1 (1978): 41–62.

50. For those interested in such detail, the term "shekel" was a unit of weight in the third millennium for measuring payment of gold or silver. In *Genesis* 23:13, 15–17 a description of Abraham buying a field describes shekels as the unit of payment: "The land is worth four hundred shekels of silver . . ." *Facts About Israel* (1985), p. 74.

51. Eliyahu Kanovsky, *The Economic Impact of the Six Day War* (New York: Praeger, 1970); and Marion Mushkat, "The Socio–Economic Malaise of Developing Countries as a Function of Military Expenditures: The Case of Egypt and Israel," *Co–existence* 15:2 (1978): 135–45.

52. Antoine Mansour, "Monetary Dualism: The Case of the West Bank Under Occupation," *Journal of Palestine Studies* 11:3 (1982): 103–16.

53. Arie Bregman, *The Economy of the Administered Areas, 1968–1973* (Jerusalem: Bank of Israel, 1975).

54. *Facts About Israel* (1985), p. 64.

55. According to the *Statistical Abstract of Israel, 1987* (p. 185), 5.2 percent of the Net Domestic Product is generated by agriculture, forestry, and fishing, 22.3 percent by industry, 6.1 percent by construction, electricity, and water, 14.1 percent by commerce, restaurants, and hotels, 8.1 percent by transport, storage, and communication, 13.4 percent by finance and business services, 9.0 percent by ownership of dwellings, 24.1 percent by public and community services, and 3.9 percent by personal and other services.

56. *Facts About Israel* (1985), p. 65.

57. Michael Wolffsohn, *Israel: Polity, Society, Economy, 1882–1986* (Atlantic Highlands, N.J.: Humanities Press International, 1987), p. 255.

58. Wolffsohn, *Israel: Polity, Society, and Economy, 1882–1986*, p. 265.

Chapter 3

ZIONISM, RELIGION, AND THE STATE

Introduction

It was noted in earlier chapters that one of the fundamental goals of the State of Israel has been that advocated by the original Zionists: a Jewish majority in a Jewish state. But what does this mean? We have already seen instances in which terms which on the surface may appear to have a clear and unambiguous meaning may not be, upon closer examination, as clear and obvious as we had thought. This is very much the case in discussion of concepts such as Zionism, broader discussions of the nature of Judaism, or the relationship between religion and politics generally.

In this chapter we shall narrow our investigation from that of Chapter Two. There we dealt to some degree with both the majority (Jewish) and non–majority (Arab Moslem and Christian) populations in Israel. Here we concentrate our attention solely on the Jewish input into the political system, both because this is characteristic of an over-whelming majority of the population and because in Israel, unlike most democratic states, religious questions become political questions and are, therefore, quite germane to our analysis here.

We have already had occasion to see that not all Jews are alike, that there are differences between and among them along a variety of lines, including those implied by culture, geographic origin, and so on. If this is true, then it also follows that the *political* orientations of all Jews may not be the same. That is, the relationship between religion and politics may reflect many of the differences between and among different segments of the Jewish population as a whole. This is, in fact, the case in contemporary Israeli politics.

Our task in this chapter will be to examine in greater detail some of the fundamental concepts which have already been introduced, thereby permitting us to understand more fully those aspects of them which may *not* be as we might have imagined them. By now the reader should be familiar with the concept of "Zionism" and its historical context. But more needs to be said about the use of the concept in contemporary political discourse, something which may not be the same as that initial context might have implied. How exactly is the concept of "Zionism" used today? Could it be interpreted in a way different from its meaning at the turn of the century?

Similarly, although all students may come to the study of Israeli politics with a general understanding that Israel is a "Jewish State," the *a priori* assumptions included in this "understanding" need to be examined. We may approach the study of Israeli politics, then, with an awareness that Israeli Jews are politically different from Israeli non–Jews, but we *also* need to be aware of the fact that some Israeli Jews are different from other Israeli Jews. The kind of distinction we made in the last chapter between the Ashkenazim and the Sephardim *is* politically important. So too are differences between Orthodox Jews and Conservative Jews, and between Conservative Jews and Reform Jews. Hassidic Jews are different from all of these groups,[1] and so on. Before we can feel confident that we understand sufficiently all of the "non–political" dimensions of Israeli society, we must spend some time discussing these religious and ideological characteristics of Israeli life.

The Concept of Zionism

As was mentioned in the first chapter, the core of Zionism originally contained two objectives. First, it sought to promote the return of Jews to the Land of Israel, and the revival of Jewish society, culture, language, and other institutions. Second, it sought to establish a publicly recognized, legally secure home for the Jews in Palestine, their "historic homeland," where they would make up a Jewish majority in a Jewish state, and thus be able to guarantee future generations freedom from persecution.[2] Zionism has been succinctly defined as "the Jewish people's movement of national liberation."[3] The creation of the State of Israel in 1948 was really the climax of the Zionist movement.[4] Although Zionism may well be "Jewish nationalism" or "Jewish national liberation," it has been suggested by others[5] that it is much more complex than "conventional" national independence movements and ideologies. It evolved outside of the territory toward which it was directed, and the target of the movement, the Jewish population, was scattered all over the world rather than being concentrated in one geographic area. Such factors were bound to leave their imprint.

While these two major principles were the core of "classical Zionism" in its most simple formulation, it is instructive to examine Zionism as it exists in the contemporary world. Have its central principles changed over the last hundred years? Have recent geopolitical or military events altered its substance or general nature? Has Zionism become what some have called a "civil religion"[6] in Israel today? It is to a discussion of these questions that we shall turn our attention in this section.

One of the prime goals of the Zionist movement since the creation of the State of Israel in 1948 has been to encourage immigration from a

variety of sources. Nearly 1,700,000 Jews have indeed migrated to Israel since then. Between independence and the end of 1951, nearly
700,000 immigrants arrived. Israel has become the home for over
400,000 Jews from Arab nations. Some of them, such as Egypt, Morocco, Libya, and Syria, have seen virtually their entire Jewish populations depart since 1948. One of the most dramatic such instances was
"Operation Magic Carpet," which transported 110,000 Jews from Iraq
to Israel over the course of a single year.[7]

More recently the issue of Soviet Jewry has become an extremely
visible one, as the Soviet government has begun to permit more Jewish
emigration. Although the population of Soviet Jews in Israel has increased, particularly after 1967, it has not been of the magnitude hoped
for by Israeli leaders. To a substantial degree this is a function of the
"dropout" problem discussed in Chapter 2.

With all this immigration, however, Israel today is still the home to
only twenty percent of world Jewry. Of the approximately 11,000,000
Jews living outside of Israel today, nearly 50 percent are in the United
States, 8 percent in Latin America, 6 percent in Western Europe, 28
percent are scattered throughout Asia, North Africa, and the Middle
East.[8] In the process, the country's population mix has worked to further fragment the actual operation of Zionism as a unifying and emo-
tive concept.

One offshoot of contemporary Zionism is an emphasis on expanded patterns of Jewish settlement. That is, the "Jewish people in a
Jewish land" theme advocated by "classical Zionism" is the model accepted by these people. But their belief is that the "Jewish Land" over
which Israel had control when the fighting stopped in 1949 was insufficient. Perhaps the best example of this viewpoint is the group known as
Gush Emunim ("Bloc of the Faithful") which has as its purpose to effect

> immediate, massive Judaization of Judea and Samaria[9] through the es-
> tablishment of hundreds of settlements, promoting a revival of Zionism
> as an ideological and cultural movement which would not only bring
> millions of Jews into an enlarged Israel but—and above all—refurbish
> Jewish consciousness in Israel and the Diaspora.[10]

Conversely, a more "mainstream" current of "traditional" Zionist philosophy is "socialist Zionism." Its focus is less on geographical boundaries than on how the settlements are to be organized and operated.
Socialist Zionism is

> based on a pioneering concept of social behavior, which involved per-
> sonal asceticism, voluntarism, collective orientation, and egalitarianism.

Central to this approach was the twin emphasis on **idealism** and **collective materialism** . . .[11]

This socialist Zionist philosophy was very significant in Israel's early years, especially among founders of the state such as David Ben–Gurion, Golda Meir, and Levi Eshkol. The predominance of this philosophy helps to explain why their political party, Mapai, dominated Israeli politics for nearly thirty years. Changing migration and demographic patterns, in turn, help to explain why this strand has also seen its position progressively erode, of late.

The idea of revisionist Zionism, usually identified with Vladimir Jabotinsky (1880–1944), has emphasized *national redemption* in place of *social redemption*, stressing the need to attain sovereignty. There is greater emphasis on the role of the military, and although "revisionists" believe in an "equalitarian distribution of resources at the level of basic human needs, or a limited welfare state," they also advocate a strong free enterprise system.[12] "Neo–Revisionism," which appeared after the creation of the State of Israel in 1948, continues to emphasize the importance of reestablishing the "Malchut Israel" (Kingdom of Israel) in *the whole* of Mandatory Palestine. It also advocates taking a strong and even militant stand against the Arab powers of the region.[13] This interpretation of Zionism was most influential on a significant block of contemporary Israeli political leaders, including Menachem Begin and Yitzhak Shamir.

Yet a fourth branch of the "traditional" inspiration is "religious Zionism." Motivated by the same nationalistic goals as "regular" Zionism, it seeks to revive traditional Judaism and make it an integral part of the state. Its goals go beyond simply reviving Jewish political independence; it seeks to revive *Jewish* political independence.[14] This has provided its own set of conflicts, some of which we will cover later in this chapter when we discuss Judaism and the interplay of religion and politics in modern Israel.

The interaction of religion and Zionism has led to some interesting, if not paradoxical, confrontations. A relatively small segment of very religious Jews, for example, argue that the very idea of a "Jewish State" is blasphemous. Perhaps the best known of the groups advancing this position is *Neturei Karta* ("Guardians of the City"), who contend that the establishment of a secular State was an "act of rebellion against God," because Jews are "enjoined to wait for God to reestablish a Jewish state." They conclude therefore that "Zionism is the great heresy of modern Judaism," and that the Holocaust, in fact, "was God's punishment for the Zionist heresy, inflicted on the Jewish people for abandoning their true religion and substituting secular nationalism."[15] A logical outcome of this argument is a rejection of anything having to do with the state, including refusal to use money, to serve in the army, and so on.

Most religious Jews, however, do not see an inherent contradiction between Judaism and Zionism. In 1967, for example, the (Sephardic) Chief Rabbi of Israel went so far as to issue the equivalent of a policy paper prohibiting along religious grounds any evacuation of Judea and Samaria.[16] The Gush Emunim, mentioned above, is also typical of these groups. Even one of the mainstream "religious" parties, Mizrachi, is an avowedly religious Zionist organization, having constituted itself as a separate party within the World Zionist Organization as early as 1902.[17]

Many Zionists of today do see a need to separate or "compartmentalize" the concept of Zionism from the question of religion in the state. Some argue that religious Zionism is a noble goal and support the coexistence of religion and Zionism, but argue that this does not imply that religion and Zionism are related. Their goals are different and should not be merged or synthesized. One of the best known contemporary Zionists of this persuasion is the scientist and philosopher Yeshayahu Leibowitz (1903–), who has declared that his Zionism is based upon "being fed up with being ruled by Gentiles," rather than having a direct link with religious doctrine. He further contends that "Zionism is the desire of Jews for political independence in their own land," and "has nothing to do with the cultural, historical, or spiritual essence of Judaism. Hence the State of Israel cannot and ought not concern itself with the problems of Judaism."[18] As might be guessed, the "compartmentalized" notion of Zionism is not acceptable to most religious Zionists.

A general label of "new Zionism" has been placed upon a variety of ideas which can be described as being a rather "loosely–knit belief system which combines secular and religious elements . . . [combining] some broad historiographical strands which deal with the meaning of anti–Semitism and the Holocaust."[19] It is difficult to be specific as to exactly what would and would not be included in all of the "new Zionist" variations. They would undoubtedly entail some discussion of Jewish identity, Jewish land, and Jewish vulnerability without a Jewish state, but the exact balance of these three themes would vary.

It is the political manifestations and interaction of these contending notions of Zionism which has been blamed for many of the tensions at work in the Middle East today. As tersely put by one critic: "My proposition is that the fundamental problem in the Arab–Israeli conflict is the Zionist character of the State of Israel."[20] The thrust of the argument is that the root cause of conflict in the Middle East is not the Moslem–Jewish religious division, but rather the tension caused by substantial Jewish immigration and eventual majority status in a land previously inhabited by an Arab majority. Uri Avnery has written in this vein that:

> The early Zionist settlers were convinced that they were saving not only themselves and their people, but also the Arab peoples around them. They were perplexed, astounded, and progressively angered when the Arab world rejected them instinctively, as though obeying a biological command.
>
> Today the Arab body continues to reject the re–territorialized Israeli nation planted in its midst. Israel, fighting back and winning, has by now nearly forgotten that all it was fighting for initially was acceptance by the body.
>
> The Arabs see Israel not only as an unwanted transplant but as a spreading malignancy that threatens their very existence. The Israelis see the Arabs surrounding them as an eternal menace, eternally rejecting them: 'The Arabs will never make peace.'[21]

Zionism is seen by most Israelis, then, as a philosophy of nationalism and protection for an otherwise vulnerable Jewish majority whose only salvation is a Jewish State with a Jewish majority. Over the years a number of variations on this general theme have arisen stressing culture, economic policy, national security, and so on. It is clear, however, that whatever the variation, the concept of Zionism has been, and continues to be, critical to the State of Israel by providing, despite its permutations, a sense of identity, continuity, and purpose to an otherwise disparate population.

The Religious Communities of Israel

As indicated earlier, one of the most common misperceptions of Israel held by students new to the subject is the assumption that "Israel is a Jewish State, therefore all Israelis must be Jewish." The visibility of Israel's Arabs has been low, but contemporary political tension has made their presence more visible.[22] In fact, nearly 18 percent of the population within the pre–1967 borders, according to recent census data, are non–Jewish. Of these 769,900 non–Jews, roughly 13.1 percent are Christians, 77.2 percent Sunni Moslem, and 9.6 percent Druze.[23] There are very small communities of Greek Catholic, Greek Orthodox, Armenian, Protestant, and Maronite followers as well.[24]

The 1948 Declaration of Independence guaranteed freedom of religion to all citizens. The individual religious communities are free to exercise their faith and administer their internal affairs. Each major community has its own religious courts and the Ministry of Religious Affairs, which is responsible for overseeing the needs of all religious communities in Israel, respects their jurisdictional authority. These bodies have primary responsibility for religious questions, along with personal matters that may be regulated by the religious communities, such as marriage and divorce. Indeed, one of the ironies in Israel is that Christians and Moslems are provided greater degrees of freedom and self–regulation than are some Jewish communities. Specifically, some Reform Jewish leaders argue that they are subject to greater regulation by the Orthodox Jewish majority in Israel than are the non–Jewish sects.

Judaism in Israel

Just as it is a mistake to assume that all Israelis are Jews, so too it is a mistake to assume that all Israeli Jews are alike. In fact, there are several different "trends" in Judaism today, and in many cases the tensions which exist between and among these different "trends" are greater and perceived as more threatening than the tensions which might exist between Jews and non–Jews.[25] This is largely because the various Jewish sects see themselves as competing with each other for influence among the same population, rather than being fearful that the existing non–Jewish communities in Israel will successfully recruit from the Jewish population.

Judaism, unlike various Christian sects, can be referred to as "non–denominational."[26] That is, the same general prayer book is used in religious services throughout the world. However, there *are* differences in the way various groups of Jews practice their religion. There are primarily three major branches of Judaism which exist today: Orthodox, Conservative (or "Traditional"), and Reform (or "Progressive"). The *Orthodox* group tend to be most rigorous in following Jewish religious law, called *halacha*. This often implies interpreting religious laws literally and placing the importance of such law above the conveniences of day–to–day life.[27] *Conservative* Judaism also argues that halacha should govern one's life, but is more flexible about accepting adaptations of halacha and is more receptive to making "reasonable" accommodations. *Reform* Judaism allows and encourages even more adaptation and modification of halacha to respect different individual patterns of living. Reform Jews tend to place greatest emphasis upon Jewish ethics, rather than specific religious edicts, and argue that there should be greater freedom for Jews to decide for themselves how strictly they will follow halacha.[28]

What ends up happening, of course, is that disagreements over interpretation and application develop among these different groups. It has frequently been the case, to cite but one example, that Orthodox leaders have condemned Reform Jews as "no longer being real Jews." They suggest that the Reform wing has so adapted Judaism to be "relevant" to the contemporary world that it has lost a portion of the essence of its theology. Their basic argument has been that both Conservative and Reform Judaism "were responses to Judaism's minority status in a Christian setting, and that they therefore have no place in a Jewish state."[29] When Reform Judaism decided that women could serve as part of the *minyan*[30], Orthodox Judaism responded that the Reformers had deviated so far from traditional interpretations of halacha that it could no longer be accepted as "real" Judaism.

One issue that has proven to be particularly divisive concerns the role of women on (Jewish) religious councils in Israel. In one celebrated instance, an Orthodox woman who was a Labor Party representative to the Yeroham City Council was proposed as one of the Council's candidates for membership on the Yeroham Religious Council, the body that provides religious support services, enters into contracts, and holds property on behalf of the religious community in its district. The Minister for Religious Affairs and the local rabbinate opposed her nomination. She, in turn, appealed on the grounds that opposition to her holding the position was gender-related, referring to a letter addressed to her on May 6, 1986, by the responsible official in the Ministry for Religious Affairs, in which she was told in plain language it was impossible for a woman to be a member of a religious council.[31] The Supreme Court of Israel ruled that since the sole duty of the Council was to supply support services for religious activities, and not to give halachic, or authoritative theological rulings, the only criteria for membership on a council is: (a) that a person must be religious, or at least not anti-religious, and (b) that a person must represent a body or community having some religious interest. The person need *not* have qualifications in law or halacha. On those grounds, the Supreme Court overturned the actions of the Ministry of Religious Affairs and ordered the woman be given her position on the Religious Council, since excluding a person from membership on a Council by virtue of her gender alone violated Israeli law.

The result of this kind of issue is a tension between and among various sects which is often more divisive than that between Jews and non-Jews. The Ministry of Religious Affairs, controlled by Orthodox

Jewish religious political parties almost continually since 1948 as one of their demands for support for coalition governments of the day,[32] has essentially given the non–Jewish religious groups a free hand in their internal governance. However, the Ministry has been much more restrictive in its dealings with the Reform community in Israel, limiting its ability to build synagogues, and requiring that all marriages, divorces, and births be registered in accordance with Orthodox, rather than Conservative or Reform, religious law.[33] Indeed, even rabbis are affected by this policy: Orthodox leaders do not recognize the legitimacy of Conservative and Reform rabbis. As well, Conservative and Reform synagogues receive less state support than do Orthodox ones.[34]

The very question of "Who is a Jew?" has also proven to be an exceptionally divisive and contentious issue in Israeli politics since independence.[35] This deceptively simple question asks which set of rules will decide what constitutes "Jewishness."[36] Will conversions, marriages, and divorces be undertaken according to Orthodox rules as defined by the halacha, or according to the rules of *any* of the major Jewish groups? The answer, more often than not, has been that the Orthodox rules are the rules recognized by the State.

One of the most controversial rulings in this realm by the Supreme Court of Israel was the 1962 "Brother Daniel" case. Briefly, Brother Daniel was born and reared as a Jew in Poland prior to the Second World War. He subsequently converted to Catholicism and became a monk. Later, however, he desired to immigrate to Israel and claimed under the Law of Return that he had that right since he was Jewish by birth, arguing that the sole determining criterion should be the fact that he was born to a Jewish mother. The religious parties, who argued against his case, suggested that although by a strict definition he was Jewish (because he had a Jewish mother), the fact that he had willingly converted to another religion meant that he had given up his claims as a Jew. If he wanted to come to Israel as a Jew, in other words, he would have to "re–convert" to Judaism under the supervision of an Orthodox Rabbi.[37] In the end, the Court denied his request.

A more recent variation occurred in 1986. In this case the Israeli Supreme Court ruled in favor of a new immigrant from the United States who had challenged the Ministry of Interior's labeling her a "convert to Judaism" on her identity papers. The immigrant, Shoshana Miller, was converted to Judaism as a Reform Jew. The Reform movement is not authorized to conduct conversions in Israel, but Ms. Miller claimed that since she had been converted in the United States, she entered Israel "as a Jew." The three–judge Supreme Court panel ruled that although the Population Registry is allowed to specify religious affiliation on an immigrant's identity card, it is not authorized to include "any other details, such as how people achieved their status." The Court ruled that doing so might "undermine the unity of the Jewish people," and added that "such differentiation runs contrary to the spirit of Judaism."[38]

In recent years this general question has surfaced again and again in Israeli politics. Most recently the issue and the nature of religious–political interaction became highly visible during the coalition–formation period immediately following the 1988 Knesset (parliamentary) elections. At that time the Orthodox parties appeared to be the key to the formation of a majority coalition, for either Yitzhak Shamir and his Likud Party or for Shimon Peres and his Labor Party. Their demands, as we shall chronicle in far more detail in Chapter Five, all focused on the principle of turning State policy in a more Orthodox direction. An editorial at the time criticized the Orthodox opinion:

> The Orthodox and *haredi* [ultra–Orthodox] insistence on placing outside the law Jews whom they consider halachically impure is threatening the unity of the Jewish people. That threat should serve to arouse all Israeli patriots who are aware of the overriding importance of that unity, and all the more so in these difficult days. Prime Minister Yitzhak Shamir played the innocent when he told a delegation of the British United Israel Appeal that 'we have no intention of intervening in the internal affairs of our fellow Jews abroad. We are not questioning the legitimacy of any Jew outside Israel.' The amendment to the Law of Return, or the 'conversion law,' which our Orthodox spiritual warriors are demanding, cannot be interpreted in any way other than placing into question the Jewish legitimacy of those whom Shamir condescends to include in the category 'our fellow Jews.' It is only out of respect for Shamir that we say 'playing the innocent' rather than accusing him of insensitivity or of outright, conscious wickedness.[39]

The fact that the support of the Orthodox religious political parties has been absolutely necessary for governments to stay in power has meant over the years that more often than not the government has sided with the Orthodox in these questions. As things turned out in 1988, however, both Likud and Labor found the demands of the religious parties— that the Law of Return be amended so that only Orthodox converts to Judaism would be recognized as "real" Jews eligible for immigration under that law—so distasteful that they joined together in another "National Unity Government," something they both had pledged during the campaign they would not do, in order to avoid the necessity of yielding to the Orthodox demands.

Religion and Politics: Issues

Among the most intensely felt attitudes in the Israeli political world
are those which deal with the interaction of religious and political
values, the former also being among the most private values an individual can hold and the latter by definition requiring public articulation
and behavior. In the extreme, they can lead to the imposition of one's
opinions upon another. As one analyst has put it:

> The State of Israel is poised atop a delicate balance of concessions made
> to the secularists and the religious as the demands of each threaten to
> topple the government. At the extreme of the religious position are those
> Orthodox who see in the establishment of a Jewish state an opportunity
> to recreate a nation based upon, and entirely faithful to, Jewish law and
> tradition. The opposite standpoint is taken by those secularists who ar-
> gue that Israel is no more than the homeland of a people having common
> historic roots.[40]

Reflecting the heterogeneity of Judaism itself is the broad range of differences within Israeli public opinion about what the relationship between religion and politics should be. In one recent study it was apparent that the populace was clearly split on whether the government
should "see to it that public life is conducted in accordance with Jewish
religious tradition." A depiction of the distribution of public opinion
would reflect an almost–evenly divided population, in a roughly symmetrical distribution, similar to that reflected in Figure 3.1.

The problem is that despite the symmetry of the relationship illustrated in Figure 3.1, the *policy relationship* is not so symmetrical. Non–
religious Jews should not be surprised, one observer has written, "that
while they respect the Orthodox and their needs, such consideration is
not always mutual. 'Live and let live,' pleads the non–Orthodox Israeli
Jew, not grasping that this is a secular concept at total odds with pure
religious faith."[41] In other words,

> whereas even the most anti–religious Jew respects the fact that the reli-
> gious Jew has inviolable boundaries of behaviour beyond which he can-
> not go, such as eating non–kosher food or desecrating the Sabbath, reli-
> gious leaders tend to assert that such limits do not exist on the other side.[42]

It is this belief on the part of the religious leaders—that non–religious
Jews have no finite limits on their behaviour—that prompts them to
want to use the instruments of the state to *legislate* these limits. And, of
course, the values that are used to determine what these limits should
be come from religious orthodoxy.

FIGURE 3.1
Religion and Politics

Should the Government See To It That Public Life Is Conducted in
Accordance with Jewish Religious Tradition? (1981)

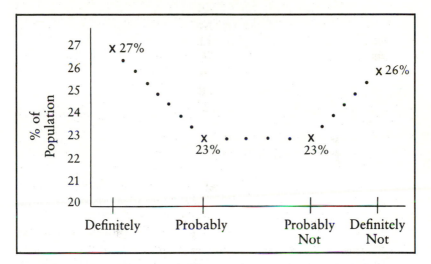

Source: Based Upon Asher Arian, Politics in Israel *(Chatham, N.J.: Chatham House Publishers, 1985, p. 217.)*

Although the public is divided on what the government's role should be in seeing that daily life is conducted according to Jewish religious tradition, it is clear that the bulk of Israeli society does not *itself* observe Jewish religious law to the letter. In fact, as illustrated in Table 3.1, 77 percent of the population responded that they observe Jewish religious law "only somewhat" or "not at all."

Despite the fact that a vast majority of the population is not Orthodox in the sense of their observation of Jewish religious law, there have been few sustained efforts to *decrease* the degree to which Jewish religion is reflected in the law of the state. If anything, Judaism is reinforced in the practices of the state in a number of ways. National holidays are Jewish holidays, not Christian or Moslem, although members of those communities are certainly permitted to practice freely their own. Public transportation does not run on the Jewish Sabbath, movie theaters are closed, as are restaurants, from sunset Friday until sunset Saturday—and do not reopen until the Sabbath is officially declared over.[43] In 1982 a major controversy developed regarding El Al, the national airline. The religious parties likewise wanted the airline to be

TABLE 3.1
Observance of Jewish Religious Law
(1981)

To the letter	9%
Quite a bit	14
Only somewhat	43
Not at all	34

Source: Adapted from Asher Arian, Politics in Israel (Chatham, N.J.: Chatham House Publishers, 1985, p. 217.)

grounded on the Sabbath, since it was owned and supported by the Government. The airline protested, arguing that it would lose too much business if that were the case. After a great deal of debate and a near–toppling of the Government, the authorities gave in to the demands of the religious parties and ceased El Al's Sabbath operations.[44]

One scholar has suggested that there are three levels of interaction between the state and religion in Israel: the symbolic, the institutional, and the legislational.[45] On the *symbolic* level are the many images of Jewish religious tradition which appear in Israeli life. The seven–branched candelabrum, or menorah, is the official symbol of the country and appears on stamps, money, and in a number of official contexts. On the *institutional* level we can identify a number of different types of religious institutions which are funded by the state or which have official governmental status. The Ministry of Religious Affairs underwrites a number of them and the Government has traditionally respected an Orthodox monopoly in this regard. The primary issue has been the amount of autonomy granted to religious institutions, as well as "the extent of the state's right to supervise the activity and influence the structure and policy of these institutions."[46] In terms of *religious legislation* there exist a number acts of cooperation, including a wide body of "Sabbath law," closing cinemas, regulating hotel and restaurant behavior, bus lines, and so on. This kind of legislation also includes rules governing marriages and divorces, and even includes laws governing pig–farming.

There are several reasons why the vast non–Orthodox majority has never been able, or inclined, to push for the separation of church and state. First and foremost is politics. All Israeli governments since Independence have been coalition governments which customarily include religious party representation. As one scholar has noted,

> A significant aspect of the religious problem in Israel is the ability of the religious parties, with the backing of only fifteen percent of the electorate, to impose the rule of the Torah (religious law) on the Jewish community. The mechanism through which the religious parties have exercised their influence has been the machinery of government.[47]

This means that the major parties have been forced to depend upon the religious parties for their support in order to stay in power, and one of the major demands of the religious parties in return for this support has been the maintenance of the "status quo" with respect to the role of religion in the state.[48]

An additional reason for this lack of separation between religion and the state has been the feeling on the part of many non–Orthodox Jews that while *they* might not be Orthodox themselves, it is appropriate for the state to at least be sympathetic. After all, if the Orthodox population cannot receive governmental support in Israel, where can it ever expect to? This explains the almost–contradictory data presented in Figure 3.1 and Table 3.1. There are clearly many individuals who are not personally observers of Jewish religious law, but who still feel that it may be appropriate for the State to promote adherence to Judaism (the 50% indicating "definitely" or "probably" that public life be conducted in accordance with Jewish religious tradition).

In more recent years, especially since 1977 when the government of Menachem Begin came to power with the assistance of Agudat Israel (an "ultra–orthodox" religious party) there has been a greater frequency of highly contentious and controversial religious policy issues introduced into the political agenda.[49] Although examples occurred in 1977, perhaps the clearest instance appeared in the 1981 coalition agreement when Agudat Israel convinced the government to take positions on the following:

1. strengthening government policy against abortion;
2. strengthening the protection of Jewish gravesites against the activities of archaeologists, road builders, and property developers;
3. strengthening policy against autopsies;
4. facilitating the excuse of women from military service;
5. strengthening policy forbidding work on the sabbath and religious holidays;
6. applying religious law to the state's determination of who is a Jew and insisting that only conversions carried out by Orthodox rabbis will be recognized;

7. opposing the activities of Christian missionaries;
8. strengthening regulations against the production or sale of non-kosher food; and,
9. forbidding swearing in the name of God in court proceedings.[50]

Again in 1988, following the elections to the Knesset, the ability of the Orthodox religious parties to play a crucial role in the creation of a government coalition gave them great leverage in forcing the government to accept more Orthodox interpretations of social policy, although eventually the religious parties were so unrelenting in their demands that they ended up alienating themselves from the other significant actors in the coalition–formation process. Although we shall present a more detailed analysis of the role of the Orthodox religious parties in this coalition–formation illustration in Chapter Five, it is enough to note here that the religious parties *were* significant. Their demands upon Mr. Shamir, the Prime Minister–designate were so strong that they forced him to form a coalition with Shimon Peres, leader of the Labor Party and his chief opponent for political leadership in Israel, rather than join with them as was his initial inclination.

Zionism, Religion and the State

We began this chapter by noting that while one of the fundamental goals of Israel's founders had been that of a Jewish majority in a Jewish state, there have obviously been problems with its realization. It is often the case that terms which on the surface may appear to have a clear and unambiguous meaning may not be, in fact, as clear and obvious upon closer examination as we had thought. Terms such as "Zionism," and "Judaism," therefore, must be looked at more carefully in this light. Not all Zionists are cast from the same mold for there can be, have been, and clearly are today quite significant differences among them. "Zionism" can variously have a cultural, economic, military, or religious interpretation, to name but a few of the possible variations. And although we offer no definitive positions on whether one or another of these is more "correct," it *is* the case that as students of Israeli politics we must be careful about understanding what assumptions we and others are using.

Similarly, we saw that "To Be a Jew" means different things to different people. Some might interpret "Jewishness" as an ethnic or historical label. For others, it has very rigorous and strict behavioral implications. Views having to do with the relationship between a "Jewish

State" and the "Jewish Religion" vary considerably, from the ultra–Orthodox who wish to institutionalize "theopolitics,"[51] to those who desire a complete and strict separation of the two.

Our task here has not been to evaluate these positions, to suggest that some views of Zionism are more correct than others, or that certain relationships between religion and politics are more valid or more legitimate. Rather, the goal of this chapter has been to impress upon the student that the political world in Israel is made even more complicated than it might otherwise be by virtue of the existence of these sources of potential political division. Not only does Israel have the "normal" political issues which must be addressed by any state—such as economics, foreign policy, social welfarism, and the like—it also has to address questions such as "Who is a Jew?," or "What should the government do to promote or restrict the role of religious orthodoxy?" What we shall later see is the fact that these issues surface over and over as *political*, rather than exclusively religious, matters.

NOTES

1. For a discussion of the distinction between Hassidic and Orthodox Jews, and the nature of Hassidism generally, see Harry Rabinowicz, *Hasidism and the State of Israel* (Rutherford, N.J.: Fairleigh Dickinson University Press, 1982).

2. One of the most impressive and thorough histories of this period is that of Walter Laqueur, *A History of Zionism* (New York: Holt, Rinehart, and Winston, 1972).

3. Jacob Tsur, *Zionism: The Saga of a National Liberation Movement* (New Brunswick, N.J.: Transaction Books, 1976), p. 9. A very sophisticated discussion of Zionism as a national movement, comparing it to nationalism found in African states, can be found in Dan V. Segre, *A Crisis of Identity: Israel and Zionism* (Oxford, Oxford University Press, 1980), pp. 1–13.

4. Tsur, *Zionism*, p. 10.

5. Ofira Seliktar, *New Zionism and the Foreign Policy System of Israel* (Carbondale, IL: Southern Illinois University Press, 1986), pp. 5–6.

6. Charles S. Liebman and Eliezer Don–Yehiya, *Civil Religion in Israel: Traditional Judaism and Political Culture in the Jewish State* (Los Angeles: University of California Press, 1983).

7. Tsur, *Zionism*, pp. 77–79.

8. Ibid., p. 82.

9. "Judea" and "Samaria" are geographical names referring to the territory which is discussed in the Bible as the "traditional" land of the Jews. The Judean and Samarian Mountains make up the bulk of the land in what today is called the "Occupied Territory" of the West Bank.

10. Segre, *A Crisis of Identity*, p. 154.

11. Seliktar, *New Zionism*, p. 115.

12. Ibid., p. 80.

13. Ibid., p. 91.

14. Segre, *A Crisis of Identity*, p. 153.

15. Liebman and Don–Yehiya, *Civil Religion*, p. 17.

16. Seliktar, *New Zionism*, p. 97.

17. Liebman and Don–Yehiya, *Civil Religion*, p. 189.

18. Ibid., p. 192.

19. Seliktar, *New Zionism*, p. 74.

20. Norton Mezvinsky, "The Zionist Character of the State of Israel," in Gary Smith, ed., *Zionism: The Dream and the Reality—A Jewish Critique* (New York: David and Charles, 1974), p. 244.

21. Uri Avnery, *Israel Without Zionism: A Plan for Peace in the Middle East* (New York: Collier Books, 1971), pp. 251–52.

22. Smooha, *Social Research on Arabs in Israel, 1948–1977: Trends and an Annotated Bibliography* (Ramat Gan: Turtledove Publishing, 1978).

23. *Statistical Abstract of Israel: 1987* (Jerusalem: Central Bureau of Statistics, 1987), p. 30.

24. *Facts About Israel* (Jerusalem: Ministry of Foreign Affairs, 1985), pp. 86, 89.

25. Two very good general studies are Sheva Abramov, *Perpetual Dilemma: Jewish Religion in the Jewish State* (Rutherford, N.J.: Associated University Presses, 1975), and Clement Leslie, *The Rift in Israel: Religious Authority and Secular Democracy* (New York: Schocken, 1971).

26. *Facts About Israel*, p. 90.

27. There are significant differences *within* Orthodoxy, too. The "Jewish Fundamentalists" have played a very significant role in recent Israeli politics, both in terms of domestic policy demands and in terms of demands having to do with foreign policy, especially in the Occupied Territory of the West Bank. The latter point will be further developed later in this book. For a detailed discussion of Jewish fundamentalism in Israel, see the recent volume by Ian Lustick, *For the Land and the Lord: Jewish Fundamentalism in Israel* (New York: Council on Foreign Relations, 1988).

28. This is a summary of a presentation of trends in modern Judaism presented in *Facts About Israel*, p. 90.

29. Norman Zucker, *The Coming Crisis in Israel: Private Faith and Public Policy* (Cambridge: M.I.T. Press, 1973), p. 90.

30. The quorum traditionally made up of ten adult males required for the purposes of formal worship.

31. See Asher Felix Landau, "The Woman and the Religious Council," *Jerusalem Post*, Monday, June 6, 1988, p. 5.

32. On the role of religious parties, see Gary Schiff, *Tradition and Politics: The Religious Parties of Israel* (Detroit: Wayne State University Press, 1977).

33. Indeed, one of the leaders of the World Reform Judaism movement once commented that it was ironic that Reform Jews had greater freedom in Europe and America, non–Jewish states, than they had in Israel, a Jewish state. Interview with Moshe Kol, at the Knesset, Jerusalem, June 1975.

34. Charles Liebman and Eliezer Don–Yehiya, *Religion and Politics in Israel* (Bloomington, IN: Indiana University Press, 1984), p. 19.

35. For a very interesting discussion of the matter, see the essay "What Does It Mean to Be a Jew?" by Eliezer Schweid in his book *Israel at the Crossroads*, translated by Alton Winters (Philadelphia: Jewish Publication Society of America, 1973), pp. 9–42.

36. Benjamin Akzin, "Who is a Jew? A Hard Case," *Israel Law Review* 5:2 (1970): 259–63; or Oscar Kraines, *The Impossible Dilemma: Who is a Jew in the State of Israel* (New York: Bloch, 1976).

37. See the fuller discussion of this case in Asher Arian, *Politics in Israel* (Chatham, N.J.: Chatham House, 1985), p. 220.

38. "Israeli Court Upholds a Convert," *New York Times*, December 3, 1986, p. 1.

39. Editorial in *Ha'aretz*, November 24, 1988, as reprinted in "Israel Press Highlights," (New York: Institute of Human Relations) November 28, 1988, p. 1.

40. Zucker, *The Coming Crisis*, p. 2.

41. Danny Shapiro, "Israel and Religious Orthodoxy," *Jerusalem Post*, June 6, 1988, p. 8.

42. Ibid.

43. Although the "religious" definition of the end of the Sabbath is when three stars can be seen in the sky, in fact there are timetables printed indicating the start and end of Sabbath so that merchants and businesspersons are not at the mercy of visibility!

44. See the discussion of the El Al issue in Ira Sharkansky, *What Makes Israel Tick? How Domestic Policy–Makers Cope with Constraints* (Chicago: Nelson Hall, 1975), pp. 67–69.

45. What follows is a discussion based upon that offered by Liebman and Don–Yehiya, *Religion and Politics*, pp. 15–30.

46. Ibid., p. 19.

47. Ervin Birnbaum, *The Politics of Compromise: State and Religion in Israel* (Rutherford: Fairleigh Dickinson University Press, 1970), p. 269.

48. For a full discussion of the "Status Quo" agreement and problems of religion and politics in Israel, see Liebman and Don–Yehiya, *Religion and Politics*, 31–40, "The 'Status Quo' Agreement as a Solution to Problems of Religion and State in Israel."

49. See the chapter "Israel After Begin: The View From the Religious Parties," by Gary S. Schiff, in Steve Heydemann, ed., *The Begin Era: Issues in Contemporary Israel* (Boulder: Westview Press, 1984), pp. 41–52.

50. Sharkansky, *What Makes Israel Tick?*, p. 60.

51. This word is used frequently in Zucker's *The Coming Crisis in Israel*.

Chapter 4

THE CONSTITUTIONAL SYSTEM AND ISRAELI PARLIAMENTARY GOVERNMENT

Introduction

By this juncture the formal creation of Israel and its contemporary social, economic, and religious features should be familiar to the reader. Our focus now can shift to a description of the constitutional principles and major structural components of the Israeli political system. Merging the societal with the structural will in turn facilitate our understanding of the system's subsequent evolution since 1948.

The establishment of a written constitution is considered essential for any modern nation–state. Constitutions have been seen as "power maps,"[1] playing an important role in a political system by providing broad guidelines for permissible and impermissible political behavior. In addition, a constitution provides the yardstick for judicial review and the set of standards for monitoring legislative or executive actions.

At the same time we acknowledge the importance of written constitutions, we must recognize that *written constitutions* do not guarantee *constitutional government*. A written constitution is a document which contains an expression of the fundamental principles of the regime, as well as a description of the political structures and processes according to which the regime must operate. Constitutional government, to be more precise, refers to a government of limited power, a regime in which there are boundaries beyond which the government simply may not go in its behavior. It is therefore possible, using this distinction, to have constitutional governments with formal written constitutions (the United States or France), constitutional government without formal written constitutions (Israel or Britain), "unconstitutional" governments with formal written constitutions (the U.S.S.R.), and "unconstitutional" governments without formal written constitutions (Nigeria after the recent military coup). The point to note here is that it is possible to over–emphasize the importance of a written piece of paper, since the actual *behavior* of a regime may be more important than the extent to which it has created a set of legal documents.[2]

The political culture which has developed in Israel over the past four decades has been less concerned with formal structures.[3] Israel has no explicit Bill of Rights or specifically created constitution to provide clear and unambiguous guidelines for governmental power. Yet, the Israeli polity is a stable democracy. How this condition of stability has come about in a culture of such remarkable diversity will be a central focus of this investigation.

The Debate Over Creating a Written Constitution

The United Nations Resolution of November 29, 1947—which advocated the partition of Palestine into two independent states, one Arab and one Jewish—required the states to adopt written constitutions.[4] In addition to requiring the creation of a constitution, the Resolution stipulated a number of other points, including:

1. establishment of a legislature elected by secret ballot and universal suffrage, and an executive responsible to the legislature;
2. settling international disputes peacefully;
3. accepting an obligation to refrain from the threat or use of force;
4. guaranteeing equal non–discriminatory rights in religious, economic, and political areas, to all persons, including human rights, freedom of religion, language, speech, education, publication, assembly, and association; and,
5. preservation of freedom of visiting and transit for residents and citizens of the "other" state in Palestine, "subject to considerations of national security."[5]

In the Declaration of the Establishment of the State of Israel, which was proclaimed on May 14, 1948, the United Nations Resolution was reiterated, and a commitment was undertaken to have an elected "constituent assembly" meet to adopt a constitution not later than October 1, 1948. This commitment was not kept because of Israel's national war for survival following the Arab military invasion. During this period of time, however, the Provisional State Council did undertake a number of discussions and appointed a committee to work on a written constitution.

In July, 1948, the Provisional Council of State appointed a committee of eight as a Constitutional Committee, "to assemble, study, and catalogue pertinent recommendations and material, and to prepare a draft constitution which, together with minority opinions in the committee, shall be submitted to the Constituent Assembly for its consideration."[6] This Committee was not asked to consider whether a constitution *should* be written; its recommendations were based upon the premise that the document *would* be written. On November 18, 1948, the Provisional Council of State passed the Constituent Assembly Elections Ordinance, calling for the election of a Constituent Assembly. Two months later the Council passed the Constituent Assembly (Transition) Ordinance, transferring all of its powers to the Constituent Assembly. The Constituent Assembly was elected on January 25, 1949, and on March 8, 1949 it transformed itself into the First Knesset.

During the three weeks of its existence the Constituent Assembly, before it became the First Knesset, enacted the Transition Law (February 16, 1949). This law was, in fact, a mini–constitution, containing chapters on the Knesset, the President, the Government, and other provisions.[7] But the Assembly never fully debated, much less adopted, a written constitution. The Assembly did table a draft constitution authored by Dr. Leo Kohn, a political advisor to then–Prime Minister David Ben–Gurion,[8] but did not take it up again until it met as the First Knesset.[9]

Between May and December of 1949 the Knesset Committee on Constitution, Law, and Justice devoted eight special sessions to the question of a constitution.[10] A number of arguments were put forward against a written constitution. Among the leading opponents was David Ben–Gurion, who, with other leaders of the Mapai party, argued that there was no reason to rush into a task that clearly needed to be handled with care and precision.[11] Opponents of a written constitution also looked to England for a precedent, arguing that if the British, with their history of stable democratic government, did not need a written constitution, then perhaps Israel could survive without one, too. Supporters of a written constitution, on the other hand, retorted that the parallel with the "unwritten" British constitution was a fallacious one because Britain was an established democracy with "built–in conventional safeguards." Israel, in their estimation, had "not yet developed sufficiently powerful and respected conventions to safeguard its system. Therefore, it was argued, Israel needed a written constitution."[12]

Beyond this, Ben–Gurion contended that Israel's population was in such a state of flux, already having doubled by 1949 and now on the verge of tripling, that writing a constitution might not be such a good idea. He suggested that "it was rather 'basic laws' without special status that were needed."[13]

> At the present time, the population of Israel represents only a small segment of world Jewry. But the aim of the State of Israel is to take in as many Jews as possible from the Diaspora countries. What right has such a State to adopt a constitution which will be binding on millions of men, women, and children yet to settle within its borders.[14]

Consequently, he declared that "no written constitution be adopted until Israel's population stabilized and the threat of Arab invasion vanished."[15]

Another major stumbling block to a written constitution, likewise foreseen by Ben–Gurion, concerned religious groups in the polity. The question of the degree to which religious principles should be entrenched in an Israeli constitution was one which bothered many citizens, both religious and non–religious, and was clearly one for which a solution could not be readily discovered.[16] The two "camps" involved disagreed profoundly. Those referred to as "secularists" advocated Israel developing a constitution similar to those of other Western, liberal states. On the other side, spokesmen for the religious faction claimed that the Torah and its tradition should make up any written constitution, which would be superior to any man–made legislation, "since it was of Divine origin." Because it was felt that constitutions are items upon which consensus should be developed, rather than items to be unilaterally imposed, it was decided that it would be better to put together, piece by piece, legislation that would eventually form Israel's constitution.[17]

On June 13, 1950, the Knesset voted by a 50–30 margin to postpone indefinitely the adoption of a formal written constitution and decided instead to allow for its gradual creation, with the individual pieces to be designated "Fundamental Laws." The Resolution read:

> The First Knesset directs the Constitution, Law and Justice Committee to prepare a draft constitution for the State. The Constitution shall be constructed article by article in such a manner that each shall in itself constitute a fundamental law.
>
> Each article shall be brought before the Knesset as the Committee completes its work, and all the articles together shall comprise the State Constitution.[18]

An additional point that is still perceived by many to be part of the June, 1950, understanding was the assumption that at some point in the future the entire body of Fundamental Laws would be consolidated into a single document to be known as the Constitution of Israel.

The outcome of the 1950 Resolution has continued to be subjected to broad interpretation. Ben–Gurion and his supporters interpreted the vote as opposition to an "entrenched" constitution and as a vote for complete constitutional flexibility, meaning there would be no laws of a "privileged position." Since the Resolution said nothing about the time frame within which the Fundamental Laws had to be written—although since the Resolution stipulated that this would be done by the First Knesset there was an implied time parameter—Ben–Gurion and his supporters were in no hurry. Indeed, the first of the Fundamental Laws was not passed until eight years later.[19]

There were, on the other hand, a number of leaders in Israel who, for a variety of reasons, supported the creation of a written constitution. One argument, of course, was that Israel had already committed itself to write such a document. Not doing so would be a breach of faith with major international actors, primarily the United Nations and those countries which had supported the creation of the State of Israel. Further, many saw the "Fundamental Laws" as not being the functional equivalent of a constitution, since they would be passed by simple majorities of the Knesset, and thus could be reversed by the same majorities. They argued instead that a constitution should be a more "special" and inflexible document than the Fundamental Laws would be. It should also require more than simple majorities—at least two–thirds or three–fourths of the legislature, for example—to come into existence.

In addition, a number of other arguments were put forward in favor of a written constitution, including: that a constitution would provide a firm basis for the government of the state, defining rights of the citizens, limiting powers of authorities, and regulating relations between the branches of the government; that since virtually every other country in the world had a constitution Israel should have one, too; that a constitution has both educational and patriotic significance for the country; and, that a constitution would be a symbol of national unity, which was especially important to Israel when it was welcoming immigrants from all over the world.[20]

In the end, the forces advocating inaction prevailed, as might have been predicted. Since the Resolution of June 13, 1950, the Knesset has passed a number of Fundamental Laws, but it has yet to "complete" its work and consolidate all of the Fundamental Laws into a single document. Some legal scholars have accordingly questioned the legitimacy of the Fundamental Laws because, unlike the First Knesset (which did not pass any Fundamental Laws), the Second and subsequent Knessot[21] did not have the same authority to enact "superior law" which was given to the First Knesset by the Constituent Assembly. They claim that only the First Knesset was a continuation of the Constituent Assembly. When it failed to adopt a written constitution, there was no duly authorized body to carry out that task.[22] Technically, then, the Fundamental Laws cannot be considered constitutional.[23] Others respond that since the powers of one democratically elected legislature are passed to the next democratically elected legislature, all Knessot have had constitution–making legitimacy.[24] After four decades of debate, it seems safe to say, no consensus is discernable.

The Structures of the Israeli "Constitution"

A well–known scholar of Israeli politics has written that it is not clear whether the classification "Fundamental Law" includes "only such legislation as has formally received that designation, or whether it may be used to define any law dealing with constitutional matters."[25] Fundamental Laws, except for their unusual titles, do not carry any specific features distinguishing them from other Acts of the Knesset. As another analyst has noted:

> Since the resolution of 1950 did not define the term "Basic Law," many considered it to apply to all laws of fundamental constitutional content passed by the Knesset, like, for example, the Law of the Return (1950), which provides that every Jew has the right to immigrate to Israel, or the Nationality Law (1952) . . . At one point Knesset Chairman Kadish Luz cited twenty–two 'laws of a constitutional nature' in addition to the two formal Basic Laws then on the statute books, and asserted that the task laid down in the 1950 resolution had already been largely accomplished.[26]

We noted earlier that with only a few exceptions Fundamental Laws can be changed at any time by a simple majority of the Knesset. One example of these exceptions can be found in "Fundamental Law: The Knesset," which has clauses that can only be amended by absolute Knesset majorities (61 votes out of 120), and one clause that would require a two–thirds vote to amend, regardless of the number of members present. While a section in the Judiciary Law makes its structure and powers totally immune from Emergency Regulations, it is the only "constitutional" legislation protected in this way. In fact, on those occasions when the Knesset has passed laws which have conflicted with Fundamental Law: the Knesset, and the Supreme Court of Israel has struck them down as unconstitutional, the Knesset has simply reiterated those same laws with an absolute majority and the legislation has then been interpreted as amending the Fundamental Law.

Thus far, eight "chapters" of an Israeli constitution have been written, each called a Fundamental Law. These laws are acts of the Knesset which have been passed by a regular majority (a majority of those present and voting), not an absolute majority. Fundamental laws are endowed with a "special" position when compared to regular legislation, but since they are simple decisions of a majority of those present and voting they can, in principle, be modified or done away with by a simple majority as well. The eight Fundamental Laws which have been passed by the Knesset are: (1) The Knesset (1958); (2) Israel Lands (1960); (3) The President of the State (1964); (4) The Government (1968); (5) The

1975); (6) The Army (1976); (7) Jerusalem: Capital of
d (8) The Judiciary (1984).[27] Three other fundamental
mptroller," "Citizens' Rights," and "Legislative Pro-
the process of being prepared. These eleven Fundamental Laws coll..tively make up Israel's "Constitution."[28]

In addition to Fundamental Laws, a number of other pieces of legislation have been passed by the Knesset over the years that have taken on
a quasi–constitutional status in terms of both their legal importance
and their contribution to the country's political culture. Included
among them would be the Law and Administration Ordinance (1948),
which established a massive body of Ottoman and British law as Israeli
law; the Law of Return (1950), which laid out the fundamental principles of the rights of Jews to immigrate to Israel and the responsibilities
of the state to help them in this effort; the Equal Rights for Women Law
(1951), giving women equal political and legal rights in the state; the
Nationality Law (1952), which regulated the naturalization of non–
Jews; the Judges' Law (1953), setting up a framework for the appointment of judges; and the Courts Law (1969), which established several
different systems of courts for different classes of litigation.

The first of the Fundamental Laws to be passed, Fundamental Law:
The Knesset, dealt with the relations between the branches of government. The Knesset was entrusted with electing the head of state, the
President, for a five year term. The President is responsible only to the
Knesset, and it alone has the power of removal from office for miscon-
duct or incapacity. Special majorities, however, are required to elect
and remove the President. Although the President has a legal obligation
to sign legislation from the Knesset, he has no veto power; nor can he
refuse to sign a legislative act. The President also plays a role in the
formation of the Government. According to Fundamental Law: the
Government, it is the job of the President to "entrust to one of the
Members of the Knesset the duty of forming a Government." Before
this Fundamental Law was passed, there was much debate in Israel over
whether the Prime Minister had to be a member of Knesset; since 1968
the question has been moot.[29]

The Presidency itself was first created in the February, 1949, Transition Law. The intention was to model it after the British head of state,
but in a republican rather than monarchical form of government.
Chaim Weizmann, the first President of Israel, advocated an American–
style "strong" presidency. His conception lost out to that of David
Ben–Gurion, who advocated a "weak" head of state and a "strong"
Prime Minister. The following anecdote illustrates the result: In 1951
the visiting American Secretary of Labor passed on a message from

President Truman to President Weizmann expressing Truman's disappointment that Weizmann "had not taken a stronger position concerning the protection of Arab refugees. 'I am only a constitutional President,' replied Dr. Weizmann, 'and it's outside my province. My handkerchief is the only thing I can stick my nose into. Into everything else—it's Ben–Gurion's nose.'"[30] Such colorful anecdotes are no longer common because the constitutional relationship of the President and the Prime Minister is well known, yet the dual roles are maintained: When Egypt's President Sadat undertook his extraordinarily courageous trip to Jerusalem in November, 1977, after his arrival at Ben–Gurion Airport he travelled to Jerusalem in a limousine with Yitzhak Navon, the President of Israel, and not with Menachem Begin, the Prime Minister, because Navon was the President, or Head of State. He negotiated, however, with Menachem Begin, the Prime Minister and Chief Executive of the government.

The Role of the Courts in the Creation of a Constitution

Due to the absence of a written constitution the Supreme Court of Israel has often had no concrete source of law higher than acts of the Knesset upon which to base its decisions. [31] This means that when the Court has handed down decisions it has always done so with questionable legitimacy.[32] The real reason for this may have more to do with politics than with principle. One of the rationales offered in opposition to the establishment of a written constitution was suggested by the Mapai party: A written constitution would lead to an activist court and the development of American–style judicial review.[33] Many political leaders were hesitant to accept an arrangement which would result in taking political power away from the legislature and placing it in the hands of a non–elected judiciary.

Thus the theme of a Knesset hesitant to divest itself of any political power is one that appears recurrently:

> The idea of the sovereignty of the Knesset (on the British model) had great appeal to the strongest political party in the Knesset. Those who opposed the adoption of a written formal constitution and promised, instead, a flexible Israeli constitution were probably inspired by this political consideration.[34]

The importance of the principle of legislative supremacy—that the Knesset is the ultimate source of constitutional dogma by a majority

vote—has several implications for the role of the Court. First, the jurisdiction of the Court is *limited by* the Knesset; the Court is not in a
position *to limit* the jurisdiction of the Knesset.[35] Second, when the
Court has chosen to adjudicate, its decisions are based upon the principle of legislative sovereignty. Only very rarely has it questioned
Knesset legislation in a specific instance, and never has it questioned the
ability of a *majority* of the Knesset to do anything it wanted. Third,
because of the principle of legislative supremacy the Court cannot "say
what the law is,"[36] which the Court has argued is the role of the
Knesset. Thus, the absence of a formal, written constitution combined
with the principle of legislative supremacy have resulted in a Court with
strictly limited abilities to shape the "constitution" of the nation. On
those occasions when the Court has been willing to become more active
its rulings have been limited and politically very cautious. As a group,
the Court has expressed the belief that its function is to uphold the law,
rather than to make it.[37] A few examples of this attitude will be examined here.

The earliest instance of the Court avoiding political cases was
Jabotinsky v. Weizmann (1951). This was also the first time the term
"justiciability" was used by the Court.[38] The question under review
concerned the mechanics of forming a new government. One of the
President's powers as set forth in the Transition Law was to form new
governments when the need arose. After consulting with the representatives of the political parties, the President was to assign the task of
actually forming it to a Knesset member who was prepared to undertake the effort. In this case, after receiving a Knesset vote of non–
confidence David Ben–Gurion had resigned as Prime Minister. The
President, Chaim Weizmann, consulted with party leaders and subsequently asked Ben–Gurion to try to form a new coalition. Ben–Gurion
refused. At that point, the President quit trying, and Ben–Gurion introduced a motion of dissolution calling for the election of a new Knesset.[39] Suit was brought by members of the Opposition, claiming that
Weizmann had failed to fulfill his duty to "entrust a member of the
Knesset" with the task of forming a government by prematurely permitting Ben–Gurion to move for its dissolution. Their argument was
that Jabotinsky, the leader of the Opposition, might have been able to
form a coalition if he had been given the opportunity.

In rendering its verdict the Court ruled that the entire question was
"political," and therefore "not justiciable."

> The whole subject of the duty of forming a Government . . . is nonjusti-
> ciable and beyond the scope of judicial determination . The relationships

involved are in their very nature outside the field of judicial inquiry; they are relationships between the President of the State, the Government and the Knesset, that is to say the executive and parliamentary authorities . . . The remedy must be found through parliamentary means . . . in the reaction of the Knesset to (the) Government . . .[40]

The principle established was very clear: Henceforth the Court would avoid "political" questions which dealt with issues best resolved by the legislature itself, including questions dealing with the legislature's scope of authority.

The later case of *Basul v. the Minister of Interior* (1965) concerned a legislative act dealing with the prohibition of pig raising in certain areas of Israel which were to be designated on a map. At the time the bill was passed, however, the Knesset had not yet completed the design of the necessary map, so the law could not be enforced. A Moslem petitioner, resenting pig raising in his area, appealed to the Supreme Court, claiming that the prohibition against pig raising should still apply because it was the Knesset's fault that it did not have the map completed, rather than a problem with the law itself. The Justice, J. Berinson, who authored the majority opinion dismissing the case, claimed:

I doubt whether we [the Court] have the power to deny the validity of a law duly passed by the Knesset, even if it contains an error of fact or is based on faulty premises. In other words, it is doubtful whether a Court can look beyond the law and examine its correctness or compliance with the facts . . . The Knesset is the legislative authority in the State and, as such, is sovereign.[41]

Once again the Court's reluctance to strike down legislation reflected its desire to support the Knesset and its belief that parliament should be supreme in the political system. The Court has followed a doctrine of deferring action in cases that are labelled as "political," and has disclaimed the power to amend or annul a law of the Knesset, believing that legislative supremacy is the very "keystone" of the Israeli constitutional system.[42]

In the case of *Shalit v. the Minister of Interior* (1969), the view that the Court's function does not include making policy was further substantiated. The case involved the request of a Jewish father and an agnostic mother of non–Jewish heritage that their children be registered as "of Jewish nationality but without religion."[43] The registration officer refused to register the children as Jews, claiming that according to Halachic[44] rules "a child born to a non–Jewish mother cannot be registered as a Jew."[45] The father petitioned the Supreme Court, with the majority eventually ruling by a five–to–four margin—after two years of reflection and consideration—that the registration officer had to enroll the children in accordance with the information of the declarant "unless he had reasonable grounds to believe that the declaration was not correct."[46] The important principle in this case is that the Court refused to *make* law and interpret the question on religious grounds (i.e. should the Orthodox rules about the mother's religious background be the deciding factor?), but simply said that the law of the Knesset indicated that the Minister of Interior was to register children according to parents' information.

Probably the most famous decision by the Supreme Court of Israel—often compared to *Marbury v. Madison* in the United States—was the case of *Bergman v. the Minister of Interior* (1969). The plaintiff, Dr. Aaron Bergman, had brought suit before the Court seeking to prevent the Minister of Finance from acting under a provision of the Financing Law of 1969 that provided for governmental financing of political parties in election campaigns.[47] Dr. Bergman claimed that the Financing Law unfairly discriminated against new political parties since it provided governmental financing only for those parties that already had seats in the (outgoing) Knesset. Bergman argued that such an inequity required the Court to invalidate the Financing Law by reason of Section Four of Fundamental Law: The Knesset, which provides that

> The Knesset shall be elected by general, national, direct . . . equal elections in accordance with the Knesset Elections Laws. This section shall not be varied save by a majority of the members of the Knesset.

Bergman argued that the Financing Law was in conflict with Section Four in that it produced an election that was not "equal."[48] In addition, he contended that the Financing Law could not be regarded as a valid amendment to the Fundamental Law since the Financing Law *was passed by less than the majority of the total membership of the Knesset*, as required for a valid amendment under the terms of Section Four.

The Court's decision would clearly establish the principle of judicial review, but like the *Marbury* decision did so in a way that was politically acceptable at the time. Justice Landau, speaking on behalf of the Court, declared an Act of the Knesset void for the first time in modern Israeli history. The Court sided with Bergman and ruled that the Financing Law was "incompatible with the equality in Section Four of the Basic Law: A Knesset elected under the Financing Law would not by terms of the Law be elected in an equal election."[49] Accordingly, the Financing Law was struck down. In fact, the Court went even further

and provided the legislature with detailed advice as to ho
repair the inequality in the Financing Law, advising the Knesset ...
could either re–enact it with a special majority to essentially "override"
the Fundamental Law, or it could be amended "so as to remove the lack
of equality" by providing support for new political parties.[50]

The role of the Court, then, in the creation of the Israeli constitution has been as minimal as possible. The Court has consistently ruled
that the will of a simple majority of the sitting Knesset is sovereign, save
in those instances in which a Fundamental Law has explicitly required
special majorities for legislation designed to amend the doctrines of the
Fundamental Law. This has meant that the "constitution" has continued to grow through a slow, additive process of Knesset actions on new
Fundamental Laws.

Israel as a Parliamentary System

Many scholars argue that the British model is the "mother" of parliamentary government and that all parliamentary systems belong in
one way or another to the British "family." This notion has received a
good deal of attention in the Israeli context. Although there are many
aspects of Israel's parliamentary system that do bear some resemblance
to the British model,[51] there are also a good many structures that are
significantly different. One of the most respected studies on the subject
has concluded that while Britain's "legacy" to the Knesset was "not
negligible," major influences in the formation of the Knesset came primarily from the Zionist and Palestinian Jewish Communities, as well as
British, American, French, Yugoslav, Russian, and Turkish sources.[52]

There are a number of similarities between the Israeli parliament
and the British or "Westminster Model." The "Westminster Model" is
composed of four characteristics.[53] First, the chief executive position is
not held by the same person as the head of state. Second, the executive
powers of government are exercised by the chief executive and his or
her cabinet. Third, the chief executive and the cabinet are all members
of the legislature. Fourth, the chief executive and the cabinet are responsible to, and can be removed by, the legislature.

All of the above are characteristics of the Israeli polity. First, there
are two executives in Israel, the President and the Prime Minister, not
one as is found in the person of the President of the United States.
Second, the "real" powers of the government are exercised by the Prime
Minister and the Cabinet, while the President serves a primarily symbolic function even though, as we noted earlier, this relationship led

initially to political machinations on the part of both Ben–Gurion and Weizmann before a firm relationship was established. Third, the Prime Minister and most of the Cabinet[54] come from the legislature, unlike the relationship found in a "presidential" system in which there are specific prohibitions against membership in both branches of government. Fourth, and finally, the Knesset has the power to vote the sitting Government out of office at any time.

The Knesset is constitutionally the supreme political authority.[55] There is no executive veto of its actions and, within limits, the courts will not tamper with legislative actions by declaring them unconstitutional. Unlike the United States, in Israel there is no widespread American–style system of judicial review.[56] The Knesset cannot be dissolved and new elections cannot be called by either the head of state or the chief executive, as we would find in other parliamentary systems. Only the Knesset can cut short its electoral mandate from the voters and dissolve itself and call for new elections.

The role of the president is clearly a secondary one in the political system, as would be expected from the "Westminster Model." The President acts on the advice of the Prime Minister and on his own has very little discretionary power. As Sager reminds us:

> Just how limited the president's discretion can be in the determination of the premier designate was illustrated by the sequence of events that led up to the change of Government in 1983. After Prime Minister Begin declared his intention to resign, but before doing so, the *Herut* Central Committee nominated Yitzhak Shamir to succeed him, and Mr. Shamir at once met with the coalition partners of the outgoing Government and secured the necessary Knesset majority by a signed agreement. On Mr. Begin's resignation, shortly afterward, the president duly went through formal consultations with the parliamentary Groups, while his choice of Mr. Shamir to form the new Government was in fact a foregone conclusion.[57]

In short, Israel can be considered to be a parliamentary political system, but it is not a clone of Britain.

Concluding Comments

Israel *is* a good model of a constitutional, parliamentary political system, but it does have some idiosyncratic characteristics. These characteristics will be the subject of our study throughout the next several chapters. We will see that the Knesset is elected by the people and that the leader of the executive branch, the Prime Minister, is chosen by a majority in the legislature. The Prime Minister stays in office only as long as he or she can command a legislative majority. In the Israeli case, this entails the construction and maintenance of coalition governments.

As with other parliamentary political systems, then, it is the cabinet, not the legislature, which is the day—to—day focus of public attention and which is the "engine" which drives the machinery of government. Because of the strong party discipline which exists in Israel the role of the individual Member of Knesset in the legislative process is very limited. In other words, it is the political party which constitutes a key link between society and the polity. It is to this area that our narrative now must turn.

NOTES

1. Ivo Duchacek, *Power Maps: Comparative Politics of Constitutions* (Santa Barbara, Calif.: Clio Press, 1973).

2. Leonard Ratner, "Constitutions, Majoritarianism, and Judicial Review: The Function of a Bill of Rights in Israel and the United States," *American Journal of Comparative Law* 26:3 (1978): 373–97.

3. Martin Edelman, "Politics and Constitution in Israel," *State Government* 53:3 (1980): 171–82.

4. See paragraph 10, section B, Part I of the United Nations General Assembly Resolution 181 (II) of November 29, 1947, *Official Records of the Second Session of the General Assembly, Resolutions, September 16–November 29, 1947, January 8, 1948*, p. 135.

5. Ibid., 134–37.

6. Asher Zidon, *The Knesset: The Parliament of Israel* (New York: Herzl Press, 1967), p. 285.

7. A full text of the Law of Transition can be found in David Ben–Gurion, *Israel: A Personal History* (New York: Funk and Wagnalls, 1971), p. 336–38.

8. Although the new constitution was not yet written, Ben–Gurion had the title of Prime Minister because the Israeli political system was to be generally modelled after the British "Westminster" system, and that system called its chief executive—also unwritten in law—the Prime Minister.

9. Oscar Kraines, *Government and Politics in Israel* (Boston: Houghton Mifflin Company, 1961), p. 28.

10. A very good discussion of the major background issues of the argument for and against a written document can be found in Yehoshua Freudenheim, *Government in Israel* (Dobbs Ferry, N.Y.: Oceana Publications, 1967), pp. 24–37.

11. Ben–Gurion, *Israel*, pp. 331–34.

12. Ervin Birnbaum, *The Politics of Compromise: State and Religion in Israel* (Rutherford, N.J.: Fairleigh Dickinson University Press, 1970), p. 74. See also E. Rackman, *Israel's Emerging Constitution, 1948–1951* (New York: Columbia University Press, 1955), p. 111.

13. Samuel Sager, *The Parliamentary System of Israel* (Syracuse: Syracuse University Press, 1985), p. 36.

14. Zidon, *The Knesset*, p. 291.

15. Kraines, *Government*, p. 29.

16. One of the best general discussions of this type of tension over the degree of religious institutionalization of the state can be found in Birnbaum, *The Politics of Compromise*.

17. Asher Arian, *Politics in Israel* (Chatham, N.J.: Chatham House, 1985), p. 179.

18. Kraines, *Government*, p. 30.

19. Sager, *The Parliamentary System of Israel*, p. 39.

20. Zidon, *The Knesset*, p. 289.

21. The plural of "Knesset" is "Knessot."

22. Melville Nimmer, "The Uses of Judicial Review in Israel's Quest for a Constitution," *Columbia Law Review* 70 (1970): 1219.

23. Ibid., pp. 1239–40.

24. Claude Klein, "A New Era in Israel's Constitutional Law," *Israel Law Review* 6 (1971) : 382.

25. Zidon, *The Knesset*, p. 297.

26. Sager, *The Parliamentary System of Israel*, p. 40.

27. Ibid.

28. Michael Wolffsohn, *Israel: Polity, Society, and Economy, 1882–1986* (Atlantic Highlands, NJ: Humanities International Press, 1987), p. 6.

29. Although it is worth noting that *cabinet* members do not have to be members of Knesset, many Members of Knesset, upon appointment to the cabinet, resign their seats to devote their full attention to their cabinet duties, allowing their party colleagues to take their place in the legislature. This method of succession is explained in Chapter Seven.

30. Kraines, *Government*, pp. 124–25.

31. Max Goldweber, "Israel's Judicial System," *Queen's Bar Bulletin* (April, 1960), p. 204.

32. Meir Shangman, "On the Written Constitution," *Israel Law Review* 9 (1974): 352. See also Joseph Laufer, "Israel's Supreme Court: The First Decade," *Journal of Legal Education* 17 (1964): 44.

33. Klein, "A New Era," p. 382.

34. Ibid., p. 383.

35. J. Sussman, "Law and Judicial Practice in Israel," *Journal of Comparative Legislation and International Law* 32 (1950): 30.

36. Ariel Bin–Nun, "The Borders of Justiciability," *Israel Law Review* 5 (1980): 569.

37. Shimon Shetree, "Reflection on the Protection of the Rights of Individual: Form and Substance," *Israel Law Review* 12 (1977): 42.

38. Alfred Witkon, "Justiciability," *Israel Law Review* 1 (1966): 40.

39. Yaacov Zemach, *Political Questions in the Courts* (Detroit: Wayne State University Press, 1976), p. 44.

40. Ibid., p. 45.

41. Witkon, "Justiciability," p. 54.

42. Eliahu S. Likhovski, "The Courts and the Legislative Supremacy of the Knesset," *Israel Law Review* 3 (1968), p. 351.

43. Felix Landau, *Selected Judgments of the Supreme Court of Israel*, Ministry of Justice, 1971, p. 35.

44. Religiously orthodox.

45. Landau, *Judgments*.

46. Zemach, *Political Questions*, pp. 130–31.

47. Nimmer, "The Uses of Judicial Review," p. 1221.

48. Zemach, *Political Questions*, p. 58.

49. Nimmer, "The Uses of Judicial Review," p. 1221.

50. Zemach, *Political Questions*, p. 60.

51. Leslie Wolf–Phillips, "The 'Westminster Model' in Israel?" *Parliamentary Affairs* 26 (1973): 415–39.

52. Samuel Sager, "Pre–State Influences on Israel's Parliamentary System," *Parliamentary Affairs* 25 (1972): 29–49.

53. Gregory Mahler, *Comparative Politics: An Institutional and Cross–National Approach* (Cambridge, Ma.: Schenkman Publishing, 1983), p. 133.

54. Fundamental Law: The Government (1968) states that the president ". . . shall entrust to one of the Members of the Knesset the duty of forming a Government." This made formal what prior to 1968 had been only a convention—that the Prime Minister would have to be a member of Knesset itself. Prior to that year when the "Fundamental Law: The Government" was passed, there was considerable debate as to whether the President could invite a non–member of the Knesset to be Prime Minister. However, as we have already noted, with the exception of the Prime Minister, cabinet members do not have to be members of Knesset, and many MKs resign from the Knesset after being named to the cabinet to allow party colleagues to inherit their seats in the legislature.

55. Benjamin Akzin, "Israel's Knesset," *Ariel* 15 (1966): 5–11.

56. Likhovski, "The Courts," pp. 345–67.

57. Sager, *The Parliamentary System of Israel*, pp. 196–97.

Chapter 5

POLITICAL PARTIES AND INTEREST GROUPS

Introduction

The underlying factor in contemporary Israel that explains most actions in the political system is that of the political party. The Israeli political system has been referred to as a "parteienstaat par excellence,"[1] and the description is appropriate. Political parties played an important role in Israel's achieving statehood. One could even say that the State of Israel "was actually brought into existence by political parties, which were organized and developed entities . . . years before the coming of statehood."[2] Indeed, contemporary Israeli political parties are a direct link to the past in that virtually all have roots in some prestate political form.[3]

The political party system, as will be seen below, could almost be classified as "overdeveloped." Indeed, in the 1988 election for the Twelfth Knesset, twenty–seven different party lists were presented to the voters of Israel,[4] and many of these lists represented temporary electoral coalitions of up to five separate political party organizations. Many Israelis believe, in fact, that the system would be better off with only three or four parties, and see no real need for so many party organizations. These suggestions often include a "left," a "right," a "religious," and perhaps the Communists as a fourth party. They argue, for example, that there is no need for four individual "religious" parties. As we shall see later in this chapter, however, not all "religious" parties are the same.

There are, of course, several reasons why the independent party organizations continue to function—and even thrive—in spite of the fact that they may be losing their autonomy of action within the legislature. Perhaps the most important is that party organizations engage in considerably wider ranges of activity than mere legislation. They do not, in other words, confine their behavior to only the "obviously" political. Israel's parties "have been more than electoral mechanisms and formulators of governmental policies."[5] Parties "occupy in Israel a place more prominent and exercise an influence more pervasive than in any other state with the sole exception of some one–party states."[6]

Political parties in Israel work for their members in a variety of ways to maintain public support. One classic study of party activity, to a very large extent still quite accurate today, beautifully captured the party–member relationship:

> A person who subscribes to the party's daily newspaper, is given medical care in a party sponsored clinic, hospital, or convalescent home, spends his evenings in a party club, plays athletic games in the party's sports league, gets his books from the party's publishing house, lives in a village

or in an urban development inhabited solely by other adherents of the party, and is accustomed to look to the party for the solution of many of his daily troubles—is naturally surrounded and enveloped by an all–pervasive partisan atmosphere.[7]

It thus becomes clear that an understanding of political parties is absolutely essential for a clear understanding of the operation of the Israeli political system.

Ideology in Israel

"The style of Israeli politics is ideological."[8] Ideology refers to a set of values and beliefs pertaining to political behavior, the political "oughts" or "shoulds." In particular, Israel was born of both socialist and Zionist ideologies,[9] each of which has endured to this day. In addition to these fundamental philosophies, however, a number of other ideological and policy issues have developed over time which have become the focus of much debate and discussion. Israel's political culture, in fact, "demonstrates a fascinating mix of ideology and pragmatism."[10]

Many years ago a path–breaking study of political ideology in Israel was undertaken. At that time, five major issues were seen to be crucial in determining party platforms:

1. Private enterprise (a) vs. socialism (b);
2. "Activist" Arab policy (c) vs. restraint (d);
3. Torah–oriented life (e) vs. secularism (f);
4. Pro–Soviet Union (g) vs. pro–West (h);
5. Zionist (i) vs. non–Zionist (j).[11]

Based upon these five issues, thirty–two different platforms were mathematically created, of which nineteen were logically impossible or ideologically incompatible. (An example of an incompatible ideological mix would be a pro–Soviet, private enterprise, Torah–oriented, non–Zionist platform.) Ten of the remaining hypothesized platforms corresponded with political parties of the time, and three were logically possible but had yet to be offered as political alternatives.

With the exception of the Soviet question (4) which is not really a matter of contention in Israel today (with the exception of a Moscow-oriented Communist Party), the other four issues remain active and continue to be the cause of further party fragmentation.[12] In research done on the Knesset, Members were asked to position the various political parties of the time along the remaining four scales, which they were able to do without trouble. The results of their efforts are shown in Figure 5.1

FIGURE 5.1
Party Ideologies

Abbreviations of Party Names

Herut	H	Agudat Israel	AI	Mapai	Ma
Liberals	L	Ind. Liberals	IL	Mapam	Mp
State List	S	Citizens' Rights	CR	Ahdut HaAvodah	Ah
Free Center	FC	National Religious		Rafi	Ra
Moked	M	Party	NR	Rakah	R

"Economic Policy"

R   M   Mp   Ah   Ra   Ma   S   CR   IL   NR   AI   FC   L   H
_____
Socialism   Private
                                                       Enterprise

"National Security"

R   M   Mp   Ah   Ma   Ra   CR   IL   NR   AI   L   FC   S   H
_____
Negotiate/   Hard Line
Compromise

"Religion"

```
          CR  IL  L  S
R  M  Mp  Ah  Ra  Ma  FC  H                            NR  AI
```
_____
Secular   Religious

"Zionism"

```
  Ma  Ra  Ah
  AI  NR  FC
  H  L  IL  S  CR                           M            R
```
_____
Zionist   Anti-Zionist

Source: Adapted from Gregory Mahler, The Knesset *(Rutherford: Fairleigh Dickinson University Press, 1981), p. 49.*

It is clear from the responses that these Members feel it *is* possible to position parties along a number of different ideological scales in a way that adequately represents their different issue positions and thereby gives them their distinctive identities. It is also clear from the legislators' responses that although many of the "center," "left," and "religious" parties have similar views, they *do* diverge enough for the legislators to feel comfortable rating them separately.

As we shall see, one result of the *several* distinctive ideological bases in Israel has been an ongoing proliferation of political parties. Two parties may agree on one, two, or even three major issues, but differ on the fourth, thus preventing the two from permanently merging. In a similar manner, although the total number of positions on four bipositional issues ("yes"/"no," "for"/"against") is only sixteen, some of which may be logically contradictory or incompatible, the various degrees of opinion and intensity of belief for each of the four issues leaves open the possibility for *more* competing party organizations to form. At the same time, conversely, some political parties have become firmly identified with specific ideological positions. For example, the Mapam party is still identified as having a predominantly Marxist ideology.[13]

What should be clear from Figure 5.1 is how extraordinarily tenuous some of the coalition governments in Israel have been. For example, the last two Knesset elections have resulted in Likud–Labor "Grand Coalitions," or "Governments of National Unity" including both Likud (H, L, FC, and S in the Figure) and Labor (Ma, Mp, Ah, and Ra) as government partners. The very general illustration in Figure 5.1 demonstrates how difficult it is for these two partners to *be* partners: they disagree, sometimes fundamentally, on *many* issues, including economic policy, how flexible Israel should be in negotiations with Arab powers, what policy should be in regard to settlements on the West Bank, what influence the Orthodox religious groups should have in politics, and so on.

Party ideology has been most important in times of elections. "Israeli voters tend to report that ideological considerations are important" in motivating their votes.[14] To some extent, of course, this depends upon how one defines "ideology," because in one sense *all* of Israeli politics is "ideological." On the other hand, if we define "ideology" in a more specific sense, including policy positions on a wide variety of individual issues, then it is possible to conclude that electoral campaigns have become less ideological over the years. Many argue in fact that ideological differences between the parties have decreased to such an extent that general party image and the popularity of individual party leaders have taken the place of ideology as the reason why people vote as they do.[15]

Over the years, the predominant coalition of political ideologies in Israel has been seen as having shifted "to the right,"[16] toward a more conservative and hawkish position. This was offered as one of the reasons for Likud's victory and the (Labor) Alignment's loss in the 1977 election; the Alignment ideology had become "stale" and had fallen out of step with public opinion.[17] To some extent, the creation of pre—electoral "blocs" between and among several different political parties has tended to force some of the parties to relax their ideological rhetoric. Parties seeking to hold political office must operate in the "real world," and this sometimes necessitates their making political deals with parties which take opposing ideological positions, requiring some compromise and modification of "pure" ideological standards.[18] Indeed, one example of this is the National Unity Governments formed after the 1984 and 1988 elections, spanning parties from the "left" and the "right," which resulted in a "markedly low ideological content of the Coalition Agreement."[19]

The Functions of Parties

Quite apart from the fact that we may credit the various organizational ancestors of contemporary political parties for assisting in the formation of the State of Israel, contemporary political parties perform a significantly greater number of important functions for the political system. Although we do not mean to suggest that all Israeli parties perform all of these functions (or that they all perform them equally well) it can be suggested that *most* parties perform *most* of these functions *most* of the time.

First, parties act as "personnel agencies," or mechanisms to assist in the recruitment of political leaders.[20] It is very clear that in Israel one does not become active in politics at the national level without operating within a party framework. "Independents" are not elected to the Knesset, and as will be clear in Chapter 7, the Knesset does not encourage the participation of independent, non—party Members. Individuals seeking political office in Israel *must* operate using the vehicle of a political party. This assertion is further substantiated by the fact that when individuals break away from established political parties, they do not compete in the political arena as "independents." Rather, they establish their own political parties and continue to operate in the party—dominated environment. An overarching explanation for this is the country's electoral system. The Israeli formula of proportional representation makes it literally impossible to run for office without a party label. The nature of the electoral system likewise gives party leaders a great deal of leverage over individual Members even after elections.

The second function of political parties is to help organize groups and articulate political demands.[21] Parties seek the support of various constituencies when elections for the Knesset are at hand, and they work full–time between elections to continue generating public support for their organizations. Translated into action this means that parties publish newspapers, operate medical clinics, subsidize housing, run job placement services, and provide a wide range of additional specialized services to their members.[22] Beyond this, when parties see new issues looming on the public agenda, they seek to stake out an advantageous position in relation to their own platform and those of their rivals. Parties will act to mobilize groups around "their" issues, and will speak out in an effort to attract even more popular and electoral support. This is especially true in relation to issues of social class structure.[23] In this respect political parties in Israel can be seen to act as *movements*, in addition to being "simply" political parties in the conventional sense of the word. It is really difficult for citizens of other democracies, in which political parties serve primarily an elective function, to appreciate the extent to which parties in Israel touch a *wide range* of aspects of an Israeli citizen's life.

A third function involves providing an ideological or perceptual frame of reference for voters. The world is a complicated place, and very often citizens (and voters) are not sure how to perceive events happening around them. Parties perform a useful function here by staking out positions on a wide range of issues, offering general and detailed explanations for why those opinions are the "correct" opinions to hold, thereby making the political world a more understandable place for individuals who might not otherwise grasp many of the finer points of contemporary political discourse. In this sense parties perform a crucial role in the function of "political socialization," the process by which individuals develop their beliefs, attitudes, and values related to the political world. Along with the family, schools, ethnic groups and group leaders, occupational colleagues, peers, the media, and community leaders, the political party plays a significant role in serving as a point of orientation as the individual develops his or her views about how and why the political world operates as it does.[24]

Finally, parties serve as so–called "linkage mechanisms," helping to tie the individual to the political system within which he or she resides. Although there are formal mechanisms in the Israeli political system which "link" members of the public to governmental structures, specifically elected representatives, there is a great deal of ambiguity about the role of the representative. Since Israelis vote for political parties, not individual candidates, and since there are no geographical districts in Israel, individual Israelis are left not having "their own" representatives. It is, instead, through the political party that Israelis relate to the political system as a whole. Israeli parties are what is termed "mass" parties—they are based upon mass membership and are truly run by the rank–and–file of the party—and it is the party which provides the opportunity for the individual to feel that he or she has a real "say" in the political process.

Party Organization

Political parties in Israel are much more "tightly" organized than are those in most other countries. To be sure, in all parliamentary systems of government we are likely to find what is called a high degree of "party discipline," a term which refers to the likelihood that members of a political party in a legislature will debate, vote, and generally behave in a manner that follows the instructions of their party leader. The nature of the electoral system, which will be discussed in the next chapter, makes party discipline even *more* intensely felt in Israel. Because party discipline and continuous, formal organizational structure are so important, it becomes especially critical for party organization to accurately reflect the views of its membership.

In the words of one analyst, political organizations in Israel can be characterized by a "tendency toward mass–membership parties with extreme oligarchical tendencies."[25] Political parties are organized on both a national and local level, and as the following general illustration indicates, are highly active organizations.[26] Every four years a party convention is called and local party chapters choose delegates to attend it. For example, in the case of the Labor organization approximately 3,000 delegates were chosen to attend its national convention in 1981.

TABLE 5.1
Levels of Party Organization

Party	Convention Size	Center Size	Leadership	Executive
Labor	3,000	880	61	n.a.
Mapam	901	601	401	101
Liberal	801	429	196	35
National Religious Party	902	688	264	76

Source: Derived from Arian, Politics in Israel, *p. 112*

The National Convention will meet—usually in Jerusalem or Tel Aviv—over a two or three day period, and will hear speeches from a variety of party and national leaders. It will, subsequently, choose from among its delegates a smaller body, often called the Party Center (880 for Labor). The Center meets twice a year during its four year term between national conventions, at which time it reviews actions taken in its name and hears reports from party leaders. This Center elects from among its members a Central Committee, referred to as the Party Leadership (61 for Labor) which meets six times a year to discuss party business. From among its own members the Central Committee selects an Executive Committee (of approximately a dozen members), which meets twice a month. One person is elected from the Executive to be the Director–General (sometimes called Secretary–General) of the party.

Party activism extends from the top on down to the rank–and–file. The local level usually does not have as complex an organizational structure as the national party, but consists of a general membership, a Central Committee, an Executive, and a Secretary–General. They may meet as often as once every two weeks, which, considering the vast range of party concerns previously detailed, is not particularly frequent. Local parties, as national parties, have to discuss and resolve policy concerning the housing of party members, taxes, employment, newspaper editorials, management policy of local health clinics, strategy in sports leagues,[27] and the like. Individuals who cannot imagine what a party would have to talk about if it met on a weekly or biweekly basis are thinking of parties in the American model—where parties are almost exclusively electoral machines—and not in the Israeli context, where parties do much more than simply confine their activities to the electoral calendar.

Parties and Issues

Political parties in Israel are conventionally grouped into four categories: "left," "center," "right," and "religious." This quadripartite classification has occasionally been upset by the existence of parties that do not "fit" the system, such as the Democratic Movement for Change. Here we shall briefly describe the major parties which exist in Israeli politics, adding some historical perspective. Given the overwhelming number of parties that have floated into and out of existence in the electoral arena, we shall concern ourselves here with parties that have won seats in the Knesset in recent years. (See Figures 5.2a and 5.2b)

FIGURE 5.2a
The Evolution of Israeli Political Parties: Pre-State–1977

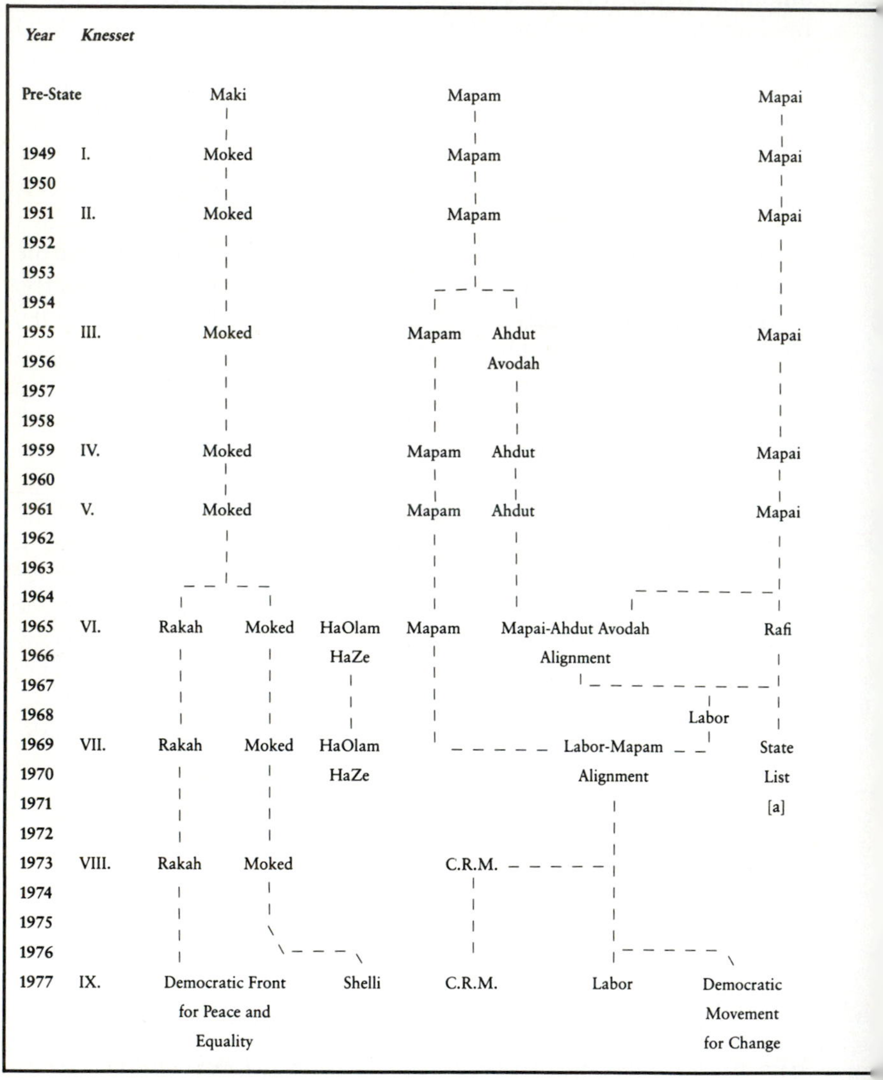

Year	Knesset						
Pre-State		Maki			Mapam		Mapai
1949	I.	Moked			Mapam		Mapai
1950							
1951	II.	Moked			Mapam		Mapai
1952							
1953							
1954							
1955	III.	Moked			Mapam	Ahdut	Mapai
1956						Avodah	
1957							
1958							
1959	IV.	Moked			Mapam	Ahdut	Mapai
1960							
1961	V.	Moked			Mapam	Ahdut	Mapai
1962							
1963							
1964							
1965	VI.	Rakah	Moked	HaOlam	Mapam	Mapai-Ahdut Avodah	Rafi
1966				HaZe		Alignment	
1967							
1968							Labor
1969	VII.	Rakah	Moked	HaOlam		Labor-Mapam	State
1970				HaZe		Alignment	List
1971							[a]
1972							
1973	VIII.	Rakah	Moked		C.R.M.		
1974							
1975							
1976							
1977	IX.	Democratic Front	Shelli		C.R.M.	Labor	Democratic
		for Peace and					Movement
		Equality					for Change

Note: [a] Merged with Likud, 1973

Source: Statistical Abstract of Israel.

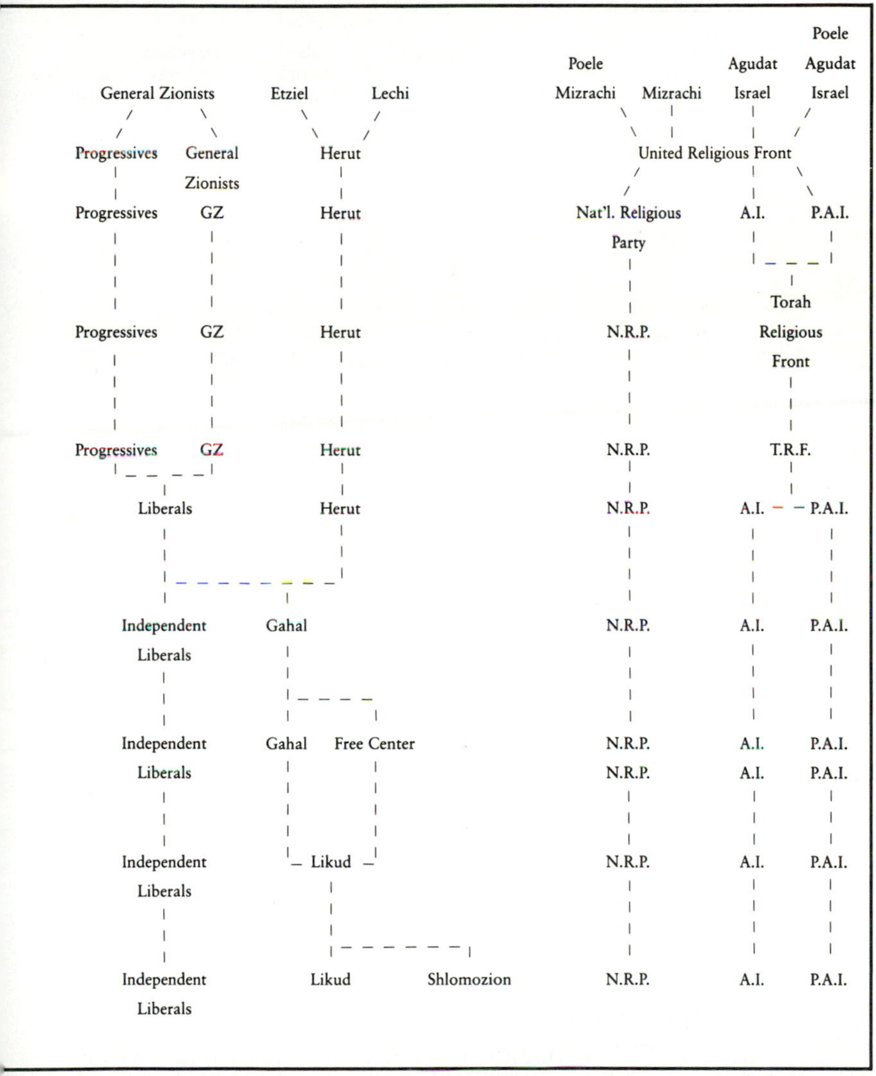
General Zionists
Etziel
Lechi
Poele Mizrachi
Mizrachi
Agudat Israel
Poele Agudat Israel
Progressives
General Zionists
Herut
United Religious Front
Progressives
GZ
Herut
Nat'l. Religious Party
A.I.
P.A.I.
Torah Religious Front
Progressives
GZ
Herut
N.R.P.
Progressives
GZ
Herut
N.R.P.
T.R.F.
Liberals
Herut
N.R.P.
A.I.
P.A.I.
Independent Liberals
Gahal
N.R.P.
A.I.
P.A.I.
Independent Liberals
Gahal
Free Center
N.R.P.
A.I.
P.A.I.
N.R.P.
A.I.
P.A.I.
Independent Liberals
Likud
N.R.P.
A.I.
P.A.I.
Independent Liberals
Likud
Shlomozion
N.R.P.
A.I.
P.A.I.

FIGURE 5.2b
The Evolution of Israeli Political Parties: 1977–1988

	Democratic Front for Peace and Equality	Shelli	Citizens Rights Movement	Labor-Mapam Alignment	Democratic Movement for Change	Ind. Liberals
1977	(5)	(2)	(1)	(33)	(15)	(1)
(9th Knesset)	I	I	I	I	I	I
	I	I	I	I	I	I
1978	I	I	I	I	I	I
	I	I	I	I	I	I
1979	I	I	I	I	I	I
	I	I	I	I	I	I
1980	I	I	I	I	I[c]	I
	I	I	I	I	[d]	I
1981	(4)	(0)[c]	(1)	(47)	(2)	(0)
(10th Knesset)	D.F.P.E.	Shelli	C.R.M.	Labor	Shinui	I.L.P.
	I		I	I	I	I
1982	I		I	I	I	I
	I		I	I	I	I
1983	I		I	I	I	I
	I	[e]	I	I	I	I
1984	(4)	(2)	(3)	(44)	(3)	(0)[a]
(11th Knesset)	D.F.P.E.	Progressive List for Peace	C.R.M.	[f] / Labor Mapam	Shinui	I.L.P.
1985	I	I	I	(6)	I	I
	I	I	I	I	I	I
1986	I	I	I	I	I	I
	I	I	I	I	I	I
1987	I	I	I	I	I	I
	I	I	I	I	I	I
1988	(4)	(1)	(1)	(5) (3)	(39) (2)	– – – – – [i]
(12th Knesset)	D.F.P.E.	Democratic Arab Party	P.L.P.	C.R.M. Mapam	Labor Shinui	

Notes: [a] Ran with Labor   [b] Most of party rejoined   [c] Party dissolved
         [g] Created with ex-   Likud   [i] Merged with Shinui
             NRP and ex-PAI   [h] Merged with Labor in 1986
             Members

Source: Statistical Abstract of Israel.

The Labor or Alignment Bloc

The *Maarach* ("Labor Alignment") has seen much change over the years.[28] The largest party of the "Labor" bloc is *Mapai*. (Mapai is an acronym for the "Party of Israeli Labor": *Mifleget Poalei Israel*). The party dates back to the 1930's and was especially prominent during the first three decades of Israeli history.[29] Such names as David Ben–Gurion, Levi Eshkol, and Golda Meir represented mainstream Mapai

	Likud	Shlomo-zion	Flatto-Sharon	Kach	National Religious Party	Agudat Israel	Poale Agudat Israel
	(43)	(2)	(1)	(0)	(12)	(1)	(1)

Tehiya

[b][c]

(2) Telem	(3) Tehiya	(48) Likud	(0):[c]	(0) Kach	(6) N.R.P.	(3) Tami	(4) A.I.	(0) P.A.I.

(1) Ometz	(5) Tehiya	(41) Likud	(3) Yahad	(1) Kach	(4) N.R.P.	(1) Tami	(2) A.I.	(4) Shas	(2) Morasha[g]

[h]

(0) Ometz	(3) Tehiya	(40) Likud	(2) Moledet	(2) Tsomet	[j] Kach	(5) N.R.P.	[0] Tami	(5) A.I.	(6) Shas	(0)[k] Morasha	(2) Degel HaTorah

[d] Most of party rejoined Labor

[e] Many from Shelli Organization

[f] After Labor joined the "National Unity Government" in 1984, 6 Mapam members left the Labor Alignment

[j] Ruled ineligible to compete by the Courts

[k] Split in 1988; some members returned to NRP

political sentiment. The Mapai organization developed from early socialist Zionist roots, played a central role in the creation of the State of Israel, and dominated Israeli politics through the 1977 Knesset election. It is still seen as representing moderate socialist economic policy, not going as far as some European socialist parties in nationalizing major industries, but instead supporting a mixture of private enterprise and government ownership. As can be seen in Figure 5.2, Mapai has survived many splits and mergers over time.[30] But survival has not guaranteed domination. Leaders of the Labor bloc in the era since the departure of Golda Meir have now come from other factions.

The *Achdut Ha'Avodah* party ("Unity of Labor") has been another major segment within the Labor bloc. Achdut could be described as slightly more socialist than Mapai, perhaps less pragmatic. In 1948 Achdut joined with other socialist movements to form *Mapam*, but broke away in 1954 and remained independent until 1965, when it joined with Mapai to form Maarach. Former Prime Minister Yitzhak Rabin is a member of the Achdut faction.

Mapam is probably the most "left" of the Labor bloc. It was founded in 1948 from a merger of the Achdut Ha'Avodah and other left wing groups, most notably HaShomer HaZair ("The Young Watchmen"). Mapam has been most vocal and ideologically consistent in its advocacy of a classless society and equal rights for Arabs in Israel. The six member Mapam faction left the Labor alliance in 1984 following the Labor Party leadership's decision to enter into a National Unity Government with Likud and spent the remaining years of the Eleventh Knesset as an independent party. Mapam ran on its own in 1988, winning three seats in the Knesset.

If Mapam is on the "left" of the Labor bloc, then *Rafi* is on the "right." In 1965 when Achdut Ha'Avodah merged with Mapai, David Ben-Gurion left the new Alignment and formed Rafi as an expression of a lack of support for the more doctrinaire socialist policies of Achdut. This faction has tended to support more militant positions on foreign policy issues, has been less prone to make territorial concessions in negotiations, and is generally more inclined to favor military responses to Arab disturbances.[31] The majority of Rafi's members reunited with Mapai in 1968, primarily out of a realization that as a small party Rafi could not be as influential and successful as its founders had wished. Some members refused to return to Labor, and instead formed a new party, the *State List*. Former Prime Minister Shimon Peres is a member of the Rafi faction.

From 1948 through 1977 Labor, in one form or another, dominated Israeli politics, consistently winning a plurality of the seats in the Knesset. At times it had a strong coalition position with minimal assistance from a few ideologically proximate partners. At other points it had to cast the coalition nets wider in order to achieve the degree of political support that was necessary for the time, requiring a greater ideological range to be represented in the coalition, and correspondingly leaving Labor less ideological flexibility in the policy formation process. Since 1977 Labor has either shared power with Likud or played a secondary role in a "National Unity" government, participating in the cabinet but not being the leader in the coalition–formation process and not occupying the office of Prime Minister.

The Center and Right Blocs

The *Likud* ("Gathering"), like the Maarach, is an umbrella organization made up of several different parties that has changed its name and shape many times during the course of Israeli history.[32] Here we need to mention Herut, the Liberals, the State List, and the Free Center parties. In so doing it will become even clearer that in Israel the term "coalition" encompasses both *inter* and *intra-* party behavior.

In the same way that Mapai has dominated the "left," *Herut* ("Freedom") has dominated the "center" and "right" in Israel. Herut appeared at independence as a political merger of many of the para–military, "right wing" and extremist pre–state organizations, including the Irgun Zvi Leumi. From its inception Herut was perceived as a nationalistic party,[33] which "emphasized the firm assertion of the claim of the Jewish state to the whole of historic Palestine."[34] Herut was a "hawk" on military issues. Economically, its orientation was toward private enterprise and less government intervention in the economy.[35] Herut was also the party of Menachem Begin and Yitzhak Shamir.

The *Liberal Party* was created in 1961 through a merger of the Progressive and General Zionist parties. Although economically compatible with Herut, its pre–state roots were based in the General Zionist movement rather than the para–military organizations which led to the formation of Herut. In 1965 the Liberal Party and Herut merged to create *Gahal* (an acronym for "Bloc of Herut and Liberals"—or "Gush Herut ve Libralim.")[36] It was at this point that some Liberals broke away to form the *Independent Liberal Party*, which proceeded to join Labor parties in coalition governments on several occasions. The Independent Liberals are much more ideologically "centrist" than either the Liberals or Gahal, supporting civil rights, less influence in politics for religious groups, and more equality for Arabs in Israel.[37] For several elections the ILP regularly won four to six seats. But it was virtually wiped out in the 1977 election for the Ninth Knesset, primarily due to its association with Labor coalition governments, dropping from four seats in the Eighth to one in the Ninth.[38] In the elections for the Tenth Knesset in 1981 the ILP received less than one percent of the vote (0.6%) and no seats in parliament. In 1984 the ILP did not submit a list of candidates, and instead was offered a position on the Labor list.[39] In 1988 the ILP joined with former members of the *Democratic Movement for Change/Shinui* and the *Center Liberal Party* to form the

New Independent Party. The new bloc won two seats in the Twelfth Knesset.

Two disenchanted members of Likud, Geula Cohen and Moshe Shamir, formed *Tehiya* ("Zionist Revival Movement") as a faction of Likud in 1979 because of their opposition to the Camp David agreement, particularly its provisions on eventual Palestinian autonomy in the West Bank and Gaza. Its goals are Israeli sovereignty over Judea, Samaria, and Gaza, an extensive settlement program, greater economic independence from the United States, and the uniting of religious and non–religious camps within Israel. Tehiya won three seats in 1981, five in 1984, and three in 1988.

Other small parties have been active in the Likud over time, in addition to those discussed above. The *Free Center* and *State List Party* factions are both much smaller components. Free Center broke away from Gahal following the 1965 election, and although it remained in the opposition until it re–joined the Likud in 1973, it voted for Labor policies on occasion, as did the Independent Liberal Party, although it did not actually join the coalition. The State List Party was originally formed by members of Rafi who did not want to rejoin the Labor bloc in 1968. State List formally joined Likud in 1973. The *Greater Israel Movement* was a part of the Likud bloc in 1973. In 1977, General Ariel Sharon led a group of extreme conservatives out of the Likud party and established his own, *Shlomozion* ("Peace for Zion"), which rejected any negotiations over the West Bank and was seen as an extremely militant party. Immediately after the 1977 election General Sharon pledged his support for Menachem Begin, and Shlomozion joined the Likud bloc once again, although it was not totally absorbed because many in Likud were uncomfortable with the controversial General (nor did Sharon want Shlomozion to be absorbed by Likud). Shlomozion ran again in the election for the Ninth Knesset in 1981, won two seats, and subsequently disbanded as an independent party and its members for the most part rejoined Likud. Lastly, two new right–wing parties won seats in 1988, *Tsomet* ("Crossroads") and *Moledet* ("Homeland"). Both are viewed as "extremist" in so far as their views on Palestinians and their support for increased Jewish settlements in the West Bank are concerned.

The Religious Parties

There are two major religious political organizations in Israel today: the *National Religious Party* (Mafdal: an acronym for "Mifleget Datit Leumit"), and the *National Torah Bloc* (Agudat Israel, and Poalei Agudat Israel).[40] The National Religious Party (NRP) was formed in

1955 from the merger of two pre–existing Orthodox religious parties, *Mizrahi* and *HaPoel HaMizrahi*. The NRP is an Orthodox party which supports the governing of the State of Israel according to Orthodox religious law. For example, it insists that all government–supported facilities have kosher[41] dietary facilities, that the Sabbath be respected by government owned and licensed services (such as bus lines or the national airline), and that Orthodox women be exempt from military service. It also seeks to establish a Constitution based on Jewish religious law, or Torah. It is, however, committed to democratic government and does not support a shift to the almost pure theocracy advocated by some of the more radical religious groups.

The NRP has been characterized by a great deal of internal division over the years.[42] Throughout the 1970's, seven factions competed in party leadership elections,[43] perhaps most vocal being the "Young Guard," which lobbied for younger leadership and a greater sharing of power by the older, established party leadership. The NRP splintered on several occasions in the 1980's, most notably with the breakoff of a Sephardic orthodox religious party, *Tami*, in 1981.[44] Tami won one seat in 1984, but none in 1988. The NRP itself won six seats in 1981, four in 1984, and five in 1988.

Agudat Israel and *Poalei Agudat Israel* ("Poalei" means "labor" wing of the party) are both considered "ultra–Orthodox" in outlook. They have traditionally been distinguished from the NRP "by both their more extreme attitude in religious matters and by their traditional rejection of the secular ideological basis of Zionism."[45] Until the actual establishment of statehood in 1948, Agudat opposed Zionism as a movement.[46] Once the State was created, however, they supported it while advocating a strong degree of religious guidance and state adherence to religious dogma. Agudat Israel is guided by a Council of Torah Sages, a group of senior rabbis, which dictates the religious lines the party should follow. The difference between Agudat Israel and its labor branch "lies mainly in the sociological basis of their support, Poalei Agudat Israel being historically the party of highly orthodox working–class people."[47] Agudat Israel received four seats in 1981, two in 1984, and five in 1988.

On two occasions Agudat Israel and Poalei Agudat Israel have joined together as one "Torah Religious Front" in the Knesset and submitted a uniform slate of candidates at election times, convinced that they could perform better as one (slightly larger) combined Orthodox group than as two much smaller ones. Both times, however, the alignment did not last as the parties disagreed about one unforeseen policy question or another, and they ended up going their separate ways.

In the election of 1984 there were several more splits among the religious parties, in both the NRP and the Agudat blocs. The *Morasha*, an electoral alignment of the Poalei Agudat Israel and another religious group, the *Matzad* ("Rally of Religious Zionists"), captured two seats. Morasha was "essentially a single–issue party—unimpeded Jewish settlements in the Occupied Territories and no withdrawal by Israel."[48] Morasha merged with a dissident NRP faction in 1986, and in 1988 the new Morasha party ran again, but this time won no seats in the new Knesset. The *Sephardi Tora Guardians*, called *Shas* for short, was another new party that emerged in 1984 as a Sephardic breakaway from Agudat Israel. Essentially the same thing happened to the NRP with the formation of Tami. The Sephardic members of Agudat Israel complained that all of the Agudat's Knesset seats were held by Ashkenazim, who in general supposedly exerted a disproportionate influence within the party. When the Council of Torah Sages did not respond to the Sephardic complaints, Shas was created to provide an alternative. It won four seats in 1984, compared to two won by Agudat Israel, and in 1988 captured six to Agudat's five, more accurately reflecting Ashkenazic–Sephardic proportions in the population than had been the case in the past. A new Orthodox party called *Degel HaTorah*, primarily made up of former NRP members who supported stronger government action promoting Orthodoxy, won two seats in 1988.

Reform Parties

Two parties, both of which have "left" or "labor" roots, should be mentioned in the context of reform. The *Citizen's Rights Movement* (CRM) was founded in 1973, prior to the elections for the Eighth Knesset. Organized by Members who had once been in Labor, it was led by Shulamit Aloni, whose disagreements with then–Prime Minister Golda Meir centered on the Labor government's attitude towards the National Religious Party and the "Who is a Jew" question. The CRM emphasized the need for electoral reform (to be discussed more fully in Chapter 6) and objected to the growing influence of religious parties in Israel, "especially in matters of divorce, marriage, and personal status."[49] The CRM was also considered to be "dovish" on issues related to the Occupied Territories and negotiations with the Arab states.

The CRM enjoyed an unexpected political success in 1973, winning three seats in the Knesset to the surprise of just about everyone—including its founders. It did not fare as well in subsequent elections, however. In 1975 CRM joined forces with Arye Eliav, another ex–

Laborite who had left in a dispute over Mapai's policies towards Arabs, to form *Yaad*. Yaad broke up that same year, however, with CRM going on its own and Eliav and others joining forces to create an association which the CRM considered to be too far to the left. The CRM had weaker performances in the 1977 and 1981 elections (winning one seat in each), but then won three in 1984, and five in 1988. Its revival is attributed to its being seen as one of the few "realistic" alternatives to the two major parties that is neither Orthodox nor "hard line" on national security issues.

A second "reform party" worthy of note is the *Democratic Movement for Change* (DMC), which appeared prior to the elections for the Ninth Knesset (1977).[50] Although it attracted supporters from across the Israeli ideological spectrum, ranging from Herut to the Free Center to members of the CRM, its membership was drawn primarily from former Labor adherents. Lifelong supporters of Labor were now presented with an unusually attractive alternative: a party that was essentially of the same general ideology as Labor, but which had electoral reform as its major campaign platform, an issue that was bound to appeal to a population tired of what it perceived as an old, corrupt leadership. The DMC won 11.6 percent of the vote in 1977, accounting for the vast majority of the 15 percent decline in Labor's total support compared to 1973. Most commentators, in fact, credited the DMC with Likud's winning a plurality in the 1977 election, which in turn led to the end of Labor's monopoly on the office of Prime Minister.

After a protracted and complex period of negotiations, DMC joined the Likud Government that fall (even though Mr. Begin had a minimal coalition government sworn in that June, four months earlier). Although DMC had agonized over joining Likud, the conclusion reached was that it could be more effective as a junior member of a government coalition than it could be as a junior member of the opposition. As things turned out, the DMC did not survive the Ninth Knesset; it factionalized and dissolved before the next elections, and its plans for electoral reform (also discussed in the next chapter) never came about.

Shinui ("Change") was a reform party which had joined with the DMC at its inception. Organized in 1974, it had representation in the Ninth Knesset (1977) as a part of the DMC. In 1981, after the demise of the DMC, Shinui ran on its own and won two Knesset seats. In 1984, again on its own, Shinui won three. As indicated above, in 1988 Shinui—along with some former members of the DMC and the Independent Liberal Party—ran as the *New Liberal Party*, also known as *Center–Shinui*, and won two seats.

Far Left, Communist, and Arab Parties

On the far left are situated *Shelli* and *Rakah*. Shelli is an association of three different organizations: the Israeli Communist Party (or *Moked*: "Focus"), which itself is not Moscow–directed and best known for its opposition to the Government policies regarding the Occupied Territories and its overall attitude towards peace in the Middle East; *Ha'Olam Ha'Zeh*, an organization headed by Uri Avnery; and a group known as the *"Black Panthers,"* best remembered for their role in public demonstrations through the 1970's. Shelli (an acronym for "Shalom Lemaan Israel," or "Peace for Israel") was led for a time by the one–time Secretary–General of the Labor party, Arye Eliav.[51] Shelli broke up after the 1977 election. Although there are, in fact, two communist parties in Israel,[52] only one, Rakah (an acronym for the "New Communist Party," or "Reshuma Kommunistit Hadash") is pro–Moscow, anti–Zionist, and predominantly Arab. It also operates peacefully in the Israeli electoral system.[53] The Rakah party evolved into the *Democratic Front for Peace and Equality* in 1977.

The Democratic Front for Peace and Equality (DFPE) has recently taken up where Rakah left off. The DFPE is also a predominantly Arab party which has survived in the Israeli electoral climate for many years. The DFPE has consistently opposed Israeli policy in the Occupied Territories, advocates withdrawal to the pre–1967 borders, and supports the creation of a Palestinian state on the West Bank.[54] The DFPE won four seats in the 1984 Knesset elections and five in 1988. The DFPE today includes the Israel Communist Party (Rakah) and the Black Panthers.

There have been a number of other "Arab" parties which have submitted lists of candidates during the years since Israeli independence. Two or three of these parties have won seats at many Knesset elections, taking anywhere from one to five places in total.[55] One of them has been the *Progressive List for Peace*. Formed in 1984, it represents both Jewish leftists and Israeli–Arab nationalists. This party was briefly banned by the Central Election Commission for advocating recognition of the PLO, the establishment of a Palestinian state in the West Bank and the Gaza Strip, and including on its party membership rolls "subversive elements." The Central Election Commission further charged that "'key persons on the list' were identified with 'enemies of the state.'" This action was condemned by Uri Avnery, co–chairman of the PLP and a former leader of Ha'Olam Ha'Zeh, as "scandalous," and was subsequently overturned by the Supreme Court, which permitted the PLP to participate in the national elections. The PLP won two seats in the 1984 election and one in 1988. The *Democratic Arab Party* won one seat in 1988. Also notable has been the *United Arab List*, which generally supported Labor governments through 1977 and Labor policies thereafter, although it was never formally a party of any ruling coalition. A substantial proportion of Arab votes have been directed to other parties which have put forward Arab candidates, including the DFPE, Mapam, and Maarach.

Maverick Parties

Although, as indicated above, individuals in the Israeli political system are virtually forced to operate through the party structure to run for Knesset seats, there have been some noteworthy "maverick parties" in recent years that deserve brief comment here. We have already mentioned General Sharon's *Shlomozion*, which appeared in 1977, later supported Mr. Begin's coalition government, and then ran again as an independent party organization in 1981. Shlomozion rejected negotiations on the status of the West Bank and generally took a "hard line" on all "Arab issues." After the elections for the Ninth Knesset in 1981, in which it won two seats, it disbanded as an independent party and its members for the most part rejoined Likud.

Rabbi Meir Kahane formed a political party called *Kach* ("Thus"), which ran unsuccessfully in 1977 and 1981. The American–born Kahane was best known as an "ultra–rightist" on issues of nationalism and anti–Arabism who indeed has advocated expulsion of the Arab populations of Israel and the Occupied Territories. Many Israelis abhor Kahane, comparing him to European fascists of the 1930's. Indeed, Kach was banned by the Central Election Commission prior to the 1984 election on the grounds that it "advocated racist and anti–democratic principles," and that it "openly supported terror."[56] However, the Israeli Supreme Court overturned this ban in time for it to compete, citing the need for a free exchange of ideas—all ideas—in any election. In 1984 Kach received enough votes to win Kahane a seat in the Knesset. Because he was democratically elected, the courts since then have supported Kahane's right to make speeches and introduce legislation, no matter how repugnant they may seem to Parliament. Prior to the 1988 election legislation was passed banning parties which promulgated racism, once again disestablishing a party that, by some accounts, had begun to attract an alarmingly large electoral following (particularly among younger voters and West Bank settlers).

Ezer Weizman, a former General, military hero, Cabinet member, and leading negotiator at the Camp David Summit with Begin and Sadat, created a new party called *Yahad* ("Together") for the 1984 elections. Basically a group of ex–Likud adherents, they followed him out of the Likud after an intra–party struggle with General Sharon. Yahad advocated a peace settlement with the Arabs, won three seats in the 1984 election, and then merged with Labor in 1986.

Finally, but certainly not least, a new party, *Telem* (an acronym for "Movement for State Renewal"), was created in 1981 to serve as an electoral vehicle for former Defense and Foreign Minister Moshe Dayan. In 1977 Dayan had left the Labor Alignment to serve as Menachem Begin's Foreign Minister. By 1981 Dayan had departed the Begin cabinet and there seemed no future for him in either his old party, Labor, which he had deserted, or Likud, which had not become his new one. Accordingly, he formed a party of his own and received enough support in 1981 to win two seats. After Dayan's death in October of 1981, Yigal Hurewitz (a former Finance Minister in the Begin Government) changed the name of the party to *Ometz* (which was an acronym for "Courage to Cure the Economy"). Ometz won one seat in the 1984 election, but none in 1988.

What we see in this brief examination of the Israeli party system, then, is an almost bewildering array of political opinions and options. If the descriptions of political parties seem to be a bit "short" on ideology and "long" on personality, that is a fair conclusion to draw. The nature of the electoral system, the subject of our discussion in the next chapter, tends to permit—and even encourage—a proliferation of what we have called here "maverick parties." It is relatively easy for a well–known political leader with a solid base of support to break away from his former party and to form a party of his own, with little that is ideologically new except himself or herself as the party head. This is precisely why it is difficult to pinpoint the differences in substance between many of the parties, because often there are very few substantive differences at all. What we find is a series of personal followings that form individual parties that then establish coalition blocs on the basis of ideology and programmatic preference.

Interest Groups

Interest groups are commonly defined as collections of like–minded individuals. There are many different kinds of interest groups, some highly organized, others less so. Some are large, others are small. Regardless of their size or level of organization, interest groups are important because of the manner in which they can influence the behavior of a government. Not only do interest groups communicate the views of the public, they also help to communicate the views of the government to different sections of the public. Thereby, interest groups serve as "linkage mechanisms" in the democratic machinery of government. It should be noted, however, that interest groups in Israel do not have the level of activity, or importance, that they do in many other democratic polities, because many of the most important functions performed by interest groups elsewhere are performed by the political party organizations in Israel. In a sense, then, political parties have essentially usurped much of the traditional role played by interest groups.

The largest single interest group in Israel is the *Histadrut*, or General Federation of Workers, which was established in 1920. The Histadrut is often referred to as a national labor union, but it is much more than that. It owns, builds, rents, and sells property, runs housing projects, administers medical clinics, owns newspapers and publishing houses, supervises schools, and in general is responsible for a wide range of social services. Through the 1977 Knesset election the Histadrut had very strong and close ties with the government. Primarily this was achieved through an explicit overlap (or "interlocking directorate") of personnel in leadership positions of each. In the process, Histadrut actually "inspired" many important pieces of legislation dealing with labor and employment, such as the Hours of Work and Rest Law, the Youth Employment Law, and the Labor Exchange Law.[57]

Under Likud governments the Histadrut has lacked the direct governmental access or general influence that it once had with Labor. The policies of Likud have been considerably less sympathetic with the union cause. In recent years, partly as a result of this trend, Likud supporters have been increasing in numbers within the Histadrut. In the last two Knessot, with "national unity" coalitions made up of Likud and Labor, the Histadut's level of influence has still not reached that which it once enjoyed when Labor formed center–left coalitions with parties that were *more* socialist than itself.

Another interest group that must be considered when examining Israeli politics is the *military*. The study of civil–military relations has demonstrated that the military do influence public policy in Israel.[58] Since an overwhelming percentage of Israel's adult population is either on active service or in the reserves, opinions of the military have a way of finding their way into politics. This is particularly noticeable when one examines the political recruitment process. There has been no shortage of examples—Dayan, Rabin, Weizman, Sharon—of individuals who have achieved fame through their military exploits, then exchanged that fame for a position on a party's electoral list, or simply gone out and formed their own. On the whole, studies of Israeli army officers "have indicated that their political attitudes and orientations are as diverse as those of the population at large. They do not constitute a distinct or separate ideological bloc."[59]

International Jewry constitutes yet a third group which exercises an influence in Israeli politics. Diaspora Jewry has on many occasions expressed its policy preferences through a variety of mechanisms, including formal organizations such as the Jewish Agency, the World Zionist Organization, and the American Jewish Committee, as well as through direct communication between them and Israeli politicians.

It is very clear that international Jewry was very important in terms of its response to the 1988 election in which its American component (at least) exerted great pressure on Yitzhak Shamir to deter him from forming a Likud–Orthodox coalition that would force a ruling on the "Who is a Jew?" question. The eruption of this long–simmering controversy—with the Orthodox parties wanting Shamir to introduce legislation recognizing only *Orthodox* Jewish conversions and marriages, among other rituals—generated a tremendous amount of concern in Jewish communities outside of Israel and is an excellent case study of how overseas Jewish communities can influence domestic Israeli politics.

The fact of the matter is that the Israeli government receives a great deal of money through these international interest groups, and thus is very sensitive about avoiding actions which might cause an erosion of this international support.[60] For example,

> Because of the prestige and wealth of its members, the American Jewish Committee has been especially cultivated by Israel's leaders. It is the only private organization with which the Israeli government has reached a quasi–official agreement defining a "proper" relationship with diaspora Jewry.[61]

Finally, but not least, *ethnic groups* have begun to influence government policy in a direct way. For many years, as we have already seen, the Ashkenazim completely dominated the political arena. Sephardic Jews were a substantial minority (although rapidly approaching majority status), but were systematically excluded from positions of leadership in the party organizations, governmental bureaucracy, and elected office. In recent years the Sephardic groups have begun to speak out, to organize, and to lobby for their own interests. Their common concerns and platforms have to do with equal *opportunity*, with the claim that they have not had the education and career opportunities of other segments of society, as well as all of the concomitant benefits that such opportunities include. We have already seen how new political parties, such as Shas and Tami, have been created to specifically represent the interests of the Sephardim.

One result of this activism by Sephardic groups is that the larger parties, especially Labor and Likud, have been compelled to increase overtures to them. Likud recognized prior to the 1977 election that the Sephardim were an untapped electoral resource and it became identified as the party of Sephardic interests. Labor, in recent years, has tried to make inroads in this Likud constituency, but with minimal progress. In brief, the Sephardim have been recognized as a significant interest group and are now receiving the kind of electoral attention that they felt in the past they deserved.

Concluding Comments

We have seen in this chapter the extremely heterogeneous and pluralistic forces at work in Israel today. The country is indeed a democratic system, with all of the noise and fuss that the best conceptions of "democracy" and "pluralism" suggest. The Israeli party system, as we will see in the next chapter, is strongly influenced by the electoral system. But parties in Israel are much more than electoral machines.

Although the *raison d'etre* of any political party involves elections, and while that is certainly the case in Israel, political parties there are involved in many aspects of the lives of Israeli citizens. In this chapter we have seen how parties are organized, what they stand for, and how they have survived and, indeed, proliferated, over the years. We have also seen their all—encompassing role in socialization, recruitment, interest articulation, interest aggregation, and policy—making. Our next step is to examine how parties operate in the electoral arena.

NOTES

1. Emanuel Gutmann, "Israel," *Journal of Politics* 25 (1963): p. 703.

2. Scott Johnston, "Politics of the Right in Israel," *Social Science* 40 (1965): p. 104.

3. For a description of the history of parties in Israel, see Benjamin Akzin, "The Role of Parties in Israeli Democracy," *Journal of Politics* 17 (1955): pp. 507–45.

4. Election data from 1988 can be found in Chapter 6.

5. C. Paul Bradley, *Parliamentary Elections in Israel: Three Case Studies* (Grantham, N.H.: Thompson and Rutter, 1985), p. 11.

6. Akzin, "The Role of Parties," p. 509.

7. Ibid., p. 520.

8. Asher Arian, *Politics in Israel: The Second Generation* (Chatham, N.J.: Chatham House Publishing, 1985), p. 8.

9. For discussion of some of these ideological bases of the Israeli system, see Daniel Elazar, "Israel's Compound Polity," in *Israel at the Polls: The Knesset Elections of 1977*, ed. Howard Penniman (Washington, D.C.: American Enterprise Institute, 1979), pp. 1–38.

10. Arian, *Politics in Israel*, p. 8.

11. Thomas Goodland, "A Mathematical Presentation of Israel's Political Parties," *British Journal of Sociology* 8 (1957): pp. 263–66.

12. See, for example, Zeev Ben–Sira, "The Image of Political Parties and the Structure of a Political Map," *European Journal of Political Research* 6:3 (1978): pp. 259–284.

13. Asher Arian, "The Electorate: Israel, 1977," in *Israel at the Polls: The Knesset Elections of 1977*, p. 64.

14. Arian, *Politics in Israel*, p. 134.

15. Ibid., pp. 253–54.

16. Arian, "The Electorate," p. 71.

17. Myron J. Aronoff, "The Decline of the Labor Party: Causes and Significance," in *Israel at the Polls: The Knesset Elections of 1977*, pp. 120–21.

18. Asher Arian, "Conclusion," in Ibid., pp. 287–88.

19. Bradley, *Parliamentary Elections*, p. 188.

20. One of the classic studies of this phenomenon outside of the Israeli context is Austin Ranney's *Pathways to Parliament: Candidate Selection in Britain* (Madison: University of Wisconsin Press, 1965).

21. Amitai Etzioni, "Agrarianism in Israel's Party System," *Canadian Journal of Economics and Political Science* 23:3 (1957): pp. 363–75.

22. A good illustration of this can be found in Paul Burstein, "Political Patronage and Party Choice Among Israeli Voters," *Journal of Politics* 38 (1976): pp. 1024–32.

23. See, for example, Burstein, "Social Cleavages and Party Choice in Israel: A Log–Linear Analysis," *American Political Science Review* 72 (1978):

pp. 96–109, or M. Roshwald, "Political Parties and Social Classes in Israel," *Social Research* 23:2 (1956): pp. 199–218.

24. For a more thorough discussion of the process of political socialization in Israel, see Gregory Mahler, *The Knesset: Parliament in the Israeli Political System* (Rutherford: Fairleigh Dickinson University Press, 1981), pp. 113–30.

25. Arian, *Politics in Israel*, p. 103.

26. A fascinating account of recent trends in "democratization" in the Israel Labor Party can be found in the article by Myron Aronoff, "Better Late than Never: Democratization in the Labor Party," in Gregory Mahler (ed.), *Israel After Begin* (forthcoming).

27. In recent times, however, competition in sports leagues has become so intense that teams have even been known to recruit players who are not from their own party if they think it will help their chances of winning!

28. Peretz Merhav, *The Israeli Left, History, Problems, Documents* (New York: Barnes and Co., 1980).

29. For a fuller discussion of the background of Mapai, see Aronoff, "The Decline of the Israeli Labor Party," pp. 115–23, or Efraim Torgovnik, "Party Organization and Electoral Politics, The Labor Alignment," in *Israel at the Polls, 1981: A Study of the Knesset Elections* (Washington, D.C.: American Enterprise Institute, 1986), pp. 36–48. For a full history see Peter Medding, *Mapai in Israel: Political Organization and Government in a New Society* (Cambridge: Cambridge University Press, 1972).

30. For a more detailed description of both the pre–state background and the more modern history of the Alignment parties, see Arian, *Politics in Israel*, pp. 73–79. See also Myron Aronoff, *Power and Ritual in the Israeli Labor Party: A Study in Political Anthropology* (Assen, Amsterdam: Van Gorcum, 1977).

31. Alfred Katz, *Government and Politics in Contemporary Israel, 1948– Present* (Washington, D.C.: University Press of America, 1980), p. 30.

32. For a good brief history of the Likud, see Ilan Greilsammer, "The Likud," in *Israel at the Polls, 1981*, pp. 65–92, or Arian, *Politics in Israel*, pp. 79–86.

33. Bradley, *Parliamentary Elections in Israel*, p. 15.

34. Benjamin Akzin, "The Likud," in *Israel at the Polls: The Knesset Elections of 1977*, p. 93.

35. David Nachmias, "The Right Wing Opposition in Israel," *Political Studies* 24 (1976): pp. 268–80.

36. Akzin, "The Likud," pp. 96–97.

37. Katz, *Government and Politics*, p. 42.

38. Elyakim Rubinstein, "The Lesser Parties in the Israeli Elections of 1977," in *Israel at the Polls: The Knesset Elections of 1977*, pp. 185–88.

39. Arian, *Politics in Israel*, p. 86.

40. A good general discussion of the religious parties is to be found in Shmuel Sandler, "The Religious Parties," in *Israel at the Polls, 1981*, pp.

105–27. See also Gary Schiff, *Tradition and Politics, The Religious Parties of Israel* (Detroit: Wayne State University Press, 1977), or Stephen Oren, "Continuity and Change in Israel's Religious Parties," *Middle East Journal* 27 (1973): pp. 36–54.

41. This refers to Jewish dietary laws, and means *"fit, proper, or in accordance with the religious law.* Any food that satisfies the requirements of Jewish law is *fit* for eating; it is *kosher . . .* Kosher does not stand for an ethnic way of cooking food nor for certain tastes. It is a religious term with very specific religious meaning. Its applicability is determined by set religious criteria. Either a food is kosher or it is not." Haim Donin, *To Be a Jew: A Guide to Jewish Observance in Contemporary Life* (New York: Basic Books, 1972), p. 97.

42. Yael Yishai, "Factionalism in the National Religious Party: The Quiet Revolution," in *The Elections in Israel—1977*, ed. A. Arian (Jerusalem: Jerusalem Academic Press, 1980), pp. 50–60, or Shimshon Zelnicker and Michael Kahan, "Religion and Nascent Cleavages: The Case of Israel's National Religious Party," *Comparative Politics* 9 (1976): pp. 21–48.

43. Bradley, *Parliamentary Elections*, pp. 54–55.

44. Ibid., pp. 104–5.

45. Rubinstein, "The Lesser Parties in the Israeli Elections of 1977," p. 180. See also Eliezer Don–Yehiya, "Origins and Developments of the Agudah and Mafdal Parties," *The Jerusalem Quarterly* Summer, 1981, pp. 49–64, and Rael Isaac, *Party and Politics in Israel: Three Visions of a Jewish State* (New York: Longman, 1981).

46. David Schnall, "Native Anti–Zionism: Ideologies of Radical Dissent in Israel," *Middle East Journal* 31 (1977): pp. 157–74.

47. Rubinstein, "The Lesser Parties," p. 180.

48. Bradley, *Parliamentary Elections*, p. 154.

49. Katz, *Government and Politics*, p. 35.

50. For a fuller examination of the Democratic Movement for Change, see Efraim Torgovnik, "A Movement for Change in a Stable System," in *Israel at the Polls: The Knesset Elections of 1977*, pp. 147–71.

51. Rubinstein, "The Lesser Parties," pp. 189–90.

52. Alain Greilsammer, "Communism in Israel: 13 Years After the Split," *Survey* 23 (1977–78): pp. 172–92, and Martin Slann, "Ideology and Ethnicity in Israel's Two Communist Parties," *Studies in Comparative Communism* 7:4 (1974): pp. 359–74.

53. For two very good studies, one current, the other more historical, of the communist party in Israel, see Moshe Czudnowski and Jacob Landau, *The Israeli Communist Party and the Elections for the Fifth Knesset, 1961* (Stanford, Ca.: Hoover Institution, 1965), and Dunia Nahas, *The Israeli Communist Party* (New York: St. Martin's Press, 1976).

54. Katz, *Government and Politics*, p. 36.

55. Samuel Sager, *The Parliamentary System of Israel* (Syracuse: Syracuse University Press, 1985), p. 60.

56. Bradley, *Parliamentary Elections*, p. 160.

57. Don Peretz, *The Government and Politics of Israel* (Boulder, Co.: Westview Press, 1979), p. 120.

58. Yoram Peri, *Between Battles and Ballots, Israeli Military in Politics* (Cambridge: Cambridge University Press, 1983). See also Amos Perlmutter, *Military and Politics in Israel* (New York, Praeger, 1969), especially Chapter 5.

59. Peretz, *Government and Politics of Israel*, p. 128.

60. The subject of financial support from these overseas Jewish communities is discussed in Chapter Two.

61. Peretz, *Government and Politics of Israel*, p. 131.

Chapter 6

THE ELECTORAL SYSTEM AND ISRAELI VOTING BEHAVIOR

Introduction

The electoral system of any country is very important in terms of both its role in the selection of political leaders and its influence on the nature and style of political discussion and activity. This is clearly the case in Israel, where the electoral system itself promotes such diverse and even contradictory phenomena as a splintering of established political parties, strict party discipline, and close overall control of individual legislators within the separate party organizations. Indeed, the very nature of the Israeli electoral system is often credited with being the prime reason for so many political parties. There are few institutional incentives for factionalized parties to remain together, and many for groups with a moderate amount of popular support to break away from parent political organizations and run for office under their own banners.

Conversely, individuals who do not wish to break away are left in a very vulnerable position in relation to their party leaders, for party leaders can use the electoral system as a lever—or a threat—to remind the rank–and–file that they would do better to act in a manner consistent with party guidelines, or face the consequences. Not surprisingly, then, there have been numerous calls for reform of the Israeli electoral system over the years. For reasons which will also become clear in this chapter, these proposals have been intensely opposed by most existing political parties, with politicians in Israel generally agreeing that reforms are not likely to come about in the very near future. The outcome of the 1988 election, however, along with the complex and protracted coalition–formation process, brought the issue of electoral reform back to the political agenda.

Proportional Representation and Elections

Maurice Duverger, a French political scientist, once wrote that there was a direct relationship between the electoral system of a nation and the number and nature of political parties which existed in it. More specifically, Duverger wrote that proportional representation elections lead to multiple political parties.[1] That is certainly the case in Israel.

Israeli elections must be held at least every four years. That is, although the maximum term of any single elected Knesset is four years, the Knesset may vote to dissolve itself prior to the normal time of expiration of its term and call for new elections. Unlike the situation in other parliamentary systems, only the Knesset, not the head of state, has the power to dissolve itself prior to the expiration of its legislated term of office. On a number of occasions in Israeli history the term of a Knesset has been less than four years; on two occasions (1949–51 and 1959–61) it was less than three. In recent years, however, the general pattern has been to approach the end of the four year term before calling for new elections.

The "Fundamental Law: The Knesset" says that "the Knesset shall be elected in general, national, direct, equal, secret, and proportional elections."[2] This means, in practice, that all citizens eighteen years of age or older can vote. The actual electoral system employs a single–ballot, national constituency, with a proportional representation electoral formula.[3] That is, the whole country is considered a single electoral district, and each voter casts his or her vote for the *party* whose platform and candidates he or she most prefers. The percentage of votes received by each party in the national election determines the percentage of seats it will accordingly receive in the Knesset.

Parties receiving at least one percent of the vote are entitled to representation. Parties receiving less than this "threshold" receive no Knesset representation. Total votes in the election (minus the votes going to parties which receive less than the one percent threshold) are divided by 120, the total seats in the Knesset, thereby establishing a "key."

Thus in the 1988 election for the Twelfth Knesset, 2,227,618 valid votes were cast after the "wasted votes" for parties receiving less than one percent were deducted. When this figure was divided by 120, the

TABLE 6.1 Knesset Elections, 1949–1988	
1	January, 1949
2	July, 1951
3	July, 1955
4	November, 1959
5	August, 1961
6	November, 1965
7	October, 1969
8	December, 1973
9	May, 1977
10	June, 1981
11	July, 1984
12	November, 1988

number of seats in the Knesset, a "key" of 18,563 votes was determined. The Likud, for example, received 709,305 votes; which yielded
thirty–eight Knesset seats, with a remainder of 3,911 votes. After all of
the parties received their initial seat distribution in this manner, and
after virtually all of the seats had been allocated, nine seats remained.
(Party seat totals are indicated in Table 6.2.)

TABLE 6.2
Results of the 1984 and 1988 Knesset Elections

Party	1984 Votes	% Votes	# Seats	1988 Votes	% Votes	# Seats	
Alignment	724,074	34.9	44	709,305	31.1	40	Likud
Likud	661,302	31.9	41	685,363	30.0	39	Alignment
Tehiya	83,037	4.0	5	107,709	4.7	6	Shas
N.R.P.	73,530	3.5	4	102,714	4.5	5	Agudah
Dem. Front				97,513	4.3	5	C.R.M.
for Peace and				89,720	3.9	5	N.R.P.
Equality	69,815	3.4	4	84,032	3.7	4	D.F.P.E.
Shas	63,605	3.1	4	70,730	3.1	3	Tehiya
Shinui	54,747	2.6	3	56,345	2.5	3	Mapam.
CRM	49,698	2.4	3	45,489	2.0	2	Tsomet
Yahad	46,302	2.2	3	44,174	1.9	2	Moledet
PLP	38,012	1.8	2	39,538	1.0	2	Shinui
Aguda	36,079	1.7	2	34,279	1.5	2	Degel HaTorah
Morasha	33,287	1.6	2	33,695	1.5	1	PLP
Tami	31,103	1.5	1	27,012	1.2	1	Arab. Dem. List
Kach	25,907	1.2	1				
Ometz	23,845	1.2	1				
* * * * * * *				* * * * * * * * *				
Eliav	15,348	.7	—	16,674	0.7	—	Pensioners
Disabled	12,329	.6	—	15,783	0.7	—	Meimad
Zionist Renewal	15,876	.3	—	4,253	0.2	—	Derech Eretz
Youth & Aliyah	5,794	.3	—	4,182	0.2	—	La'or
Integration	5,499	.3	—	3,222	0.1	—	Just Society
Tenants	3,195	.2	—	2,947	0.1	—	Yishai
Flatto-Sharon	2,430	.1	—	2,838	0.1	—	Ma'as
Atzmaut	4,887	.2	—	1,654	0.1	—	Tarshish
Income Tax				1,579	0.1	—	Quiet Force
Repeal	1,472	.07	—	1,018	0.04	—	Veterans
Homeland	1,415	.07	—	909	0.04	—	Yemenites
Amcha	733	.02	—	446	0.02	—	Ahdut (Tayyar)
* * * * * * * *				* * * * * * * *				

Eligible Voters: 2,654,613
Total Votes Cast: 2,091,402
Percent of Voters Voting: 78.8%
Total Valid Votes Cast: 2,073,321
1% "Threshold": 20,733

Eligible Voters: 2,918,439
Total Votes Cast: 2,305,567
Percent of Voters Voting: 79%
Total Valid Votes Cast: 2,283,123
1% "Threshold": 22,831

The 12 unsuccessful lists in 1988 accounted for 55,505 "wasted votes" and these were subtracted from the
2,283,123 valid votes, leaving 2,227,618 votes for subsequent calculations.

Source: The Jerusalem Post *(November 6, 1988) pp. 1, 8; Eve Jacobson, "An Introduction to the Israeli Electoral Process" (New York: American Jewish Committee,
Institute of Human Relations, 1988), p. 6.*

Seats remaining in the Knesset after the initial assignment are then distributed, in a complex process, among parties with high numbers of "surplus votes." This "surplus vote" distribution mechanism appears to be quite complex, but in actuality is not that hard to understand. The process which has been used in Israel since 1973 is called the d'Hondt system, named after the Belgian who devised it. Briefly, the system seeks to guarantee that "no reallocation of seats would reduce discrepancies in the shares of the vote received by the winners."[4] In Israel it is referred to as the Bader–Ofer system, named after the two Members of Parliament who introduced it.[5]

For many years seats were awarded purely on the basis of the size of the remainders. This, in fact, sometimes permitted parties that had not even won a single seat to win a "surplus" seat, because they had higher "remainders" (in this case, a remainder after 0 seats and before 1 seat) than the more established parties (perhaps with more votes than needed for 32 seats, but not enough votes for 33 seats). The Bader–Ofer formula does not allow this and is said to slightly favor the larger parties.

This system does not necessarily give "surplus" Knesset seats to the largest parties, or to the parties with the largest remainders, but instead puts a premium on the base of party support. The idea here is that "a party supported by a million voters must be treated differently from a party supported by 20,000 voters."[6]

The operation of the Bader–Ofer formula is reflected in Table 6.3. The "remaining seats" are distributed by setting up a table very much like that demonstrated in the Table, in which each of the parties' "remaining votes" are divided in turn by larger and larger divisors. In Table 6.3, three hypothetical parties ("A", "B", and "C") have "remaining votes" of 10,000, 8,000, and 3,000 respectively. After the division has taken place, the "remaining seats" are given, in order, to the largest dividends in the Table, so that if there were fifteen "remaining seats" to be distributed, Party A would win seven (seats 1, 3, 5, 8, 10, 11, and 14), Party B would win six (seats 2, 4, 7, 9, 12, and 15) and Party C would win two (seats 6 and 13).

During the pre–election period, the amount and degree of partisan campaigning reaches intense proportions. Election periods vary in length; when the Knesset dissolves itself and calls for new elections it sets the dates of the campaign. There is no legally mandated period, however, although campaigns generally tend to last about eight to ten weeks. Election expenses of Israel's political parties through the 1960s had been among the world's highest.[7] Reform in 1969 led to limitations on overall campaign expenses and increased government oversight of party spending during the election period. Since 1973 Israeli parties

	TABLE 6.3 "Surplus Vote Distribution" (Bader-Ofer Formula)		
	Party A	Party B	Party C
"Surplus Votes"	10,000	8,000	3,000
Divide by:			
1	(1)10,000	(2)8,000	(6)3,000
2	(3)5,000	(4)4,000	(13)1,500
3	(5)3,333	(7)2,666	1,000
4	(8)2,500	(9)2,000	750
5	(10)2,000	(12)1,600	600
6	(11)1,666	(15)1,333	500
7	(14)1,428	1,142	428
8	1,250	1,000	375
Total Seats Won	7	6	2

have been forbidden from receiving corporate contributions.[8] Parties are given free time on television and radio for campaigning, and those which already have seats in the Knesset are given substantial allowances for the electoral campaign based upon the number of seats they control at the time.[9]

The role of the media merit some discussion here. The media have begun to be recognized in the scholarly literature as playing a significant role in Israeli campaigns.[10] During the last month of the campaign in 1988, each party list was allocated ten free minutes of prime time television each evening, six nights a week, and parties already represented in the Knesset receive an additional four free minutes per seat they control.

Opinion about the level of substantive discourse presented in these advertisements varies, however, to such an extent that one wonders if the editorial–writers were in the same country watching the same television![11] Yeshayahu Ben–Porat wrote in an editorial in one major newspaper (*Yediot Aharonot*, October 9, 1988) that: "Most, if not all of the party telecasts constitute an insult to the intelligence. They are based on the assumption that the average voter is an infantile imbecile, whose vote will be determined by some jingle or electronic or graphic stunt taken from the world of video *Pacman* games." A different editorial, one by Avraham Schweitzer in *Ha'aretz* (October 7) wrote that:

A few words should be said in praise of the telecast war. Labor, the Likud, Tehiya, the CRM—and even the representatives on earth of God

Almighty, the religious parties—are all addressing the issues. Observers of the American presidential election are complaining about the absence or extreme paucity of substantive issues in the campaigns of Bush and Dukakis. That is not the case in Israel.

There is no doubt that television adds an extra dimension to the campaign. Left unresolved is the question of whether or not this extra dimension is a positive or negative one.[12]

During the actual campaign itself, walls are covered with party advertisements, while rallies and speeches abound. All registered voters are mailed an official government publication, prepared by the Central Elections Committee, which contains information provided by all political parties which have lists of candidates on file with the Election Bureau. This Central Elections Committee is made up of members of Knesset parties in proportion to their strength. The information provided to all voters includes the Hebrew letter or letters which the parties have chosen as their electoral symbols, their party platform, and a list of their candidates, in that order. (This is illustrated in Figure 6.1.)

Lists of candidates for Knesset elections may be submitted either by a party which is already represented or by a group of 2,500 qualified voters.[13] In 1948 the requirement was for a group of 250 qualified voters. This was raised to 750 in 1951, and has steadily increased ever since.[14] Individuals whose names are on party lists must formally write to the Central Elections Committee to accept their nominations. In order to submit lists of candidates to the voters, new parties must deposit a sum of money (about $2,800 in 1984[15]) with the Central Elections Committee; if it wins at least one seat its deposit is returned, if not, it forfeits a portion. This is designed to discourage truly "unrealistic" parties from campaigning. But it is clear from the number of parties that compete in Knesset elections that this device does not stop new parties from forming.

Many of the serious parties submit lists with 120 names on them, one for each seat in the Knesset, even though the parties know that none will win 100 percent of the vote. Smaller, as well as "unrealistic", parties often submit shorter lists, realizing that there is no point in their putting forward 120 names. Sometimes even the smaller parties surprise themselves, though. In the Eighth Knesset election of 1973, for example, the Citizen's Rights Movement, which was started by a former Mapai parliamentarian, submitted a list with only five names to the electorate, not really expecting that the party would win enough votes for even the first name on the list to be given a seat. To the surprise of many, the party won enough votes for the first three names on the party list to actually be given seats in the Knesset.

FIGURE 6.1
A Party Campaign Notice

The official assignment of seats in the Knesset is determined purely by position on a party list. If a party wins 25 percent of the national vote and is allotted thirty seats in the Knesset on the basis of that result (25% × 120 seats = 30 seats), the seats are awarded to the first thirty names on the party list. If a member of Knesset dies during the term, or if a member resigns for some reason, the seat is passed along to the next name on the list. The importance of rank order for an individual candidate on the party electoral list immediately becomes clear. Since most parties will put a great number of names on their lists that have no realistic chance of being elected it is of crucial importance to a serious candidate that he or she be placed in as high a position as possible on the party list.[16]

This positioning on electoral lists has a great deal of significance in the Israeli political recruitment process.[17] It also has an equal importance in terms of intraparty and interfactional argument over which individual is placed in which position. In a pre—electoral coalition, in which one electoral list is submitted for a number of parties (such as some of the pre—electoral alliances discussed in the preceding chapter) one's position on the list is as decisive for the parties as for the individuals concerned. This position is determined in a conference of party leaders, the most important party in the alignment receiving the best positions, and so on. In the case of the Labor alignment list for the Eighth Knesset, composed of the Mapai, Ahdut HaAvodah, Mapam, and Rafi "factions," the distribution of the first eight places on the combined list for Knesset was:

1. Mapai	5. Ahdut HaAvodah
2. Mapai	6. Mapai
3. Mapai	7. Mapai
4. Rafi	8. Mapam[18]

There is no overall formula for the order of party factions on the list. Each position is argued over individually among the parties involved until an agreement is reached. This type of argument can sometimes lead to near crisis for the pre—election party alignments: on one occasion the Likud alignment almost fell apart before an election because of fighting between the State List and the Free Center parties over which would receive the thirty—sixth and thirty—seventh positions on the party list.[19] Some parties, in fact, reach a compromise on list positions by determining that there shall be a rotation of office; this is especially frequent in the smaller parties which can only elect a few members. Occasionally in the middle of a parliamentary term a member of one small party bloc will resign because of a pre—election compact within his party which required that he do so halfway through the Knesset's term of office so that a member of another party faction, who was next on the party list, could assume a seat in the Knesset.[20]

A good position on the party list, which is important to the leaders of party factions who desire maximum representation in the Knesset, is likewise critical for serious candidates. On the Labor list, which won 49 seats in the Eleventh Knesset, positions 45 through 55 were in the "maximum risk" area. A higher position would have been considered "safe" since it was virtually assured before the election that the party would win that share of the vote, and a lower position was considered "unrealistic" since it was equally virtually assured that the party would *not* win *that* much of the vote.

Because their position on the party list is so critical for those who want to advance their political careers, individual Knesset members are extremely vulnerable to the party leaders and list makers. The member who is elected from a "safe" position—for example, position thirty on the Labor party list—who is too much of a maverick during the Knesset term, who votes or speaks against the party, may find his or her position on the next electoral list lowered, perhaps by only one or two positions as a warning, or possibly more. This ability to lower a member's position on the list puts a real lever in the hands of those who demand party discipline in the Knesset.[21]

Since the assignment of a "safe," as well as a "marginal," position on the party list may be entirely up to the discretion of the party leaders in a given party,[22] a safe position is usually awarded as a prize or a reward for a history of good work and loyalty. The work may involve living on a party kibbutz, working at the party's headquarters in one of the many full–time positions, or merely being active in electoral campaigns. Even being placed in an "unrealistic" or "symbolic" position can be seen as an honor for a political neophyte, for it implies that with continued good work and loyalty a higher list rank and possibly a Knesset seat might eventually be forthcoming. The party list thus becomes a prime tool in the hands of the party leaders for recruiting new members. If leaders see an individual whom they would like to nurture and encourage to become active in the party, they can place him or her in the "marginal" zone, or slightly below that, with the implicit understanding that better things are to come.

In addition to recruiting individuals with the Knesset list, the party can also use the list strategically to attract individuals or groups.[23] The group may serve as the focal point in this process, where the party may offer groups "safe" or "marginal" positions on the party list in exchange for party endorsements and support. Certain groups in the Israeli political system have sufficient power to be able to demand and receive "safe" places on the major parties' lists. For example, the Tel Aviv Women's Association has regularly demanded a "safe" place in recent elections, and has been given "safe" positions along with the right to choose its own candidate. In 1973 it chose as its candidate Ora Namir, who had no previous party political experience. She was given position fifty on the Labor party list for the Eighth Knesset, and was subsequently elected. The Jerusalem Women's Association similarly demanded a "safe" place on the Labor list, but since its electoral influence was not as great as Tel Aviv, the Jerusalem group was given a position in the low eighties—a symbolic reward only.[24]

To take an even more recent example, much was written during the 1988 Knesset campaign period about the role of women in the Israeli polity and the degree to which the electoral list system did or did not help women more than a different electoral system might. As things turned out, women ended up expressing their "disappointment" with the outcome of the list–formation process, in which fewer women ended up in high list positions than had been hoped.[25]

In the end, all types of groups are "represented" on the party list, irrespective of how individual candidates are chosen. Local party organizations vie for "safe" places along with union organizations, professional association, ethnic groups, and the like. In recent years the major parties have significantly "opened" their nomination procedures, but the basis of group representation has not changed.[26]

Proposed Electoral Changes

Over the years many efforts, some moderate and some much more extensive, have been undertaken to change the electoral system in Israel. It is clear that the process as it presently exists has had a significant effect upon election outcomes. If Israel had a single–member district electoral arrangement similar to that of the United States, it is doubtful that fifteen different parties would be represented in the Knesset. Accordingly, many Israelis—especially those in the smaller political parties—have steadfastly fought against any proposed change in the structure of the electoral system.

One of the earliest proponents of electoral change was former Prime Minister David Ben–Gurion. He favored the single–member district as practiced in Britain and the United States, claiming that the Israeli proportional representation system encouraged small factions to break away from larger parties and form new, small parties, which in turn made it more difficult for stable government coalitions to be created. In fact, in 1952 Ben–Gurion and the Mapai party proposed raising the one percent "threshold" necessary to gain representation in the Knesset to 10 percent,[27] a change which would have significantly cut Knesset representation at the time (from fifteen parties to four), and which would have a similarly radical effect today (cutting representation in the Knesset from fifteen to two). In 1958 Ben–Gurion and Mapai spoke out favoring an amendment providing for 120 single–member districts, but the bill was never passed.[28]

Although there were a number of subsequent and unsuccessful efforts, the next major attempt at reform came in April, 1974, when a bill aimed at modifying the party list system was introduced in the Knesset. The bill proposed that "a majority of Knesset members will be elected in districts by a proportional system, and a minority by a national list,"[29] and would have made the Knesset members "more responsive to the wishes of the constituents and would prevent a minority from having the power to distort the wishes of the majority."[30] This proposal, sometimes referred to as the Ya'acobi Proposal (named after its primary advocate, Gad Ya'acobi), is an imaginative proposal worth brief examination here.[31]

One of Ya'acobi's primary concerns was that the existing system overly encouraged small parties. As he wrote:

> It enables a relatively small party, by being the balancer, to dictate to the whole government positions that run counter to the wishes of the majority of the people, of the Knesset, and even of the government.[32]

Ya'acobi proposed that Members of the Knesset be elected in two ways: most—90 of the 120—from a modified proportional representation system using eighteen small constituencies; the rest, chosen from a single national district. He envisaged that voters would cast two ballots. The first would be in the eighteen five–member districts. There each of the parties would field five candidates. Voters would express their preference for a political party, and the actual number of seats would be determined proportionally. If a party won twenty percent of the vote, for example, it would receive one seat.

It is clear that one effect of this proposal would have been to raise the vote threshold from one percent to twenty. Parties receiving less than that would win no seats. This would also very likely encourage more pre–election alliances between political parties (especially small parties) that knew they alone could not win sufficient votes but felt that in combination with other parties they might stand a chance. An additional favorable result of this system is that members of the public would now have a stronger sense of who "their" representatives were.

In the second vote there would be a single national constituency, as there is today, in which the remaining 30 Members would be elected at large, with a party winning, say, ten percent of the at–large vote receiving three seats. This would enable the smaller parties to contest some of the Knesset seats; essentially there would be a 3.3 percent threshold for these seats (instead of the 1 percent threshold which exists today), since 3.3 percent of the vote would net one at–large seat.

When Ya'acobi's bill was introduced in the Knesset it passed with a bare 61 votes. Although this was a large majority in terms of those present and voting, it received the absolute minimum necessary. Any bills proposing change in the electoral system are in fact proposals for amendments to the "Fundamental Law: The Knesset" (which describes the method of election to the Knesset), and as amendments to a Fundamental Law they require an absolute majority (i.e. at least 61 votes out of 120 possible votes, *not* merely a majority of those Members present in the legislature at the time) to pass. Since Ya'acobi's bill was a private member's bill, that is a bill not introduced by a member of the Government (cabinet), when it received its 61 votes it was sent to committee for consideration, and it never reappeared.

A more recent attempt at electoral reform took place in 1977 after the elections for the Ninth Knesset.[33] The Democratic Movement for Change had demanded electoral reform as one of its primary campaign platforms, and when Menachem Begin invited them to join his Likud Coalition electoral reform was one of their two prerequisites (the foreign ministry cabinet post being the other). Since the 1977 election was the first in nearly thirty years in which Begin's party had emerged victorious, he was hardly likely to agree to change the electoral system which had put him there, and that proved to be the case. In the final coalition agreement which the DMC signed with Begin the Government agreed to set up a committee of the four coalition partners (Likud, DMC, National Religious Party, and Agudat Israel) to discuss the topic of electoral reform, although it was widely perceived that this "concession" was purely symbolic, constituting the price Begin was willing to pay to broaden the coalition. With two small religious parties on the Committee with the Likud, the DMC held no illusions about the likelihood that it could effect changes. The committee commenced to discuss the number of regions into which the country might be divided for district–based representation.[34]

To no one's surprise, the DMC's proposals for electoral reform, which it characterized as central to any reform of Israeli politics, were not put into effect by the Likud Government. The leaders of the DMC knew when they signed the coalition agreement that setting up a committee to "study" their reform proposal was comparable to putting a cat in the cage to protect the bird; Agudat Israel had openly condemned the proposal before the elections, and both Likud and the NRP were skeptical at best.

The arguments of the DMC were that the consequences of this type of change would have been enormous. To shift from an electoral system based upon proportional representation and a single national electoral list to *any* kind of district–based representation—regardless of the number of districts to be established—would have crucial consequences for party discipline in the legislature. Giving legislators a specific district and constituency to which they feel responsible would lessen the vulnerability of the individual MKs to their party leadership, if for no other reason than there would no longer be a single national party electoral list.

The theme of electoral reform has once again received a great deal of attention in the last year. In June, 1988, the Knesset began to address an electoral reform bill that could "revolutionize the country's political life." The bill proposed two possible ways for changing the Israeli electoral system, both of which would produce a 120–Member Knesset. The first would divide the country into twenty electoral districts, each electing four Members, with another forty representatives to be elected by the national proportional–representation list system as exists at the present time. A second proposal would divide the country into sixty electoral districts, each electing one representative, with the remaining sixty likewise to be elected by national proportional–representation. Both proposals were strongly opposed by the religious parties, who claimed that "the system would deprive large sections of the electorate of any share of the vote." In the final analysis, the bill was not voted on before the Knesset adjourned for the fall elections.[35]

After the 1988 election the topic of electoral reform received even *more* attention as a result of the initially unsuccessful efforts of Yitzhak Shamir and the Likud party to form a coalition government. In that election, since the Likud received a plurality of Knesset seats—that is, more than other parties but less than an absolute majority—the President gave the Likud leader, Shamir, three weeks in which to form a coalition. After a great deal of public wrangling, most of which had to do with demands by the small religious parties to expand the influence of Orthodox Judaism in exchange for their support for the coalition, the three week coalition–formation period expired without the Likud being able to establish a parliamentary majority. Shamir was simply unwilling to give in to what he—along with substantial communities in Israel and abroad—felt were unreasonable demands.[36]

Shamir thereupon returned to the President and asked for another three week "mandate," arguing that he was sure that he could succeed in a second attempt. The President agreed, but advised him to form another "Government of National Unity" with the Labor party, something that both Likud and Labor had promised their audiences during the campaign that they would not do. The President *also* advised Shamir to consider changes in the electoral system after a coalition was established, so that there would not be the number of small parties represented in the Knesset in the future, something which he felt exacerbated difficulties in the coalition—formation process.

Eventually, 51 days after the November 1 Knesset election, Shamir succeeded in forming a broad "Likud—Labor—religious unity government." Unlike its predecessor "unity government," this coalition did not include an agreement for Shamir and Labor party leader Shimon Peres to exchange offices after two years. Peres was instead appointed Finance Minister, while Likud held control over foreign policy with the appointment of Moshe Arens, a senior Likud member and former Israeli ambassador to the United States, as Foreign Minister. The entire coalition—formation process brought honor upon neither Shamir nor upon the system of forming coalitions in Israel. One editorial writer observed that:

> The Likud made exorbitant promises to (the religious parties) in order to win their support—and then systematically broke most of them. Had it not made those promises, in the field of religious legislation, settlements, and in ministries, honors and money, they would not have recommended to the President that he name Shamir to form a government, and the President would not have chosen him. Nor could Shamir have expected Labor to agree to join his government without a rotation in the premiership. The unity government could not have arisen on the conditions that it did. The government that did arise was the result of two factors: the Likud's acquiescing in most of the demands of the religious parties, and its breaking of those promises.[37]

Another major editorial focused upon the religious parties:

> Could the entire coalition—forming process have been concluded quicker and more elegantly? Certainly, but with an infinitely worse government resulting in which the Likud would have sold out completely to the insatiable greed of the fundamentalistic religious parties. There are several lessons to be learned from the turning of the tables on the religious parties (by the Likud's Prime—Minister—designate Yitzhak Shamir) and from the fact that they came into the coalition in the end on Shamir's terms and not on theirs. Despite the aura of holiness they like to radiate, our religious politicians and rabbis are supreme pragmatists. They always give in when confronted with real opposition; it is only when the secular majority rolls over and plays dead that the religious win.[38]

Such expressions notwithstanding, the mechanics of the legislative amendment process and the disproportionate role small parties have often played make prospects for electoral reform practically nil. The politics of coalition–formation seems destined to be an integral, if cumbersome, part of the Israeli political process.

Voting Behavior and Electoral Results

This is not the place for a comprehensive analysis of voting behavior in all of the twelve Knesset elections. That has been done more than adequately elsewhere.[39] Our task here is to highlight some of the major themes which have been brought to light in the substantial scholarship in this area.

To begin with, overall voter turnout in Israel is high. It has ranged from a peak of 86.8% in 1949 for the first Knesset election, to a low of 75.1% in 1951, with an average of about 80%. Even the voting turnout of the Bedouin voters in Israel is nearly 65% over time, lower than most other groups in Israel, but certainly much higher than a corresponding American figure.[40] One interesting difference between Jewish and non–Jewish Israelis has appeared in recent research: they differ significantly in their motivations for *non*–participation. Few Jewish Israelis fail to vote for ideological or political reasons, and their responses to interview questions indicated that when they failed to vote it tended to be because of "technical" factors such as illness, failure to register, or not having adequate identification when they intended to vote. Non–Jewish Israeli citizens, on the other hand, expressed a *conscious* motive in their nonparticipation: "54.6 percent of the non–Jews gave purposeful abstention as the reason for not voting, compared to 12.8 percent of the sample of Jewish voters."[41] Ascertaining bases for political preferences, however, has been a more difficult endeavor.

Ideology

Why Israelis vote as they do has been the subject of much study in recent years. Certainly one explanation has to do with *ideology*—what Israeli voters believe and what policy alternatives the political parties offer them. According to Arian: "Israeli voters tend to report that ideological considerations are important in motivating the vote. The Israeli political system is, and is perceived to be, ideological in nature; one is tempted to say that this is the ideology of the system."[42] Survey data tend to support this view. Recent opinion polls have shown that in response to the question: "Which is the most important factor in influencing a person to vote for a particular party?", 32 percent responded that their party identification was the most important factor, 10 percent that the party's candidate was most important, 53 percent that the party's platform or ideology was most important, while only four percent indicated that the party's being in government or opposition was most important (two percent offered other responses).[43]

One of the real problems with political ideology in Israel, and one dimension in which we can see its direct impact upon the electoral system and electoral behavior, has to do with the number of cross pressures that individuals face. Cross pressures can be defined as conflicting claims on a voter's loyalties, with one loyalty—or issue—pushing in one direction, and another pulling him or her the opposite way. In the United States, with its loose party discipline in the legislature, this would not be so great a problem. Although various Republicans in Congress may have different opinions on some crucial issues, they can all survive as Republicans because the national party platform is (deliberately) general and vague, and because they have a great deal of legislative autonomy (including actual voting) in Congress.

In the Knesset, however, with highly disciplined political parties that try to deliver on policy promises they make, members of legislative parties cannot disagree on important policy issues. Instead, new political parties have to be formed that represent specific policy combinations. For example, members of the National Religious Party and the Agudat bloc are in general agreement on the importance of the Torah and Zionism, but disagree on Arab and economic policies. Members of the Likud alignment, on the other hand, are in agreement that a strong national security policy is necessary, but are more divided over the role of the Torah and on various economic questions. The presence of numerous "major" issues in Israel causes a great deal of disharmony in the political system and tends to encourage the formation of more political parties with more specific combinations of policy positions.

In fact, some in Israel say that *more* parties are needed, not less, because of the great number of possible issue positions that can be taken. Although the total number of positions on four bipositional issues is only sixteen, some of which are logically contradictory or incompatible, the various degrees of opinion and intensity of belief for each issue leave the possibility open for more competing party organizations to form. Given that most of the major issues in the Israeli political arena are *not* bipositional—there being a "left," "right," and "center," as well as a number of intermediate positions—there is room for a wide range of parties to represent functionally the spectrum of views in Israeli politics.

Ethnicity

Although scholarship on Israeli voting behavior has found a number of meaningful associations in recent years, the most important has increasingly been that of ethnicity. In brief, Likud was brought to and has stayed in power since 1977 with the support of the Sephardim—Jews of Asian, African, or Middle Eastern background. Correspondingly, the Alignment is most strongly supported by European and American–descended Jews—the Ashkenazim.[44]

Interpretations of this phenomenon vary. Many suggest that for almost thirty years, while the Alignment was in control in Israeli politics, the Sephardic Jews were systematically "shut out" of top political positions in the Government, the bureaucracy, and the Knesset. This was reflected most directly in the electoral lists for the Knesset, although in the early years the Alignment "regularly won support from most groups in society."[45] Significant change in electoral behavior occurred during the 1970's. Research has shown that

> in the late 1960s both parties were predominantly Ashkenazi; by 1981 the Alignment had stayed that way, and the Likud had become predominantly Sephardi. The turnabout seems to have occurred in 1977 when a majority of the Likud vote was Sephardi for the first time.[46]

Several reasons can be advanced for the increased Sephardi vote. As their proportion of the population increased from a minority to a majority, and as awareness of their relatively lower income and educational levels grew, the Sephardim became increasingly dissatisfied with the "in" party, Labor. At the same time Likud was seeking a new constituency, and the attraction of Likud to the Sephardim proved advantageous for both parties. In the end, and for whatever reasons, "ethnic politics" has been more and more visible in Israel for the last three elections and there is no indication that this will not continue to be the case even though the Alignment has undertaken a concerted effort to break the Likud's hold on the loyalties of the Sephardim.

Voting Trends

Although there have been a large number of short–term variations in the twelve Knessot elections, most have been exhaustively chronicled and analyzed in specific monographs and essays.[47] Here we simply want to identify a few general trends in recent elections.

First, observers of elections in Israel have seen a substantial decline—and then partial recovery—of the Alignment's Knesset seats, as illustrated in Figure 6.2. This has been explained as a function of both short– and long–term factors. In 1977 the Labor leader indicated that "corruption in his party was the major cause of the Labor defeat in the election." In fact,

> during the Seventh and Eighth Knessot there were scandals in the Finance Ministry, the Bank of Israel, and personal financial illegalities committed by the Labor Prime Minister (Rabin) and his wife . . . These events simply led to the public perception of the Labor party as a whole becoming corrupt, and a good share of the public was looking for new leadership.[48]

In the longer term one could list ethnicity (already discussed in the preceding section), other demographic shifts, and changes in the general political setting as factors influencing voting behavior. Many analysts noted that the terrorist bombing of an innocent civilian's vehicle the day of the 1988 election was responsible for a last–minute swing of several percent of the vote to Likud. In sum, although Mapai was originally the overwhelmingly dominant party on the political landscape in Israel, this was at least partly because it was the government party. As the role of the government has changed, the advantages to the public of supporting Mapai, and then the Labor Alignment as a whole, have changed, and voters have proven to be much more willing to switch to other parties when given the choice in national elections.

FIGURE 6.2
Some Electoral Trends in Recent Knesset Elections

Alignment (A)		Likud (L)		Other (O)	
A 56	A 51	A 32	A 47	A 44	A 38
L 26	L 39	L 43	L 48	L 41	L 39
O 42	O 30	O 45	O 25	O 35	O 43
A					
A	A	O		A L	
A O	A L	L O	A L	A L O	A L O
A L O	A L O	A L O	A L O	A L O	A L O
A L O	A L O	A L O	A L O	A L O	A L O
A L O	A L O	A L O	A L O	A L O	A L O
1969	1973	1977	1981	1984	1988
7th	8th	9th	10th	11th	12th
Knesset	Knesset	Knesset	Knesset	Knesset	Knesset

One high–ranking Likud party official explained the decline of Mapai, the rise of Likud, and the subsequent equalization of parties in the Knesset as a function of governmental involvement in the economy.[49] In Israel's formative years political parties were extremely important in providing services to the public as extensive as employment, housing, education, and medical care. As the government itself has assumed responsibility and equalized the public's access to these services, there has been less need for citizens to belong to a major political party like Mapai, for example, to receive these benefits.

The gradual decline in the electoral strength of Mapai, the largest party in Israel until 1977 and the party organizing the government in every coalition until that time, can be explained by this phenomenon. Since Mapai was the largest party, it had the most rewards to give to its supporters. Now that these rewards—medical care, education, employment services, and the like—are being distributed equally by the government ministries, Mapai is losing the advantages that it used to hold over the other, smaller parties, and consequently voters have felt freer in recent years to shift their support, knowing that the governmental services would be theirs in any case.

In more recent years foreign policy issues, the question of settlements on the West Bank, and the general issue of national security have also come to be seen as distinguishing characteristics of the two major political parties. Likud was the party of the "strong response" to the Arab challenge, while Mapai—now Labor—was perceived as the party supporting negotiation and moderation. This has been an image that Labor has tried hard to shed, but to a large extent it has not been successful.

This has led to a gradual decline in the strength of Mapai, the Alignment, and then Labor, and an increase in the Likud. When this general pattern is combined with the change in degrees of ethnic support, and when short term issues such as corruption of the emergence of a new political party led by a charismatic leader—such as the Democratic Movement for Change—are added to the equation, some drastic changes in electoral outcomes can result.

One thing is quite clear: Although the Likud may have been seen in Israel's early years as a totally "unrealistic" alternative basis for a government—thus leading some voters to support Labor despite being ideologically predisposed not to do so—that is no longer the case today. Likud has shown that it *can* govern and that it *does* provide an ideological and programmatic alternative to the Alignment. This is a self–reinforcing phenomenon and means, minimally, that voters will continue to vote for non–Alignment parties now that they realize the Israeli political system can survive periods of alternative leadership. If anything, the elections of 1984 and 1988 support this assertion.

Significance of the Electoral Process for Israel

The current Israeli electoral system has been criticized for a number of reasons. Attitudes have ranged from the contention that the electoral list system makes the member of Knesset too dependent upon party leaders, to the view that this means that each Knesset member has no reason to want to stay in contact with the voters, to a feeling that power is too highly concentrated in the hands of a few party leaders, to a conclusion that the current system leads to unstable government and weak coalitions because it encourages too many political parties to compete.[50] The Israeli electoral system, according to one scholar,

> has been criticized on three main grounds: that in encouraging multipartism and coalition rule it impedes truly responsible government; that it facilitates undemocratic choice of candidates; and that it separates between electors and representatives.[51]

A number of these points deserve additional comment here.

It is apparent that the electoral system presently constituted encourages many different political parties to operate in the Israeli political world. We have seen how some proposed—but unadopted—electoral changes would have drastically altered the way that both the electoral and the party system would operate. The point to remember, however, is that the electoral system did not originally create the many political parties which currently exist in Israel. They themselves created an electoral system that has perpetuated their existence. As one author put it: "Israel's choice of an electoral system . . . rested on solid precedents from the prestate period."[52] Nor should we forget that there is also a positive side to multiple political parties: It more closely reflects the characteristics of the population.

We would no doubt see a quieter and calmer electoral system if Israel were divided into equal–representative districts. In that case, most likely two large parties would capture virtually all of the Knesset seats, leading to majority government. However, one of the very special—perhaps unpleasant, but special—characteristics of Israeli elections over the years has been the degree to which identifiable electoral minorities are able to succeed in attaining Knesset representation.

There can be no question that this has forced coalition governments and given many smaller, usually religious, parties undue leverage in government policy. Still, for many this is the saving grace of the Israeli electoral framework.

This situation does, of course, have implications for responsible government and the ability of elected representatives to deliver on their promises. First, no party has ever received an absolute electoral majority, thus necessitating the formation (and instability) of coalitions. Second, small electoral groups have a disproportionate influence on government policy. Where a small group becomes necessary for the creation of a coalition, that party has an undeserved influence, which has been offered as an explanation for the continuation—and indeed expansion—of legislation supporting Orthodox Jewish public policy.

In 1981 a proposal was introduced in the Knesset to raise the "threshold" for votes from one to 2 1/2 percent, a change which would have eliminated several of the smallest parties in the Knesset. The bill was barely defeated by a forty–four to thirty–seven margin.[53] Once again, for obvious reasons, strong opposition came from the smaller parties in the Knesset. In addition to many of the smaller parties, even Labor opposed the bill "because it would have eliminated the small Arab lists formed on a regional and personal basis, who traditionally supported Labor."[54] This issue is not likely to go away in future political debates in Israel.

It seems clear that it is also true that the Israeli electoral system facilitates an oligarchic choice of candidates. The proportional representation system, with electoral lists composed by national party organizations, clearly limits the ability of interested individuals to enter the political arena with any likelihood of winning at all unless they operate within the framework of an established political party. Some of the political parties have opened up their list construction procedures and now stipulate that national conventions must approve positions on the party list.[55] But in many cases the closed–door or "smoke–filled room" scenario is still apt. In the words of Sager: "Herut and the Liberals have in recent elections both entrusted the choice of head of the list and the entire task of naming the candidates and arranging their order to their Central Committees numbering, respectively, 1,000 and 240 members."[56] One thousand party members in a convention setting is not exactly a smoke–filled room, but it is also not an entirely open process.

On the other hand, although the process may not be entirely open, it is not entirely closed. The major parties make a concerted effort to recruit candidates from a variety of social, economic, ethnic, geographic, and occupational backgrounds.[57] In doing so they force themselves to be relatively "open." This process may have additional benefits, in that it may do a better job of representing some of these groups than an "open market" approach would. One study has found, for instance, that women fare better being recruited to positions on the party list than they would in a district–based electoral system.[58]

The Israeli proportional representation system is not one in which open primary elections would be appropriate. Although it is possible for single individuals to offer themselves as "one–man lists," this is not an established practice in Israeli politics. An actor who wants to have a realistic chance to be elected to the Knesset must operate from a high position on an established political party's electoral list. This does, in fact, make the system less democratic in terms of a choice of candidates, especially because individual voters must vote for lists, not individuals, and a voter who strongly wants candidate number fifty–three on the Labor list, must wait for the first fifty–two Laborites to be elected before his or her vote counts for his or her preference. This is precisely the reason for the Ya'acobi proposal for a number of smaller electoral districts. Thus there is no doubt that the electoral system *does* have a significant impact upon politics in the Israeli political system. Not only does it affect the quality and style of debate in the political arena, but it also, obviously, affects the membership of the Knesset and thereby the makeup of the governing coalition, a topic to which we now turn our attention.

NOTES

1. Maurice Duverger, *Political Parties* (New York: John Wiley, 1963), p. 239.

2. Fundamental Law: The Knesset, Section 4.

3. For a fuller explanation, see Asher Zidon, *The Knesset* (New York: Herzl Press, 1967), pp. 23–29.

4. David Butler, Howard Penniman, and Austin Ranney (eds.), *Democracy at the Polls*, (Washington: American Enterprise Institute, 1981), p. 24.

5. For an expanded explanation of this process, see Yehoshua Freudenheim, *Government in Israel* (Dobbs Ferry, N.Y.: Oceana Publications, 1967), p. 126.

6. Asher Arian, *Politics in Israel: The Second Generation* (Chatham, N.J.: Chatham House), p. 123.

7. Samuel Sager, *The Parliamentary System of Israel* (Syracuse: Syracuse University Press, 1985), 67. See in particular his section on: "Financing of Elections," pp. 67–72.

8. Ibid., p. 69.

9. Leon Boim, "The Financing of Elections," in *Israel At the Polls, 1977,* Howard Penniman (ed.) (Washington, D.C.: American Enterprise Institute, 1979).

10. For example, the article by Judith Elizur, "The Role of the Media in the 1981 Knesset Elections," discusses recent changes in election law, the image problems of the political parties, and differing patterns of media use. The article is included in Howard R. Penniman and Daniel Elazar, *Israel at the Polls, 1981* (Bloomington, Ind.: Indiana University Press, 1986), pp. 186–212.

11. Editorial comments cited here come from "The Election Campaign on Television," edited by Gary Wolf, part of the series of news releases *Israeli Press Highlights* (New York: Institute of Human Relations, American Jewish Committee, October 10, 1988), pp. 1–2.

12. An article by Joel Brinkley in the *New York Times* on October 8, 1988, p. 18, titled "Israeli TV Political Ads Lowering the Low Road" developed this theme, pointing out that the ads do help to raise issues, but that they also use character defamation, propaganda, misrepresentation, deceptive photography, alteration of pictures and quotations, and, generally, "a loose version of facts."

13. Arian, *Politics in Israel*, p. 121.

14. Zidon, *The Knesset*, pp. 23–24; Sager, *The Parliamentary System of Israel*, p. 46.

15. Arian, *Politics in Israel*, p. 121; Sager, *The Parliamentary System of Israel*, p. 46.

16. Gregory Mahler, "The Effects of Electoral Systems Upon the Behavior of Members of a National Legislature: The Israeli Knesset Case Study," *Journal of Constitutional and Parliamentary Studies* 14:4 (1980); pp. 305–18.

17. Moshe Czudnowski, "Legislative Recruitment Under Proportional Representation in Israel: A Model and a Case Study," *Midwest Journal of Political Science* 14 (1970); pp. 216–48.

18. Gregory Mahler, *The Knesset: Parliament in the Israeli Political System* (Rutherford, N.J.: Fairleigh–Dickinson University Press, 1981), p. 44.

19. One specific event like this was covered in the *Jerusalem Post*, September 10, 1973, p. 1.

20. *Jerusalem Post: Overseas Edition*, November 12, 1975, p. 3.

21. Avraham Brichta, "Selection of Candidates to the Tenth Knesset: The Impact of Centralization," in *Israel at the Polls: 1981*, Howard Penniman and Daniel Elazar (eds.) (Washington, D.C.: American Enterprise Institute, 1986), pp. 18–35.

22. Steven Hoffman, "Candidate Selection in Israel's Parliament: The Realities of Change," *Middle East Journal* 34 (1980); pp. 285–301.

23. Moshe Czudnowski, "Sociocultural Variables and Legislative Recruitment," *Comparative Politics* 4 (1972); pp. 561–87.

24. Mahler, *The Knesset*, pp. 46–7.

25. See the article "Labour Women Are Left 'Disappointed'," *Jerusalem Post* June 1, 1988, p. 14, for a discussion of the effect of this process in the recent election campaign.

26. Myron Aronoff has written a fascinating analysis of reforms in the Labor Party. See his "Better Late Than Never: Democratization in the Labor Party," in Gregory Mahler (ed.), *Israel Since Begin* (Albany: State University of New York Press, forthcoming).

27. Alfred Katz, *Government and Politics in Contemporary Israel, 1948–Present* (Washington, D.C.: University Press of America), p. 56.

28. Sager, *The Parliamentary System of Israel*, p. 63.

29. *Jerusalem Post*, April 2, 1974, p. 2.

30. Katz, *Government and Politics*, p. 58.

31. This is based upon more extended discussion in Arian, *Politics in Israel*, pp. 130–31.

32. Gad Ya'acobi, *The Government of Israel* (New York: Praeger, 1982), p. 307.

33. Avraham Brichta, "1977 Elections and the Future of Electoral Reform in Israel," in *Israel at the Polls, 1977*, Howard Penniman (ed.) (Washington, D.C.: American Enterprise Institute, 1979).

34. *Jerusalem Post: International Edition*, October 25, 1977, p. 1.

35. There was substantial coverage of the bill during its brief legislative life by the media. See *The Jerusalem Post*, June 8, 1988, p. 2.

36. This is discussed in "The Coalition Talks Drag On," in Gary Wolf (ed.), *Israeli Press Highlights* (New York: Institute of Human Relations, American Jewish Committee, December 6, 1988), pp. 1–3.

37. Dov Goldstein in *Ma'ariv* (December 22) quoted in "The New Israeli Government," in Gary Wolf (ed.), *Israeli Press Highlights* (New York: Institute of Human Relations, American Jewish Committee, December 25, 1988), p. 1.

38. Yosef Goell in the *Jerusalem Post* (December 23), quoted in Ibid., p. 2.

39. See, among many other sources, the following for references to the last few elections: Asher Arian, *The Elections in Israel—1969* (Jerusalem: Jerusalem Academic Press, 1972); Arian, *The Elections in Israel—1973* (Jerusalem:

Jerusalem Academic Press, 1975); Arian, *The Elections in Israel, 1977* (Jerusalem: Jerusalem Academic Press, 1980); Howard Penniman (ed.), *Israel at the Polls: The Knesset Elections of 1977* (Washington, D.C.: American Enterprise Institute, 1979); Arian, *The Elections in Israel—1981* (Tel Aviv: Ramon Publishing Co., 1983); Michal Shamir and Asher Arian, "The Ethnic Vote in Israel's 1981 Elections," *Electoral Studies* 1 (1982); pp. 315–31; and, Howard Penniman and Daniel Elazar (eds.), *Israel at the Polls, 1981*, op. cit.

40. Arian, *Politics in Israel*, p. 133.

41. Ibid., p. 134.

42. Ibid., p. 136.

43. Ibid., pp. 139–44.

44. Ibid., p. 140.

45. Ibid., p. 142.

46. Among the many journal articles dealing with specific electoral outcomes in the last three decades—a number of general books on Israeli elections have already been referred to—might be included the following: Alan Arian, "Were the 1973 Elections in Israel Critical?" *Comparative Politics* 8 (1975); pp. 152–65; Alan Arian and Shevah Weiss, "Split Ticket Voting in Israel," *Western Political Quarterly* 22 (1969); pp. 375–89; Yael Azmon, "The 1981 Elections and the Changing Fortunes of the Israeli Labour Party," *Government and Opposition* 16:4 (1981); pp. 432–46; Marver Bernstein, "Israel's Ninth General Election," *International Studies* 17 (1978); pp. 27–50; Don Peretz, "The War Election and Israel's Eighth Knesset," *Middle East Journal* 28 (1974); pp. 111–25; Peretz, "Israel's 1969 Election Issues—The Visible and the Invisible," *Middle East Journal* 24:1 (1970); pp. 31–71; Peretz and Sammy Smooha, "Israel's Tenth Knesset Elections: Ethnic Upsurgence and Decline of Ideology," *Middle East Journal* 35 (1981); pp. 506–26.

47. Gregory Mahler, *The Knesset*, p. 214. Following the 1977 election loss to Menachem Begin, Shimon Peres indicated that the Alignment's electoral defeat was attributable to "a number of domestic and international trends," but also cited the "failure of demoralized party activists to push hard for victory," adding that "corruption hurt us the most." See the *Jerusalem Post: International Edition*, May 24, 1977, p. 6.

48. Yechiel Kadashai, secretary and first assistant to Likud party leader Menachem Begin. Information was gathered in an interview that was held April 3, 1975, in the Knesset in Jerusalem. See Mahler, *The Knesset, p. 41.*

49. Avraham Brichta, "1977 Elections and The Future of Electoral Reform in Israel," in *Israel at the Polls: The Knesset Elections of 1977*, Howard Penniman (ed.), (Washington, D.C.: American Enterprise Institute, 1979), pp. 45–46.

50. Sager, *The Parliamentary System of Israel*, p. 48.

51. C. Paul Bradley, *Parliamentary Elections in Israel* (Grantham, N.H.: Tompson and Rutter, 1985), p. 20.

52. Sager, *The Parliamentary System of Israel*, p. 50.

53. Ibid.

54. See Steven Hoffman, "Candidate Selection in Israel's Parliament: The Realities of Change," *Middle East Journal* 34 (1980); 285–301; and Aronoff, "Better Late Than Never," op cit.

55. Aronoff, "Better Late Than Never," op. cit.

56. Sager, *The Parliamentary System of Israel*, p. 51.

57. Moshe Czudnowski, "Legislative Recruitment Under Proportional Representation in Israel: A Model and a Case Study," *Midwest Journal of Political Science* 14 (1970); pp. 216–48; and Czudnowski, "Sociocultural Variables and Legislative Recruitment," *Comparative Politics* 4 (1972); pp. 561–87.

58. Shevah Weiss, "Women in the Knesset: 1949–1969," *Parliamentary Affairs* 28:1 (1969/70), pp. 31–50.

Chapter 7

THE KNESSET AND THE GOVERNMENT

Introduction: The Setting

As indicated earlier, the Israeli government is a parliamentary system. That is, as with many other "Westminster Model" systems, the prime minister and his or her cabinet derive their authority and power from the parliament. Only after he or she has received a vote of confidence from the Knesset can the chief executive take office. Conversely, the prime minister can be turned out of office at any time by a vote of no confidence in that same Knesset. Supposedly, then, the principle of "legislative supremacy" is characteristic of the Israeli political system, with the legislature doing the "hiring and firing" of the executive branch. Furthermore, the Knesset passes all legislation, serves as the pool from which the executive branch officials are drawn, controls the life of the government (the prime minister and cabinet) by retaining the right to vote nonconfidence, elects the president for a fixed (five year, renewable once) term, and, generally, is theoretically the dominant political structure in Israel. In reality, as we shall see, this is not entirely the case.

In recent years a great deal of attention has been focused on comparative policy–making and a general tendency toward the "decline of legislatures."[1] The contention is that the increasing growth of executive government (which itself occurs for a variety of reasons)[2], is matched by a corresponding decline in legislative influence. Power in the political system is thus seen as "zero sum": every increment of growth in the executive's power is said to be matched by an equal unit of decline in the legislature's. This situation, as has been suggested, has given rise to the *de facto* existence of "cabinet supremacy" rather than the *de jure* principle of "legislative supremacy."

The principle of "cabinet supremacy" is relatively easy to express in its basic form. We have already seen that strong party discipline exists in parliamentary systems. Individual members of parliament are expected to follow unquestioningly the instructions of their party leaders. Because the leaders of the majority party or the majority coalition are almost invariably members of the cabinet, we find a situation in which the legislature, which is technically in command in the governmental structure, actually takes its orders from the leaders of the executive branch, the cabinet. Hence the notion of "cabinet supremacy."

The principle of "cabinet supremacy" has a great deal of relevance for Israeli political figures. It means that individual Members of Knesset (sometimes referred to as MKs) are *not* expected to engage in personal activities. Rather, they are expected to do what they are told by their leaders. Members of opposition parties are expected to follow their party leaders, just as members of government coalition parties are expected to follow theirs (who are usually cabinet members, as well).

Because of the many political parties active in the Israeli political system, no single party has ever had an outright majority in the Knesset. Coalitions have therefore been the rule. The existence of government coalitions is a crucial starting–point for any study of the political process. Because it has traditionally been necessary for political parties in the Knesset to form a coalition, traditionally there has been less latitude for individual party and legislative behavior than might otherwise be the case. Party discipline—the practice of having Members of Knesset vote together and support party policy—becomes the norm, and coalition lines are rigidly enforced.

The term "Government" in Israel refers to the prime minister and his or her cabinet. The cabinet meets weekly—usually every Sunday—to discuss those issues which have found their way onto the national political agenda. The cabinet operates under the principle of collective responsibility; namely, once a decision is reached, it must be supported by all members of the cabinet. Individual cabinet members' only alternative to supporting a cabinet decision is to resign.[3]

The Office of Prime Minister itself does not have the same relative weight as in Britain, for example, primarily because of the coalition nature of Israeli cabinets. One result of this is that the prime minister may make policy suggestions to his or her cabinet colleagues which will be voted down by a majority of members of the cabinet (with the prime minister voting in the minority), and with the prime minister left with only two choices: support the views of the majority of the cabinet or resign—something that would not happen in the British case.

In this chapter we shall examine the Knesset's role in the Israeli political system, along with the power held and exercised by coalition governments since 1948. Although Israel is a new nation in terms of years, a number of traditions and customs have already developed which are uniquely Israeli and worthy of note.

Legislation in the Knesset

In addition to debate and discussion, probably the most important function of legislatures is that of passing laws. The legislative process in the Knesset follows the standard parliamentary model fairly closely; only a brief discussion of the process is needed here.[4]

An initial distinction must be made between Government and Private Members' Bills (the latter are so named because they are introduced by Private Members, not members of the Government). Government bills are introduced by members of the cabinet, the Government. These bills are not all *authored* by members of the cabinet, of course, but tend to be authored somewhere in the ministries in the relatively vast governmental bureaucracy. Wherever they originate, these bills are passed up the "chain of command" in the ministry involved to eventually reach the Director General, the ministry's highest ranking civil servant. He or she would then pass the proposal along to the minister responsible for that Department, who would take the bill to the Cabinet and, after receiving Cabinet approval, would introduce it in the Knesset as a Government bill.

Private Members' Bills, on the other hand, are bills introduced by non–cabinet members, whether they are members of parties belonging to the Government coalition or members of the opposition. Numerically, private members' bills are a very small minority of the total number of bills processed by the Knesset annually. Two decades ago, out of 166 laws passed by the Knesset, 156 (94.4 percent) were introduced by the Government, six (3.2 percent) were introduced by private members, and 4 (2.4 percent) were introduced in committees.[5] This situation has improved somewhat over the years, but not as much as many legislators would like. Private Members' bills still account for somewhat less than nine percent of all legislation introduced and passed in the Knesset between 1981 and 1984. (See Table 7.1)

Private bills in the Knesset are apportioned to the parties by a "key"; each party is allowed to introduce approximately three private bills per seat it holds for each Knesset session. This means that private members who want to introduce legislation must have their proposals "screened" by their parties or parliamentary bloc. If their party leaders do not give them permission, private members cannot introduce their own legislative proposals. Once their proposals are cleared they still must go over several more legislative hurdles than Government bills before they become law.[6]

As Table 7.1 indicates, the bulk of the Knesset's output comes from Government–sponsored legislation. After it is approved by the cabinet, Government bills are "tabled" in the Knesset and entered as items for the agenda. The bills must "lie on the table" (be available for examination) for at least forty–eight hours before discussion on them begins. As with many other procedural rules in the Knesset, this forty–eight hour rule may be waived by the Knesset committee if it so wishes.

TABLE 7.1
Government and Private Members' Bills, 1981–1984

Year	Government			Private Members		
	Intro-duced	Passed	% Passed	Intro-duced	Passed	% Passed
1981–1982	57	53	93	254	3	1.2
1982–1983	48	48	100	119	10	8.4
1983–1984	72	64	89	103	9	8.7

Source: Adapted from Samuel Sager, The Parliamentary System of Israel *(Syracuse, N.Y.: Syracuse University Press, 1985), p. 175.*

The first stage in the legislative process is called the first reading. The minister in charge of the bill begins with a summation of the contents of the bill and then a line–by–line reading. After the minister has finished presenting the bill, debate begins. This first reading debate is usually a general one. When the vote comes at the end of the debate, Government bills almost invariably are passed and sent to committee. Private Members' Bills rarely meet with the same results.

The bill is then sent to whichever committee has jurisdiction. If more than one committee is involved, the bill will go to the committees one after another, in whatever sequence the Speaker selects. The committee in question may deal with a bill for three months or three hours, depending upon the importance of the bill, the committee's workload, and the willingness of the committee to cooperate with the Government's manager of the legislation. The committee has the power to revise a bill, even to the extent of virtually rewriting it if necessary. However, the Government retains the power to "recall" a bill to the Knesset floor in the exact form in which it was sent to committee if it believes that the committee has significantly altered the bill away from its intended direction.

At this stage the second reading takes place. This is the final major hurdle the bill must pass, because bills that pass the second reading invariably pass the third reading. Another debate takes place at this point, but in this debate only members of the committee may participate; all other members are in attendance only to vote on the bill, section by section.

If no amendments to the committee report are adopted, the third reading follows immediately after the conclusion of the second. If there are amendments, the third reading is postponed for one week to allow members time to consider them. However, even if amendments have been proposed, if the Government requests an immediate third reading it takes place shortly after the second. Following the third reading the bill is voted on as a whole. Since the Israeli parliamentary system is a unicameral one, bills passed by the Knesset are sent directly to the President for his signature.

The Members of Knesset

A general description of Members of the Knesset would begin much as a description of members of parliament in most other nations. It would indicate that legislators are older than the general population, have a higher male proportion, and underrepresent minorities.[7] Apart from their primarily Jewish religious affiliation, they differ from other legislators in one very important respect. A substantial number of Members of the Knesset are immigrants, although this percentage, naturally, has decreased over the years. Approximately one Member of Knesset in ten is female.[8] This figure is certainly not representative of the proportion of women in the Israeli population, but is not greatly different from that found in most European parliaments. It is significantly greater than the comparable figure of approximately 3.5 percent for the United States Congress. Most Members of Knesset are also highly educated.

Most Members came to the Knesset through the ranks of their political party,[9] with many having held some formal party position prior to running for public office, be it for the Knesset or for some local body. Most dated their association with a political party from very early in their lives and were active in its "youth group" throughout their childhood. This pattern of party activity simply continued on after childhood and led to adult political activity. Eventually the outcome was receipt of an invitation to be on the party's electoral list.[10]

Exceptions to this pattern of vertical advancement up the party apparatus are rare. Perhaps the most prominent involved former Supreme Court Justice Benjamin Halevy. Seeking to add some additional "luster" to their lists, both Labor and Likud invited him to be a part of their

1973 roster. Eventually, Halevy opted for Likud. The benefits for each were scant, however, as the Justice bolted Likud two years later to form his own—ultimately unsuccessful—political party. The phenomenon of outside recruitment or formal "co–option" is not an important feature of Israeli politics. Rise through party ranks is still the norm for the overwhelming bulk of Knesset legislators.

Legislative Behavior of Members of the Knesset

Party discipline in the Knesset, to repeat, is very strict. This is especially the case in the parliamentary vote (as it is with other parliamentary regimes). On virtually all legislation, both in committees as well as on the floor of the main hall (called "the plenum"), individual Members *must* follow the party line. Failure to vote with the party could certainly result in a change in a member's position on the party electoral list in the next election or removal from a prestigious Knesset committee. Although a Member cannot be expelled from the Knesset for going against his or her party, pressures brought upon them by the public as well as colleagues have caused more than one to resign their legislative seat.

Members of Knesset almost never vote against their parties and in this respect Israel is very much like other parliamentary systems. A Member who feels very strongly about his or her party's position on a particular issue is most likely to go to the Knesset restaurant for a long cup of coffee in the middle of a vote, so as to miss it. This can sometimes be effective, although occasionally absence in itself can be a sufficient act of insubordination to warrant punishment by party leaders. From time to time, if the vote is sufficiently close, the party leader will pull in reticent members—sometimes literally—from the restaurant or elsewhere to make sure that they vote on a given issue in the "correct" direction. The reason, of course, is that with a narrow coalition majority a Government could "fall" as a result of only one or two "undisciplined" Members.

Legislative voting is not the only dimension of activity in which the individual Knesset member is essentially vulnerable to pressure from party leaders. Debate is another example of this relationship. Debate by itself may be the central characteristic of parliamentary bodies internationally. Regardless of the true role of legislatures in the power structures of the governments in which they are found, the one thing that they always do is debate. The Knesset is no exception here. Debate may ensue from a formally introduced bill, a Motion to Add to the Agenda, or a statement by the government. Votes of confidence and non–confidence would fall into the latter category.

Knesset debates can be classified by one of two labels, personal and party. Personal debate, which is the less significant, is usually employed in either "nonpolitical" matters which the Knesset is discussing but which are not related to pending legislation or in matters of legislation on which opinions are not divided along party lines. Party debate, on the other hand, comprises the bulk of Knesset debate and takes place with respect to votes of confidence, non–confidence, foreign policy, the budget, and any matters that the Government regards as significant (which means virtually any bill introduced by the Government). When this kind of debate takes place, the standing committee called the "Knesset Committee" decides how much time to allocate for the total debate, then divides the total time by the total number of Members of Knesset yielding a time–per–member figure.[11] This amount of time is then given to the party leaders in the Knesset to do with as they please. The leaders may choose to permit everyone in their party to speak for the allotted time–per–member or they may choose to pool all the time into one longer speech. In many cases the party leader will speak, or the entire party time will be given to a senior party member who is considered the party's spokesman on the given issue. Even here the individual MK is vulnerable to party leaders' pressure. Should they behave (e.g. vote, speak) in a way that the party leader views as not being sufficiently supportive of or loyal to the party, legislators may find themselves in a position where they might not be allowed to introduce legislative proposals or speak out in debates!

A significant distinction can be drawn between "intra–" and "extra–" legislative behavior. Within the Knesset, members do not have a great deal of autonomy, nor are they expected to exercise a great deal of free will. Outside of the assembly hall and the committee rooms, however, Members of Knesset are still in a position to perform many services for the public, all of which bolster the esteem in which they are held. They respond to correspondence, provide information and policy positions to their constituents, make speeches and attend rallies, and represent the full gamut of their constituencies' needs.

It should be clear that in Israel the term "constituency" does not have the same meaning as it does in the United States or Britain. In countries with district–based voting, such as the United States, a representative's constituency is *geographically* delimited: Lines are drawn on a map and anyone living in the area concerned is a part of the representative's constituency. In Israel, on the other hand, with the electoral list system and a single national electoral district for the purposes of elections, one's "constituency" takes on a *functional* meaning. When individuals are placed on a party's electoral list, they are often put there as "representatives" of a group, and it is clear to both the candidate and the group who is on the list to represent whom.[12] A typical list might have clearly designated (although not in writing) representatives for women, teachers, blue–collar workers, farmers, Kibbutz inhabitants, Yemeni immigrants, residents of Eilat, and Arabs, to name just some of the possible functional "constituencies." Although an American's response to the system might be to ask: "How would I know who *my* representative on the Labor party list is?", to take one example, an Israeli citizen would not have the same reaction. He or she would go to any MK representing their party in the case of the smaller party lists in the Knesset. In the case of the larger party lists, he or she would go to one of the more "specialist" representatives.

Members of Knesset also perform a considerable amount of "ombudsman" work, in which they speak or act on behalf of members of the public to help resolve their problems. This is often the aspect of the job which the average Member of Knesset spends most of their time on and receives most of their glory (or scorn). Citizens write, telephone, or visit the MK and complain that they need help. Members contact the appropriate ministers, who are generally in the Knesset daily. They, in turn, contact the directors–general of the ministries involved and frequently sooner or later the problem is resolved. Actually, the MKs' success ratio in this type of activity is quite high, possibly because the political–bureaucratic system in Israel is gauged to this personalistic type of approach to problems.

In any case, once one distinguishes between intra– and extra–legislative behavior, a remarkable difference in effectiveness of individual behavior can be observed.[13] In aspects of intra–legislative behavior the individual Member is highly limited, constrained, and consequently highly frustrated and cynical. It is no surprise that of the members interviewed for a recent study,[14] over 83 percent indicated that they considered themselves accountable to their party or party leaders for what they did as a member of Knesset, and 74 percent indicated that individual Members had "little," "very little," or "no influence" in the formation of government policy.

In extralegislative behavior, however, Members of the Knesset do not feel as cynical or helpless. They indicate that they receive a great deal of mail and spend a great deal of time (many say most of their time) responding to it. They feel that Members play a very important role in the Israeli political system and enjoy helping their constituents with problems they are having.

Knesset Organization

The Knesset is the central organ of the Israeli political system. The power of the Government comes from the Knesset and its policies are all either enacted in its name or approved by its Members. The Knesset sits for two terms a year, one in the summer and one in the winter. Under "Fundamental Law: The Knesset," the two terms must total at least eight months.

Although the job of the Member of Knesset is taken seriously, Israeli legislators, like most other legislators in the world, do not have the office space, secretarial help, or legislative staff budgets of their American counterparts. When they receive mail—and they receive a great deal—they must read, act upon, and answer it by themselves. Only in 1975 was a bill passed creating a small allowance (about $140 a month at the time) to be spent at their discretion for legislative staff, secretarial help, and the like. Obviously this amount of support is insufficient to do the job that is needed. Their only supplement comes from elsewhere. Political parties receive an allowance from the treasury for each seat they control.[15] This money goes at the party's discretion toward defraying expenses, either within or outside the Knesset, and helps pay for party secretarial help and legislative staff in the Knesset. Again, if a Member of Knesset is a good party worker, it is possible that the party leader will grant some small access to secretarial help or to the party's staff workers. If the member decides not to follow party instructions to the letter, he or she must find other sources for secretarial help in the Knesset.

Members of Knesset are all afforded substantial degrees of parliamentary immunity to guarantee the freedom to perform their legislative duties without fear of possible governmental prosecution. This immunity is discussed in the "Immunity, Rights, and Duties of Members of the Knesset" Law passed in 1951, which was based on an ordinance dating back to 1949. The protection afforded is extremely broad. The law states that a

> member of the Knesset shall not be held civilly or criminally responsible, and shall be immune from legal action, with regard to any vote cast, any

oral or written expression of opinion, or any other act performed in or out of the Knesset, provided that such vote, opinion, or act pertains to, or has as its purpose, the fulfillment of his mandate as a Member of the Knesset.[16]

In order to provide comprehensive protection for individual legislators, the act extends beyond their legislative behavior. Neither Members of Knesset themselves nor their property may be searched, except by customs officials. While they hold office, Members are absolutely immune from arrest, unless they are caught committing a crime or an act of treason. If a Member is arrested, the Speaker must be notified immediately by the authorities and the Member may not be detained for more than ten days unless the Knesset has revoked his or her immunity. As with other national legislatures, the Knesset Building itself has immunity. Under the Knesset Buildings Law of 1952, the building and grounds are under the control of the Speaker and sergeant—at—arms. This, too, is designed to free Members from extra—legislative pressures and distractions, such as demonstrations and other interruptions.

Internally, the Knesset is a party assembly ("Knesset," in fact, means "assembly"). That is, as with the rest of the political process, parties organize and control activities in the Knesset to a remarkable degree. Because of party discipline the opportunities for individual legislative action in the Knesset are few, and only occur when the party leaders specifically state that their parties will take no stand on a given issue.

Leadership positions in the Knesset are chosen on a partisan basis. A classic study of Israeli politics has written that:

> To date, the Speaker of the Knesset in each instance has been elected unanimously . . . at the opening session of the Knesset. This indicated the aim of the political parties represented in the Knesset to remove the Speakership from the area of inter—party contention and to place it above interests. The individual who holds this position enjoys the confidence of the entire Knesset, irrespective of political party.[17]

While this may be a true expression of the goals of the Knesset, and although many academic studies of the Knesset continue to repeat this as if it were the truth, in real life the position of Speaker has often been a highly partisan one and Speakers in the past have been defeated in their bids for re—election because of their overly partisan behavior.

The office of Deputy Speaker is equally partisan, with the number of deputies to be chosen varying with party distributions in the Knesset.

In Zidon's words: "Deputy Speakerships have come to be regarded as one of those Knesset posts which, like committee chairmanships, are distributed as 'plums' among the major parties when a new Knesset is organized."[18] The speaker and the deputy speakers as a group are called the "Presidium," a body which is very important in internal organization and behavior. A majority of the positions in the presidium are always controlled by government–coalition parties.

In the same manner that the positions of Speaker and Deputy Speaker are highly partisan, so too are the committee chairmanships. In the Knesset, chairmanships are apportioned much as the Deputy Speakerships, with the major parties sharing control. Seats on committees are given to parties, not to individuals, and the parties then assign their own members to the committee seats. For example, the Finance Committee might have nineteen members, representing only three large "parties": Labor, Likud, and the NRP, and these parties in turn would assign their own members to the Finance Committee. Here again, not only is there interparty competition for positions, but there is *intra–party* competition as well. Even though it might be decided that the Labor Alignment would receive five positions on the Finance Committee, for example, the manner in which the various factions of the Labor Party would divide up these five positions might remain in dispute.

Committees for their part provide MKs with an opportunity to specialize in their particular interests and to keep in touch with government ministers and high–ranking civil servants in a variety of issue areas. The committees also play a role in the legislative process, although as we have already indicated this fluctuates with the willingness of the Government to accept proposed legislative changes.

As a general rule, there are between twelve and twenty members on each of the ten permanent standing committees, which are in turn appointed for the full term of a Knesset. In addition to the ten permanent standing committees, temporary committees are appointed from time to time as deemed necessary by the Knesset Presidium. Committees made up of members from more than one permanent standing committee are sometimes jointly appointed when legislation that crosses the jurisdictions of more than one permanent standing committee arises. The respective jurisdictions of the committees are basically self-explanatory (see Table 7.2).

Committee meetings are usually closed to the press and public, so that all information about their proceedings must come from the committee members themselves. The committees vary in the importance which they are perceived as playing in the legislative process. Commit-

---

TABLE 7.2
Permanent Standing Committees in the Knesset

Constitution, Law, and Justice
Economics
Education and Culture
Finance
Foreign Affairs and Security
House
Immigration and Absorption
Internal Affairs and Environment
Labor and Welfare
State Control

Source: *Sager,* The Parliamentary System of Israel *p. 116.*

tee members are divided over what the true role of the committee is, with many saying that the role depends upon the particular legislation that is before a given committee at a given time. Most Members agree, however, that

> committee action is generally 'meaningless' because the Government as a general rule takes no notice of committee recommendations, and although committees may spend a good deal of time modifying Government legislation, or drafting their own legislation, when the third reading of a Government bill comes on the floor of the Knesset, the Government bill is usually voted upon as it was originally introduced in the Knesset.[19]

There are exceptions to the general rule of committee ineffectiveness worth noting. The Finance and the Labor committees have been given a great deal of authority by both the Knesset and the Government to write laws in their own spheres of expertise. These committees, especially the Finance Committee, are thus considered quite powerful and influential, and positions on these committees are highly sought. The other committee to be an exception to the committee ineffectiveness rule is Foreign Affairs and Security. It is interesting that this committee should be considered an exception because it has few powers and is mostly involved in oversight and debate, devoting little time to drafting legislation. However, since foreign affairs and security are priority concerns, and since Members of Knesset who are on this committee are privy to more classified information than a member of the Agricultural Committee, positions are in greater demand.

As indicated previously, seats on committees are given to parties and are then reassigned by party leaders to party members. Consequently, when a member bolts the party line in a committee or speaks out of turn too often, he or she may be limited to participation in the general assembly, having been either reassigned from one committee to another, or, in more extreme cases, stripped of all committee memberships. In fact, members may have no committee memberships if their party leaders feel they do not "deserve" such positions.

The Knesset has an elaborate framework of other organizational and behavioral rules in addition to the more formal structures of the Presidium and Committees. A period of time is regularly set aside for individual legislators to ask questions of the government—the so—called "Question Time." This serves the dual functions of bringing new issues to the attention of the government as well as reminding the government that the public is watching its overall behavior. This question period can become quite animated, as opposition members endeavor to ask the government embarrassing questions. After Prime Minister Begin signed the "Camp David Agreement" (which we shall discuss in Chapter 10) opposition within his own party used the "Question Time" to express their dismay and serious concerns about its national security implications.

In addition to parliamentary questions, another practice which should be mentioned here concerns parliamentary motions. Since the Government controls the daily calendar, and thereby generally controls what and for how long subjects will be debated in the Knesset, there is need for a procedure by which subjects which the Government may *not* want to talk about can be brought to the agenda to receive public scrutiny. The Knesset has a very elaborate and highly formalized procedure by which individuals can endeavor to force the government to schedule debates dealing with certain subject areas it may prefer to avoid. "Motions to Add to the Agenda" and "Urgent Motions to Add to the Agenda" give members a potentially significant role in the process of deciding what issues are and are not discussed in the Israeli political world.[20] For example, after recent demonstrations by (Israeli Jewish) settlers on the West Bank against the "intifada," the West Bank Arab uprising, some Arab MKs sought to introduce a "Motion to Add to the Agenda" so that they could have the Knesset debate the Government's policy regarding both the settlers and the way it was handling the Arab demonstrators.

Coalition Politics and Coalition Governments

The existence of government coalitions is central to any study of Israeli politics.[21] Because it has traditionally been necessary for political parties to form coalitions, there has been less opportunity for individual party and legislative behavior. Party discipline is extremely tight and coalition lines have been rigidly enforced.

A *coalition government* is, very simply, one in which two or more non–majority parties pool their seats to form a majority alliance. There is often a formal agreement drawn up among the coalition partners, indicating, among other things, their priorities and objectives, limitations upon the freedom of speech or action of member parties, and "payoffs" to coalition partners (for example, the number of cabinet seats a party will receive for joining a coalition, or a promise that the government will act on certain legislative programs within a stipulated period of time).[22]

Since Israel's independence there has never been a "majority situation";[23] that is, one in which the party organizing the government has controlled on its own more than 50 percent of the seats in the Knesset. Israel, in fact, has been an oft–cited illustration of a "minority situation, majority government," one in which a party with less than a majority of parliamentary seats joins with other minority parties to create a majority government.[24] This has resulted in coalitions being formed not only after but also between Knesset elections. In fact, during the first eleven Knessot, through the election of 1988, there have been twenty–five coalition governments.[25]

Before we turn our attention to an examination of several major themes related to Israeli coalitions, let us briefly discuss coalition governments in the abstract. When no single party has a majority in a parliamentary political system, as indicated above, the most likely outcome is the creation of a political coalition, in which two or more parties will join together to create what was referred to earlier as "minority situation, majority government." Let us imagine a hypothetical situation with a 100-seat parliament and five political parties, as indicated in Table 7.3.

In this instance, the head of state would most likely invite the leader of Party A to form a Government, since Leader A heads the largest parliamentary group. Leader A needs to find an additional 18 seats in order to form a majority of 51 to support his Government in the legislature. In this case, Leader A could go to either the leader of Party B, or the leader of Party C to find a partner. As well, of course, Leader A

TABLE 7.3
A Hypothetical Party Distribution

Party A	33 seats
Party B	20 seats
Party C	18 seats
Party D	16 seats
Party E	13 seats
	100 seats

could go to *more* than one other party, to try to form an ABC coalition, for example.

Usually, Leader A will have to promise the leader(s) of other parties involved in the coalition some "payoff" for joining. In most instances, this payoff is a cabinet position (or more likely several cabinet positions). Sometimes the "payoff" is a promise that a certain piece of legislation that the prospective coalition partner has drafted will be passed as part of the Government's program. It should be clear, though, that the more partners Leader A has to invite into the coalition, the more different payoffs will have to be made. Thus, individuals charged with forming coalitions usually strive to form what are called *minimal winning coalitions*: coalitions which are big enough to have a majority (be a winning coalition), but no bigger than necessary so that unnecessary "payoffs" do not need to be made.

If Leader A can reach an agreement with one or more partners to form a coalition that will control a majority of the legislature, then Leader A will receive his or her vote of confidence, a vote by a majority that it supports the government, and the government can be said to be installed. If, however, Leader A *cannot* find sufficient coalition partners within a constitutionally mandated period of time, usually one or two weeks, then Leader A must return his or her "mandate" to the President and inform the President of their inability to form a government. At this point the President would seek out a different party leader to try to form a majority coalition.

Coalition majority government *tends* to be less stable than single–party majority governments in parliamentary systems. In a single–party majority system, the prime minister must impose party discipline to keep his or her party followers in line and maintain a majority. In a coalition system, the flow of power is more diffused. The prime minister must exercise party discipline over party followers, plus count on the leader(s) of the partner coalition party or parties to do the same. Downfalls of coalitions have usually come about because of differences between party leaders—in terms of our example above, because Leader B has a disagreement with Leader A and pulls the support of Party B out of the AB coalition—and *not* because of a failure of party discipline within Party A.

As might be expected, the complexity of the coalition–formation process is a direct function of the number of political parties in a legislature. In the example in Table 7.4, it is clear that Situation I is relatively simple, Situation II is more complex, and Situation III is even more complex. It should be kept in mind that in Situation III there are only eight parties represented; in some countries there are even more, and Israel is an example of this latter category. The more parties exist, the

---

TABLE 7.4

The Complexity of the Coalition–Formation Process in a 100–seat Legislature

Situation I:	Most Simple	Majority Possibilities
Party A	44 seats	AB, AC, BC, ABC
Party B	42 seats	
Party C	14 seats	
Situation II:	More Complex	Majority Possibilities
Party A	38 seats	AB, AC, AD, ABC, ABD, ABE,
Party B	20 seats	ACD, ACE, ADE, BCD, etc.
Party C	17 seats	
Party D	15 seats	
Party E	10 seats	
Situation III:	Most Compex	Majority Possibilities
Party A	30 seats	ABC, ABD, ABE, ABF, ABG,
Party B	19 seats	BCDE, CDEFGH, etc.
Party C	12 seats	
Party D	9 seats	
Party E	8 seats	
Party F	8 seats	
Party G	7 seats	
Party H	7 seats	

more possibilities there are for a winning coalition to form, and the more partners there are in a coalition, the more possibilities there are for a coalition to fall apart.

The study of what has come to be called *coalition theory* has greatly expanded over time. Indeed, in a recent study political scientists have suggested that coalition theory is now in its third generation: the first developed theories of how coalitions work; the second tried to apply the general theories to "real world" politics to see how well the models predicted what would happen; while the current generation seeks to combine the research of both the first and the second generations to make coalition theory a truly predictive model.[26]

There are, of course, a number of problems with broad theories of coalition formation. First, the theories may be more or less valid in one political system than in another. Second, the research may not be transferrable. That is, research done in Japan may not tell us a great deal about how coalitions work in Israel. Finally, the distribution of cabinet positions may be explained by many different theories, including the number of seats a party can claim to control, patronage, loyalty, payment for future support, and a variety of other reasons.

Several of these themes must be kept in mind when analyzing the formation of coalitions among Israeli political parties. First, political parties play an overwhelming role in not only the "political" but also the social and economic life, as was noted earlier in this book. Parties publish newspapers, run medical clinics, sponsor athletic and social events, and, in short, permeate every aspect of life.[27]

Second, one must note the number of parties currently active. As many as twenty–four presented themselves at elections for the First and Second Knessot.[28] Twenty–seven parties ran candidates in the Twelfth Knesset elections in 1988, and twelve won seats. The mere number of political parties that are active in the political system may affect our ability to theorize about coalition formation. It has been noted that whereas twelve cabinets had actually formed through 1965, in those twelve there were 7,873 possible winning coalitions,[29] to say nothing of the number of near–winning or minority coalitions possible. To provide a comparison, in Belgium over a comparable period of time there were fourteen actual coalitions with 463 possible winning combinations.[30]

Third, the regional military balance and national security in general has always been of paramount importance in Israeli politics. War situations, especially in 1967, greatly influenced the size of coalitions that were formed. On several occasions coalitions have been created that were larger than they "needed" to be and that included parties whose support was not really necessary in order to demonstrate to the outside world that the government in power at the time had a strong base of support.

Fourth, the concept of a "minimal winning coalition" must be treated carefully in the Israeli context. With the Knesset membership of 120, a majority would be 61 seats. However, on several occasions blocs of representatives have abstained on parliamentary votes. This has had the effect of lowering the active population of the Knesset from 120 to 100 (on the one occasion in which 20 members abstained), which in turn lowered the effective minimal winning coalition from 61 to 51.

Fifth, imperfect information occasionally increases the size of a coalition. The Israeli party system contains strong and highly disciplined parties—many political scientists argue that the Israeli system is second to none in the relative impotence of the individual members and in the strength of party leaders there.[31] A certain amount of imperfect information remains, however, because of the large number of parties and the fact that even though the parties may run for office together in a grand alliance, they will not necessarily be in agreement in all policy spheres. This means that the party that forms the governmental coalition cannot automatically count on any party's vote. One illustration not all that unusual is the elaborate "contract" among members of the eighteenth cabinet–governing coalition (1973), which defined precisely the conditions under which party members and coalition members could "vote their consciences". A similar "contract" was developed for the first Begin cabinet in 1977.[32] Labor and Likud signed comparable agreements in both 1984 and again in 1988.

Finally, the history and ideological nature of the Israeli party system must be considered. The party system has been called overdeveloped by many, and several political scientists have written that the large number of political parties is not really necessary. The abundance of political parties is usually attributed to the fact that most existed before the state did—"every one of the political parties represented in the Fifth Knesset (August, 1961), with the exception of two small Arab lists, had roots in and at least some organizational history going back to the pre–state period."[33] This history, combined with the proportional representation electoral system that encourages new parties to form by making representation in the Knesset relatively easy, has encouraged the expansion of parties, which has complicated the coalition–formation process.

The important consequences of coalitions governments for the Israeli political system are several. First, they result in an increased party discipline, and thereby less individual legislative freedom, because the

Government has to be sure that it can depend upon coalition members to support government policy.

Second, and perhaps more important, coalitions leave the government vulnerable to "blackmail." If a given coalition is a "minimal" one in which the government would lose its majority if a single party withdrew, then a relatively small coalition partner might have considerably greater leverage with the Government than its size alone would suggest. We have already seen how Israel's religious parties have had a great deal of influence over government policy. This has rarely reflected a government's ideological commitment to religious issues. Rather, it has often been because the smaller religious parties have issued ultimatums such as: "Pass/Support our policy, or we will withdraw from the government coalition and you will lose your majority and will no longer be prime minister." Prime Ministers have tended, over the years, to be quite responsive to this kind of threat.

Finally, coalitions have led to a condition termed "immobilisme"— or an inability to act on a given issue. This occurs when a problem comes up and the government knows that if it acts in one direction or another one of its coalition partners will get angry and withdraw. The only solution, then, is to do nothing. A good example was observed during the government of Menachem Begin: the Minister of Education told Begin that if the Cabinet did not approve a significant raise for teachers, he (the Minister) would leave the cabinet and take all of his party followers with him. The result would be Begin's loss of his Knesset majority. At the same time, however, the Minister of Finance indicated that if Begin gave in to the Minister of Education and altered the fiscally tight budget he had created, he would leave the cabinet and take all of *his* party followers with him, also resulting in Begin losing his majority. The outcome was Begin's decision to call for new elections and a subsequent new coalition. (After the election, when a new coalition was in place with a new budget, the teachers did receive slightly higher salaries!)

The Knesset, The Government, and Israeli Politics

The political structure of Israel tells us a great deal about Israeli society. As was pointed out earlier, it is a stable democratic polity in a part of the world in which stable democracies are not very common. Stability and democracy, of course, do not necessarily mean unanimity, and it is this characteristic of modern Israel that has led to the existence of a multiple political party system in which so much loud and often heated debate takes place.

Political parties, it has been argued, are the key to the political structures of the Knesset and the Government. Parties not only are the basis for governmental organization, they are also the vehicles through which virtually all of the "official" functions of the Knesset are undertaken. Individual legislators are to a substantial degree "at the mercy" of their party organization. Not only can they not run for office without being on a party list, once they are in the Knesset they cannot introduce bills, serve on committees, or engage in debate without a party leader's approval.

Related to this, the number of political parties has led to the development of a coalition system in Israel. This, in turn, has had two broad consequences. First, governments have on a number of occasions taken less dramatic action than otherwise might have been the case, precisely because the Prime Minister needed to worry about whether such an action would alienate one of his or her coalition partners. Second, this phenomenon has resulted in the smaller parties—most notably, of course, the Orthodox religious parties—having far more influence on government policy than their size alone would have merited. The role of the small party as the "keystone" of government coalitions has been significant in the continued visibility of the religious question in Israeli politics, and has continued to serve as a source of irritation to a substantial portion of the Israeli electorate.

NOTES

1. Gerhard Loewenberg, *Modern Parliaments: Change or Decline?* (Chicago: Atherton, 1971), p. 3.

2. Joseph LaPalombara, *Politics Within Nations* (Englewood Cliffs, N.J.: Prentice–Hall, 1974), pp. 221– 25.

3. Don Peretz, *The Government and Politics of Israel* (Boulder, Co.: Westview, 1983), p. 159, for a description of one instance in which this type of resignation caused the breaking apart of a coalition and the fall of a Government.

4. For a more detailed description of this process, see Asher Zidon, *Knesset: The Parliament of Israel* (New York: Herzl Press, 1967).

5. S. Weiss and A Brichta, "Private Members' Bills in Israel's Parliament," *Parliamentary Affairs* 23 (1969); p. 25.

6. Samuel Sager, *The Parliamentary System of Israel* (Syracuse, N.Y.: Syracuse University Press, 1985), pp. 171–74.

7. Data on demographic characteristics of members of Knesset, as well as information on their political upbringing, can be found in Gregory Mahler, *The Knesset: Parliament in the Israeli Political System* (Rutherford: Fairleigh Dickinson University Press, 1981), Ch. 5: "The Member of Knesset," pp. 106–37.

8. Avraham Brichta, "Women in the Knesset," *Parliamentary Affairs* 28 (1974); pp. 31–50.

9. Moshe Czudnowski, "Legislative Recruitment Under Proportional Representation in Israel: A Model and a Case Study," *Midwest Journal of Political Science* 14 (1970); pp. 216–48, and Czudnowski, "Sociocultural Variables and Legislative Recruitment," *Comparative Politics* 4 (1972); pp. 561–87.

10. Mahler, *The Knesset*, pp. 138–59, includes a thorough study of the political recruitment of Knesset members.

11. In order to provide the small parties (one or two members) with some debate time, Knesset rules state that no party shall have less than ten minutes time in a four–hour debate and fifteen in a five–hour debate.

12. See the article on the Labor Party convention by Myron Aronoff, "Better Late Than Never: Democratization in the Labor Party," in Gregory Mahler (ed.), *Israel Since Begin* (Albany: State University of New York Press, forthcoming).

13. For a thorough analysis of this intralegislative frustration and extralegislative effectiveness, see Mahler, *The Knesset*, Chapter 8.

14. Ibid., p. 103.

15. Ibid., p. 98; Sager, *The Parliamentary System of Israel*, pp. 68–69, 139.

16. Zidon, *The Knesset*, p. 40.

17. Ibid., pp. 53– 4.

18. Zidon, *The Knesset*, p. 55.

19. Mahler, *The Knesset*, p. 89.

20. For a thorough discussion of parliamentary questions, and the various categories of motions to add to the agenda, see Mahler, *The Knesset*, pp. 90–94.

21. This has been an extremely popular area of research in recent years. Among the many articles on this subject might be included the following: Gregory Mahler and Richard Trilling, "Coalition Behavior and Cabinet Formation: The Case of Israel," *Comparative Political Studies* 8 (1975); pp. 200–33; Dan Felsenthal, "Aspects of Coalition Payoffs: The Case of Israel," *Comparative Political Studies* 12 (1979); pp. 151–68; David Nachmias, "Coalition Politics in Israel," *Comparative Political Studies* 7 (1974); pp. 316–33; Nachmias, "A Note on Coalition Payoffs in a Dominant Party System: Israel," *Political Studies* 21:3 (1973); pp. 301–5; and K. Z. Paltiel, "The Israeli Coalition System," *Government and Opposition* 10 (1975); pp. 396–414.

22. A discussion of these "payoffs" can be found in Mahler, *The Knesset*, pp. 74–80.

23. Valerie Herman and John Pope, "Minority Governments in Western Democracies," *British Journal of Political Science* 3 (1973); p. 191.

24. Ibid.

25. See Mahler, *The Knesset*, p. 81 n. 18, for a discussion through the 8th Knesset. For a detailed historical analysis of all of those coalition–forming periods, see the same source, pp. 60–69.

26. Eric Browne and Mark Franklin, "Editors' Introduction: New Directions in Coalition Research," *Legislative Studies Quarterly* 11:4 (1986); p. 471. The entire issue of *Legislative Studies Quarterly* in which this article appears is devoted to the study of coalition theory.

27. Benjamin Akzin, "The Role of Parties in Israeli Democracy," *Journal of Politics* 17 (1955); pp. 507–45.

28. "Knessot" is plural for "Knesset." See Akzin, *op cit.*, p. 532.

29. Eric Browne, "Testing Theories of Coalition Formation in the European Context," *Comparative Political Studies* 3 (1971); p. 400.

30. Ibid., p. 402.

31. Leonard Fein, *Israel: Politics and People* (Boston: Little, Brown and Company, 1966), p. 222.

32. See the *Jerusalem Post*, March 12, 1974, p. 2; and the *Jerusalem Post: Overseas Edition*, May 24, 1977, respectively.

33. Scott Johnston, "Party Politics and Coalition Cabinets in the Knesset," *Middle Eastern Affairs* 13 (1962); p. 130.

Chapter 8

THE BUREAUCRACY, LOCAL GOVERNMENT, THE JUDICIARY, AND THE MILITARY

Introduction

Thus far our discussion of Israeli institutions and political behavior has focused upon the more "traditional" political structures: the constitution, political parties, elections and voting, the legislature, and the executive. We cannot forget, however, that the political process includes more than these "traditional" components. There are other institutions and patterns of behavior,[1] which likewise define the term "structure," that need to be considered in our study of Israeli politics. Some are inherent in modern government, such as bureaucracy; others are required in order to help control issues in daily life, such as local government. Some are formal and constitutional, such as the judiciary; others mirror the specific requirements of the Israeli political environment, like the military.

Bureaucracy, as we shall see, is a phenomenon that many have argued is inevitable in modern governmental structures. As the scope of governmental responsibilities has grown larger and larger, infrastructures have become more necessary to assist them in the development and execution of public policy. Legislatures and executives are obvious structures; bureaucratic support structures may be less so. Local government is likewise often overlooked as a significant political actor, especially in centralized unitary governments. This fact notwithstanding, however, it is true that local governments in Israel are real and very important actors in the political system and need to be covered here. In this chapter we shall examine the scope and nature of the Israeli bureaucracy and local government to determine the role each plays in the contemporary political process.

In the United States the judiciary is considered to be a natural part of the "traditional" constitutional order. The principle of judicial review was established very early in American history, and the courts—especially the Supreme Court—have been significant political structures in the American politics ever since. This is not the case in the majority of political systems in the world, however. In most parliamentary political systems the courts play virtually no political role. The dominant political principle of these regimes is that of legislative supremacy, and it is virtually impossible to have a system with both legislative supremacy *and* absolute judicial review. The Israeli system, as we shall observe, represents something of a hybrid. Clearly, the Knesset is the supreme political body. On the other hand, there has been a limited political role carved out by the Supreme Court, one that has proven to be of significance on several occasions.

Lastly, virtually all political systems have military organizations. In most stable democracies these organizations do not play a significant role in the political process. This is true for modern Israel, as well. Soldiers, like all Israeli citizens, are allowed to vote, but members of the military are not allowed to run for or to hold office in the Knesset or the Government. Nevertheless, the military is regarded as a "political actor." The principle of civilian control is important, yet the military exerts a clear influence on civilian government at all levels.

In short, our examination of political institutions and political behavior in Israel will not be complete without some discussion of these four sets of actors: the bureaucracy, local governments, the judiciary and legal system, and the military. It is to an examination of each that we now turn our attention.

The Bureaucracy and the Civil Service

Israel, like many other modern political systems, has a civil service that has grown tremendously over the years. It has become, as one author put it, "thoroughly bureaucratized."[2] In 1949 only four ministries—Foreign Affairs, Defense, Social Welfare, and Education and Culture—had an established civil service. Each of these, it should be further noted, also evolved from a pre–state organization.[3] Today, as Table 8.1 indicates, their number and size has expanded considerably. In the process the bureaucracy has also become "politicized." The fact that the figures for 1988 show a 25 percent reduction compared to 1980 is tied directly to the country's recent budget cutbacks and inflationary problems, to say nothing of Likud's ideological preferences for reduced "state–welfarism" and a less–intrusive political system.

Israel has a Civil Service Law that provides job stability and security for those who work in the government. Job security for individual civil servants, however, can cause ministers great frustration when they try to staff their offices with individuals whose support and information they seek.[4] Indeed, ministers do not have a great deal of freedom in determining the top officers of their ministries, because of the security and stability that the Civil Service Law provides to government employees. Beyond that, ministers must, generally speaking, live with the ministry employees who are civil servants.[5]

Before the formal creation of the state, the division between "party" and "state" bureaucracy was often blurred. After independence this overlap continued since the Mapai party controlled the government

TABLE 8.1
State Employees in Selected Ministries

Ministry	1980	1988
Prime Minister	866	728
Finance	7,655	6,852
Defense	2,752	2,235
Health	17,561	20,101
Religious Affairs	372	289
Foreign Affairs	913	854
Education/Culture	3,406	2,754
Agriculture	3,083	2,483
Industry and Trade	1,113	655
Justice	1,966	2,002
Labour & Welfare	4,398	3,999
Science & Development	—	53
Interior	908	749
Immigration	498	424
Construction/Housing	2,979	2,201
Israel Lands Authority	586	526
Transport	1,098	889
Railways	1,981	1,495
Tourism	—	223
Communications	14,190a	98
Energy	326	263
Economy/Planning	—	50
Police	—	35
TOTAL	66,631	49,867

Note a: Much of the Ministry of Communications became "privatized" in 1984.

Source: Statistical Abstract of Israel (Jerusalem: Central Bureau of Statistics, 1988), p. 565

and made sure that its supporters all had the most important government jobs.[6] Shortly thereafter, however, a movement was begun to establish a "neutral" civil service.[7] Eventually a formal Civil Service Commission was established in 1950, independent of other governmental agencies.[8] At the outset, the civil service was directed by the Prime Minister. Subsequently, it was moved to the control of the Ministry of Finance. This proved to be an ineffective home for the civil service and the Civil Service Department was later moved back to the Prime

Minister's Office. In the mid–1950's it was once again shifted to Finance, where it has stayed. In 1959 the Knesset passed the Civil Service (Appointments) Law, which "required civil service appointments to be made on merit and qualifications for existing positions as they become vacant and for new positions."[9]

Since independence three significant changes have taken place in the civil service. First, the civil service has become progressively less politicized.[10] To a large degree this resulted from passage of the Civil Service Law and the "institutionalization" of the civil service itself. An illustration of the decline of politics in the appointment process to the civil service can be found in the fact that "as a rule, new ministers do not even replace the director generals of their ministries, certainly not immediately."[11] Second, the level of education has significantly increased. Today, "one can barely find a civil servant . . . who was appointed in the last ten years and who does not have an academic degree."[12] Third, although the civil service has gained personnel from other Israeli bureaucracies,[13] it has also lost many to the private sector, both as a consequence of financial factors (most notably higher salaries) and because of greater independence and opportunity to exercise their own initiative outside of government.[14]

In fact, however, despite a clearly delineated civil service hierarchy it is not uncommon to hear charges of "politicization of the civil service" being directed by one political faction at another. The philosophical question of the value of a purely "neutral" civil service is one that is frequently discussed in Israel today. On one hand, most politicians agree that they do not want a blatantly political "spoils system." Merit should be a central part of the appointment and promotion process. On the other hand, government ministers must be able to work with the directors–general of their ministries, and thus feel that they should have some freedom in terms of their higher–level appointments. One scholar notes:

> . . . merit considerations are often spoken of, especially at the lower ranks of hierarchies. But as we move up the ladder of power and prestige, the prevalence of extraprofessional considerations grows. Israel is a small country, and among the few candidates for a senior position, the front runners are likely to be known. Past performance and the groups to which a candidate is affiliated cannot easily be separated in the minds of an appointment committee.[15]

In point of fact, the bureaucracy in Israel is still not completely representative of the public in purely demographic terms.[16] Higher positions are still disproportionately filled by Ashkenazic Jews, while

Sephardim tend to be found in the lower ranks of the administrative structure.[17] This practice has gradually changed over the years to one of greater equity, but the change has been long in coming and is still taking place.

Israel has furthermore been characterized as a nation without the semblance of a "coherent administrative culture." Indeed, its administrative system reflects many elements of the country's heterogeneous political culture.[18] Blatant political corruption may not be obvious and common, but "protektzia"—the use of personal "pull"—is often the currency by which the system operates. As Arian tartly put it:

> There is a plethora of rules, bureaucrats, and committees; but the political element is never far from the surface, especially if the issue is considered an important one. Lip service is paid to professionalism and nonpartisanship, but these values are likely to weaken the higher up the civil service ladder one climbs. There is a pretense of modern rational structure, and increasingly computerized techniques have been introduced; still, a solid core remains of a more personal and traditional form of dealing with the citizenry by the administration.[19]

Israel's "administrative culture" has thus been characterized as composed of four "strands."[20] One is an "indigenous Middle Eastern style," in which "business is transacted at a regal pace, in a charmingly courteous, if exasperating, fashion." This style is one in which deference to authority, status, and rank are combined to produce a bargaining situation. Next comes a remnant from the British Mandatory period. This style involves a "no–nonsense, orderly, condescending, bureaucratic approach, with little room for bargaining, local initiative, or disruption." A third is composed of "traditions brought by Jewish immigrants from their countries of origin, as varied as the contents of a spicery." This has been described as a style in which "paranoic ghetto attitudes mingle with dynamic, cosmopolitan, liberal entrepreneurship." Finally is the tradition of the Israeli "old–timers," which combines pragmatism and personal connections. This leads to getting problems resolved by taking "short cuts," operating without "appropriate" authorization, and similar actions.[21]

The "net result of these cultural strands," it has been argued, "is inconsistency, incoherence, and not a small measure of inefficiency."[22] Israelis seem to have a limitless supply of anecdotes of irrationality, incompetence, and agony caused by the national bureaucracy.[23] In *Bureaucratic Culture*, Nachmias and Rosenbloom report that based upon a survey of the population Israeli citizens do not think very highly of the bureaucracy. The public feels that the bureaucracy has a significant impact on their lives and that it is important in terms of national and social development and democracy, but quickly report that the public feels "overwhelmingly negative in their characterization of the bureaucracy's impact." The report indicates that "at least 60 percent of the public gave [the bureaucracy's] activities a negative rating," and the public perceive civil servants to be "relatively dishonest, unpleasant, inefficient, passive, slow, and unstable." As a conclusion, Nachmias and Rosenbloom indicate that "Israelis find their national bureaucracy and its employees to be undesirable features of the political community, which have a considerable, yet largely unfavorable, influence upon their society."[24]

Civil servants often participate in the political process through their testimony in the Knesset before standing committees. It is worth noting that before a civil servant from a specific ministry can appear at a Knesset committee meeting he or she must receive the permission of the appropriate minister. The minister must also approve in advance the content of the civil servant's testimony before the committee, otherwise the appearance cannot be scheduled.[25] Senior civil servants may also be invited to cabinet meetings if their expertise is needed for a policy debate.[26]

Local Government

Although they do not always receive a great deal of attention, there is a full network of sub–national governments in the Israeli political system.[27] A total of 1,409 local authorities function in Israel today; approximately one for every 2,823 inhabitants.[28] They are especially significant in four separate areas: (1) the provision of governmental services; (2) the recruitment of political leaders;[29] (3) the development and maintenance of political communications networks between the public and political leaders; and, (4) the "maintenance of necessary or desired diversity within a small country where there are heavy pressures toward homogeneity."[30]

Local governmental bodies coordinate services including water, electricity, health and sanitation, road maintenance, public parks, fire services, and similar concerns. From one–half to two–thirds of the local governments' budgets are provided by the central government, with the remainder typically raised through property taxes.[31] The Ministry of the Interior has administrative jurisdiction and works with the various local governments to coordinate policies.

Local elections are based upon direct, universal, and secret ballot. Local legislative councils have from 9 to 31 members, depending upon the population of the locality.[32] Until November, 1978, elections for these positions were based upon proportional representation, as were elections to the Knesset, and the position of Mayor was filled in the same manner as the position of Prime Minister, through coalitions in the local councils. After 1978, municipal elections combined the direct election of mayors with proportional election of city councils. The idea behind this was to minimize the political infighting which had been taking place in municipalities after local elections. Invariably coalitions would be formed as in the Knesset, based upon party representation in the municipality's legislative council. The attendant inter–party negotiation and factionalism often worked to weaken the mayor's position. Now the mayor is elected by direct vote, with the winner needing at least 40 percent of the total votes cast. If no candidate receives this, a run–off between the top two vote–getters is held two weeks after the initial election, with the winner determined at that time.[33]

For administrative purposes, Israel is divided into six districts: Jerusalem, administered in Jerusalem; Northern, administered from Nazareth; Haifa, administered in Haifa; Central, administered from Ramla; Tel Aviv, administered in Tel Aviv; and Southern, administered from Beersheba. Over the years there has come to be more and more regional differentiation in Israel, with the character of the various towns, cities, and regions more and more distinct from each other. This has developed because of geographic patterns of settlement, regional

TABLE 8.2 Local Governments in Israel	
Type	Number
Cities	37
Local Councils	125
Regional Councils	54
Local Committees	825
Confederations of Cities	32
Religious Councils	204
Other Committees/Authorities	132
Total	1,409

Source: Adapted from Daniel Elazar, Israel: Building a New Society (Bloomington: Indiana University Press, 1986), page 88.

issues, and economic circumstances.[34] Different regions have different concerns which are more or less predominant, with the southern region preoccupied with the availability of water and commercial links to the larger marketplaces of the north, while the Tel Aviv region is increasingly concerned about metropolitan growth. Some regions feel that they are slighted or underrepresented in the political arena, with Eilat and the Negev region always very sensitive about the political attention they receive.

The Judiciary and the Legal System in Israeli Politics

Although traces of many different legal systems can be found in Israeli law,[35] the legal system has been characterized as consisting of basically five components: Ottoman law which existed in Palestine until the end of World War I; British Mandatory regulations; British Common Law; Legislation of the Knesset; and religious law, coming from several different religious sources.[36] Each of these different cornerstones of the legal system merits brief discussion here.

One of the major influences on the Israeli legal system came from the Ottoman Empire. Turkish jurisprudence was the legal system in Palestine until the British Mandate began, and there are many indications of Ottoman law to be found in Israel today. The Turkish "Majelle" (Civil Code) was passed in 1869 and continued to exist in the Israeli legal system until its total repeal in 1984, although actual repeal of its sixteen volumes of over 1800 sections commenced with the Knesset's enactment of the Agency Law of 1965.[37]

Another source of Israeli legal tradition was British legislation. From 1922—the date when the Mandate officially began—until 1948, the ultimate source of Palestinian law was British legislation.[38] In a similar manner, during this period the ultimate court of appeals for Palestine was not the local Supreme Court but rather the Judicial Committee of the Privy Council at Westminster (London). Thus, much of British common law eventually found its way into Israel's legal system during this 25–year interval.

Israeli legislation is a fourth base of the legal system. The Declaration of the Establishment of the State of Israel stipulated that the People's Council, which would become the Provisional State Council, would make legislation for the new State. Among its most important acts was the Law and Administration Ordinance (1948) which reiterated that the laws in effect in Israel then—including British, Ottoman, and others—would remain in force unless they were specifically changed by future legislation. Subsequently, the Provisional State

Council became the Knesset, and the Knesset became the font from which Israeli law flowed.

Finally, religious law has played, and continues to play, a significant role in the construction and interpretation of Israeli law. During the Mandatory period the British gave each of the major religious groups some degree of autonomy over "matters of personal status," including marriage, divorce, and wills. The exercise of influence in these areas by religious courts continues today. With the perspective of history it is clear that when it passed the Marriage and Divorce Law the Knesset abdicated its right to legislate on matters of that nature.[39] All citizens of Israel are now subject to the religious laws of their individual religious communities, which have their own special networks of religious courts to handle adjudication.

While it is true that there is a "separation of power" in the Israeli political system, the nature and degree of this "separation" is uniquely Israeli. In the American political system there is a clear separation between and among the legislative, executive, and judicial branches. In Britain, the legislative and executive functions merge in the House of Commons, and the legislative and judicial functions in the House of Lords. In Israel, there "exists a certain separation among the authorities. However, the functions of policy formulation, legislation, and jurisdiction are implemented in a coordinated form."[40] The Knesset passes laws, the Government enforces them, and the Courts play a role in determining whether the actions of the Government are consistent with the intentions of the Knesset.[41] The Courts do not have the power, generally speaking, to strike down acts of the Knesset.[42]

In 1957 the Knesset passed the Courts Law, which reorganized the system of courts that had slowly evolved until that time. Since 1957, the Supreme Court of Israel has been the highest level of the judicial system. Below the high court, in terms of judicial organization, can be found municipal courts, magistrates' courts, and district courts.[43]

Municipal courts exist in each major city and have jurisdiction over relatively minor offenses committed within the city limits. Magistrates' courts have jurisdiction over the administrative districts (and in some cases, subdistricts) of Israel referred to earlier, hearing both minor monetary claims and less serious criminal charges, and may impose penalties of up to three years in prison. Appeals from these courts, as well as some initial proceedings, are heard in District courts.

District courts have both original and appellate jurisdictions. They have original jurisdiction over issues which do not come before magistrates' courts, with the exception of religious questions which are heard in the separate system of religious courts described below. Examples of original jurisdiction questions would be serious misdemeanors, felonies, and major civil cases. Appeals from District courts may be heard by the Supreme Court if the case originated in the District Court. If the case was heard in the District Court on appeal from a lower court, it may be appealed to the Supreme Court only if: (a) the District Court authorizes the appeal, (b) the President of the Supreme Court (or another Supreme Court Justice named by the President to make the decision) authorizes the appeal, or (c) if the full Supreme Court authorizes the appeal.[44]

The Supreme Court acts both as an appellate court for lower courts as well as a High Court of Justice to hear complaints against the government. Typically, panels of three justices, less than the full complement of ten, hear a case. If requested by the President of the State, cases originally heard by three Justices may be given a second hearing by panels of five or more Justices. Although the Court may not invalidate legislation passed by the Knesset as being unconstitutional, it may nullify:

a. local ordinances enacted by municipal councils on the grounds that a city is legislating in an area which is the exclusive jurisdiction of the national Parliament;
b. national administrative regulations promulgated in implementation of Knesset legislation . . . on the grounds that they violate the property or other fundamental rights of the people; and
c. decisions or other actions by public administrative officials on the grounds that their behavior is arbitrary or illegal.[45]

In addition to these, other special courts exist in Israel as well. An independent set of religious courts operate within the framework of the Ministry of Religious Affairs. These courts have jurisdiction in matters affecting personal status: marriage, divorce, and religious characteristics. Separate Jewish, Moslem, Christian, and Druze courts operate for members of those communities.

Seven rabbinical courts exist for the Jewish community in Israel,[46] appeals from which may be taken to the Grand Rabbinical Court of Appeals in Jerusalem.[47] Appeals may not be made from a religious court to a secular court. The jurisdiction of Jewish religious courts in some areas such as marriages and divorces extends to all Jews in Israel,[48] whether Israeli citizens or not, and whether they like it or not.[49] Religious courts may also share jurisdiction with civil courts in a number of areas if all parties concerned agree with the religious courts' participation in the decision.

There are four Moslem religious courts in Israel, appeals from which may be taken to the Moslem Appeals Court which sits in Jerusalem. A number of other religious courts exist for the Catholic,

Protestant, Greek Orthodox, Melkite, Maronite, and Druze communities,[50] all of whom have their own religious courts with jurisdiction over their members in matters of personal status.

In cases in which a question arises as to whether an issue falls within the jurisdiction of a religious court, a panel made up of two justices from the Supreme Court and the president of the religious court concerned sit as a panel to decide the matter.[51] The Supreme Court has heard cases in which "constitutional" questions related to religion are raised.[52] In addition to these religious courts, there are also traffic, military, labor, and small claims courts operating within the legal system.

The appointment of judges in Israel illustrates the degree of judicial independence found there. A nine–member Appointment Committee recommends individuals to the President for consideration. This committee is made up of the President of the Supreme Court and two other Supreme Court justices, the Minister of Justice and one other cabinet member chosen by the cabinet, two Members of Knesset elected by secret ballot, and two lawyers chosen by the Israeli Bar Association. Judges in Israel serve "during good behavior," either until they decide to retire (there is a mandatory retirement age of 70) or until a situation develops in which they are accused of improper behavior and then found guilty by a special court of conduct unbefitting a judge. At that point the Minister of Justice can recommend their dismissal by the President.

The role of the courts in Israel illustrates the commitment of the political system to the "rule of law," and also illustrates the singular interaction of the religious and secular realms in the polity. The courts have the power, as has been explained above, to annul any administrative action that is not consistent with legislation, or to annul any legislation which is not consistent with action by the Knesset, the source of the supreme law of the land. They have also established a clear division between religious and secular jurisdiction, a division that has been threatened by recent efforts of the Orthodox to expand *their* jurisdiction in the social realm.

The Military and the Government

Although there have been several general historical studies of the subject,[53] some have suggested that there has been a "veil of secrecy" over academic research on civil–military relations in Israel. Academics have avoided the study of the military because of both personal and political pressures. Since Israel has been at war for the forty years since independence, with five major wars since 1948 and no period of real peace, a tendency has existed not to study the military so as to avoid inadvertently "giving away" something of a military significance.[54]

When David Ben–Gurion took over the Defense portfolio in the Provisional Government of Israel in 1948, he indicated that

> I made it clear to the Provisional Government when it delegated the defence portfolio to me that I would accept the ministry only under the following conditions: (1) the army that will be formed and all its branches be subordinated to the government of the people and only to that government. (2) All persons acting on behalf of the army . . . will act only according to a clearly defined function established by the government of the people.[55]

The defense ministry created by Ben–Gurion[56] was influenced by his socialist proclivities. It was committed to the principles of a depoliticized army, the supremacy of civilian authority and direction, and a highly centralized decision–making structure.[57] The "antimilitaristic dimension of Israeli socialism" even affected the name of the organization: It would not be called an "army," but a "defense force."[58] The Israel Defense Force (IDF) was "actually the first bureaucratic structure to be successfully transformed from an autonomous pre–independence organization into a truly national institution subordinate to the government. This was achieved by taking the army out of politics."[59]

As was indicated at the outset of this chapter, the principle of civilian control of the military is widely accepted in Israel. As Peretz puts it:

> Despite efforts of army officers to influence foreign or security policies . . . civilian control of the military has remained firm. Although army officers have ascended to top political positions including the Prime Ministry, civilian political influence has always outweighed that of the military in formation and implementation of national policies.[60]

Two significant political characteristics of the contemporary Israeli military have begun to receive more attention in recent years in the literature. First, the dynamics of the IDF have changed after 1967, when much of their activities began centering around being an "army of occupation" in the West Bank, Gaza, and Golan areas.[61] Second, since the mid– to late–1960's, more and more senior IDF officers have left the armed forces and entered the political arena, making the military a regular channel of recruitment for the political elite.[62] In 1973, for example, there were five retired generals in the 21–member cabinet of Prime Minister Golda Meir, the largest number of former military leaders in the government until that time.[63] Because of the principle of mandatory universal military service, [64] all ideological groups are represented in the military, ranging from the far Left to the far Right.[65]

For obvious reasons, because of its vulnerable situation in relation to national security, the Israeli military establishment and the Defense Ministry have always played a significant role in the governmental process.[66] In the recent past, the Defense Ministry alone has accounted for almost 40 percent of the national budget and virtually 20 percent of the gross national product.[67]

Apart from the very obvious concern for national defense, one important function of the armed forces has been as a socializing institution.[68] By requiring all citizens to serve in the IDF, Israeli founding fathers "envisaged the military forces as a socializing agent, where class distinctions would be obliterated and new immigrants integrated."[69]

The Bureaucracy, Local Government, the Judiciary, and the Military

We have seen in this chapter that in addition to the more "obvious" political structures contained in virtually all constitutions—the legislature and the executive branches of government, and electoral system and voting—there are at least four other political structures which must be taken into consideration in a study of the Israeli political system: the bureaucracy, local governments, the judiciary, and the military.

Israel is not unique among the nations of the world in having a well–established bureaucracy. What we have seen here is that the bureaucracy has grown over the years, is especially well entrenched, has many of the same faults as bureaucracies in most political systems (to say nothing of those special problems caused by the heterogeneity of the Israeli culture), and is not perceived in a positive light by much of the public.

Local governments in Israel, like local governments in many political systems, are often taken for granted and are not the primary focus of political observers. But they clearly play a significant role in Israeli politics. Many of the "ordinary" and "non–glamorous" aspects of daily life, such as garbage collection, water and electricity supply, traffic regulation, and the like, are controlled by local governments, and as such they are political structures worth some passing recognition by the student of Israeli politics.

As in most parliamentary systems, the judiciary is not an integral part of the policy–making process. The principle of judicial review, although partially in effect in Israel, does not extend to a review of Knesset legislation. The political role of the courts is to ensure that the will of the Knesset is followed. Structurally, the country has an elaborate network of courts in the criminal and civil arenas. What differentiates the Israeli judicial system from most others is the series of religious courts that exist for each of the religious communities.

Finally, the military has a significant role in the Israeli political world. This is true not only because of the strategic importance of defense considerations, something to which we shall return in the next chapter, but also because of the relatively small size of the Israeli political elite and the way in which they both react to military issues and are recruited from among the military elite.

NOTES

1. This is the interpretation of the term offered by Gabriel Almond. See Gabriel Almond and G. Bingham Powell, Jr. *Comparative Politics: A Developmental Approach* (Boston: Little, Brown, and Company, 1966), p. 21.

2. David Rosenbloom and Gregory Mahler, "The Administrative System of Israel," *Administrative Systems Abroad*, Krishna Tummala (ed.) (Washington, D.C.: University Press of America, 1982), p. 24.

3. Foreign Affairs was a continuation of the Political Department of the Jewish Agency; Defense evolved from the Haganah; Social Welfare developed from the National Council of the Yishuv's Welfare Department; and Education and Culture had been the Education Department of the National Council. See Don Peretz, *The Government and Politics of Israel* (Boulder, Co.: Westview, 1979), p. 171.

4. E. Samuel, "Efficiency in the Israeli Civil Service," *Canadian Public Administration* 4:2 (1961); pp. 191–96.

5. Gad Yaacobi, *The Government of Israel* (New York: Praeger, 1982), p. 204.

6. Dan Horowitz and Moshe Lissak, *Origins of the Israeli Polity* (Chicago: University of Chicago Press, 1978), p. 196.

7. E. Samuel, "Growth of the Israel Civil Service, 1948–1956," *Revue International de Science Administrative* 22:4 (1956); pp. 17–40.

8. E. Samuel, "A New Civil Service for Israel," *Public Administration* (London) 34:2 (1956); pp. 135–41.

9. Oscar Kraines, *Government and Politics in Israel* (Boston: Houghton Mifflin, 1961), p. 208.

10. Donna Divine, "The Modernization of Israeli Administration," *International Journal of Middle Eastern Studies* 5 (1974); pp. 295–313.

11. Yaacobi, *Government*, p. 208.

12. Ibid.

13. Miron Mushkat, Jr., "Transferring Administrative Skills from the Military to the Civilian Sector in the Process of Development," *Il Politico* 46:3 (1981); pp. 427–42.

14. Yaacobi, *Government*, p. 208.

15. Asher Arian, *Politics in Israel: The Second Generation* (Chatham, N.J.: Chatham House, 1985), pp. 233–34.

16. Arye Globerson, "A Profile of the Bureaucratic Elite in Israel," *Public Personnel Management* 2:1 (1973); pp. 9–15.

17. Nimrod Raphaeli, "The Senior Civil Service in Israel," *Public Administration* 48 (1970); pp. 169–78; and Nimrod Raphaeli, "The Absorption of Orientals into Israeli Bureaucracy," *Middle Eastern Studies* 8 (1972); pp. 85–92.

18. Arian, *Politics*, p. 232.

19. Ibid.

20. The four major points which follow are based upon analysis of Gerald Caiden, *Israel's Administrative Culture* (Berkeley: Institute of Government Studies, University of California, 1970), pp. 17–19.

21. See also Brenda Danet, "The Language of Persuasion in Bureaucracy: 'Modern' and 'Traditional' Appeals to the Israel Customs Authorities," *American Sociology Review* 36:5 (1971); pp. 847–49.

22. Rosenbloom and Mahler, p. 29.

23. Brenda Danet and Harriet Hartman, "Coping with Bureaucracy: The Israeli Case," *Social Forces* 51:1 (1972); pp. 7–22.

24. David Nachmias and David Rosenbloom, *Bureaucratic Culture: Citizens and Administrators in Israel* (New York: St. Martin's Press, 1978), as cited in Rosenbloom and Mahler, p. 30.

25. Yaacobi, *Government*, p. 60.

26. Ibid., p. 222.

27. Some of the material in this section is a condensation of information presented in *Facts About Israel* (Jerusalem: Ministry of Information, 1975), pp. 102–3.

28. Daniel Elazar, *Israel: Building a New Society* (Bloomington, Ind.: Indiana University Press, 1986), p. 87.

29. Efraim Torgovnik, "Urban Political Integration in Israel: A Comparative Perspective," *Urban Affairs Quarterly* 11:4 (1976); pp. 469–88.

30. Elazar, *Israel*, p. 83. See also Morton Rubin, *The Walls of Acre: Intergroup Relations and Urban Development in Israel* (New York: Holt, Rinehart, and Winston, 1974).

31. Ernest Alexander, "The Development of an Entitlement Formula for Capital Budget Allocations to Local Government in Israel," *Planning and Administration* 7:2 (1980); pp. 13–25.

32. Kraines, *Government*, pp. 218–19.

33. Arian, *Politics*, p. 239.

34. Elazar, *Israel*, pp. 96–97.

35. Daniel Friedman, "The Effect of Foreign Law on the Law of Israel," *Israel Law Review* 10:2 (1975); pp. 192–206; Friedman, "Infusion of the Common Law into the Legal System of Israel," *Israel Law Review* 10:3 (1975); pp. 324–77; and Friedman, "Independent Development of Israeli Law," *Israel Law Review* 10:4 (1975); pp. 515–65.

36. Kraines, *Government*, pp. 137–42. The several paragraphs that follow are a condensation of much more detailed treatment of the fundamental elements of Israeli law found in Kraines' discussion. See also Henry Baker, *The Legal System Of Israel*, (Jerusalem: Israel Univeristy Press, 1968), and Izhak Englard, "The Law of Torts in Israel: The Problems of Common Law Codification in a Mixed Legal System." *American Journal of Comparative Law* 22:2 (1974); pp. 302–29.

37. Samuel Sager, *The Parliamentary System of Israel* (Syracuse, N.Y.: Syracuse University Press, 1985), p. 182.

38. Yaacov Zemach, *Political Questions in the Courts* (Detroit: Wayne State University Press, 1976), p. 21.

39. Horowitz and Lissak, *Origins*, p. 199.

40. Yaacobi, *Government*, p. 3.

41. Eliahu Likhovski, "The Courts and the Legislative Supremacy of the Knesset," *Israel Law Review* 3:3 (1968); pp. 345–67.

42. This is the general focus of the "definitive" work on this subject, Zemach's volume *Political Questions in the Courts*, op cit. See also Alfred Witkin, "Some Reflections on Judicial Law–Making," *Israel Law Review* 2:4 (1967); pp. 475–87.

43. This material is a condensation of material found in Peretz, *Government and Politics*, pp. 193–6.

44. Kraines, *Government*, p. 144.

45. Ibid., p. 148.

46. See Ervin Birnbaum, *The Politics of Compromise: State and Religion in Israel* (Rutherford, N.J.: Fairleigh Dickinson University Press, 1970), p. 210. See also M. Chiger, "The Rabbinical Courts in the State of Israel," *Israel Law Review* 2:2 (1967); pp. 147–81; and Martin Edelman, "The Rabbinical Courts in the Evolving Political Culture of Israel," *Middle Eastern Studies* 16 (1980); pp. 145–66.

47. Kraines, *Government*, p. 149.

48. See also Boaz Cohen, *Law and Tradition in Judaism* (New York: Jewish Theological Seminary of America, 1959).

49. Arian, *Politics*, p. 181.

50. Kraines, *Government*, p. 150.

51. Peretz, *Government and Politics*, p. 186.

52. See some of the discussion of the role of the Court in the shaping of the Constitution in Chapter 4 in this volume.

53. Two very good general studies of the IDF are those by Edward Luttwak and Dan Horowitz, *The Israeli Army* (New York: Harper and Row, 1975), and Gunther Rothenberg, *The Anatomy of the Israeli Army: the Israeli Defense Force, 1948–1978* (New York: Hippocrene Books, 1979).

54. Yoram Peri, *Between Battles and Ballots: Israeli Military in Politics* (London: Cambridge University Press, 1983), p. 1.

55. Amos Perlmutter, *Military and Politics in Israel: Nation-Building and Role Expansion* (New York: Praeger, 1969), p. 54.

56. Yigal Allon, *The Making of Israel's Army* (New York: Universe Books, 1970); or Allon, *Shield of David: The Story of Israel's Armed Forces* (New York: Random House, 1970).

57. Perlmutter, *Military*, p. 55.

58. Elazar, *Israel*, p. 81.

59. Perlmutter, *Military*, p. 59

60. Peretz, *Government and Politics*, 128.

61. See Abraham Becker, *Israel and the Palestinian Occupied Territories: Military–Political Issues in the Debate* (Santa Monica, Ca.: Rand, 1971), and

Nimrod Raphaeli, "Military Governments in the Occupied Territories," *Middle East Journal* 23:2 (1969); pp. 177–208. For an example of a very critical study of the IDF in this regard, see Geoffrey Aronson, "Israel's Policy of Military Occupation," *Journal of Palestine Studies* 7:4 (1978); pp. 79–98.

62. Peri, *Battles and Ballots*, p. 9. See his Chapter 5, "Generals in Mufti as Politicians," pp. 101–30. See also Amos Perlmutter, "The Israeli Army in Politics," *World Politics* 20:4 (1968); pp.606–43.

63. Peretz, *Government and Politics*, p. 127.

64. "Men under 29 and women under 26 are called up for regular service of up to 36 months for men and 24 months for women, the exact term depending on the conscript's age on recruitment . . . Married women, mothers, and pregnant women are exempted. Exemption is also granted to women on grounds of religious conviction . . . After their term of national service, men and childless women are in the Reserves until the ages of 55 and 34 respectively . . . Until they are 40, men report for 31 days' training annually, and, from then until they are 55, for 14 days." *Facts About Israel*, pp. 104–5.

65. Indeed, surveys of army officers substantiate the fact that the ideological views of ex–army officers range widely. See Peretz, *Government and Politics*, p. 129.

66. Two very good general studies of the interplay of the military and politics, both by Amos Perlmutter, are *Military and Politics*, op. cit., and *Politics and the Military in Israel: 1967–1977* (London: F. Cass. 1978).

67. Peretz, *Government and Politics*, p. 178.

68. Ayad Al–Qazzaz, "Army and Society in Israel," *Pacific Sociology Review* 16:2 (1973); pp. 143–66.

69. Peretz, *Government and Politics*, p. 147. See also Victor Azarya and Baruch Kimmerling, "New Immigrants in the Israeli Armed Forces," *Armed Forces and Society* 6:3 (1980); pp. 455–82; and Maurice Roumani, "From Immigrant to Citizen: The Contribution of the Army in Israel to National Integration: The Case of Oriental Jews," *Plural Societies* 9:2-3 (1978); pp. 1–145.

Chapter 9

THE FOREIGN POLICY SETTING

Introduction

Foreign policy is an integral part of any country's political system. This is especially true for Israel. There are several reasons for this, the most important being the continued state of hostility which exists between Israel and her Arab neighbors, her vulnerable geopolitical position, and the status of the Middle East as a focal point of superpower rivalry. The study of Israeli foreign policy thus encompasses a number of important dimensions, ranging from an examination of the geopolitical and strategic contexts within which foreign policy decisions are made to the history of Israeli and Arab foreign policies, from a consideration of military strategy and tactics to the evolving definition of what constitutes "national security." In this chapter we shall briefly examine each of these issues with an eye towards more fully understanding both the context within which Israeli foreign policy is made and the strategic considerations which constantly preoccupy decision–makers.

The Setting: The Legacy of Warfare

The foreign policy setting within which Israel has had to operate since independence unfortunately conjures up terms like hostility, suspicion, and anxiety. The central focus of the over four–decade Arab–Israeli conflict has been the Arab states' refusal (with the exception of Egypt) to accept Israel's right to exist within its borders. Since the time of its Declaration of Independence, Israel has been threatened on a number of occasions by its neighbors, with the clearly articulated purpose of these threats and the goal of wars when they occurred being the destruction of the Jewish state. Indeed, Israel has confronted since independence what has been referred to as "one long war."[1] (See Map 9.1)

As we noted in Chapter One, the Arab nations surrounding Palestine rejected all suggestions for partition into separate Jewish and Arab States. When the United Nations Special Committee recommended its *own* version of a partition plan for Palestine, in November, 1947, it was greeted with the same response. Between then and May 14, 1948, the projected date of Israel's formal independence, there was continuous preparation on the part of the Arab nations for an attack once the British completed their withdrawal from Palestine.

Not surprisingly, on May 15, 1948, the combined armies of Egypt, Jordan, Iraq, Syria, and Lebanon, assisted by forces from Saudi Arabia, launched their invasion of the new State of Israel. Over the next fourteen months many battles would be fought, sacrifices made, and tempo-

MAP 9.1
Israel in the Middle East

rary cease fire agreements come and go.[2] By July, 1949, armistices (*not* peace treaties) would be agreed to with Egypt, Lebanon, Syria, and Jordan. Their stated purpose at the time was "to facilitate a transition to permanent peace." It was destined to be an unattainable goal.

Seven years later, in October, 1956, the state of war was renewed following numerous Arab violations of the 1949 armistice agreements.[3] One of the major sources of tension contributing to this second round of warfare was Egypt's blockade of Israeli shipping through the Straits of Tiran in 1955, illegal under international law because the Straits were an international waterway.[4] This had a significant impact since it virtually closed the port of Eilat and made it necessary for Israeli ships bound for East Africa and the Far East to travel through the Mediterranean and then around Africa to reach their destinations. Israel protested the Egyptian action, but was not able to resolve this crisis either diplomatically or through unilateral action.

President Nasser of Egypt subsequently nationalized the Suez Canal itself on July 26, 1956. This action upset the British because at the time nearly 25 percent of their imports passed through the Canal and close to a third of the ships using the Canal were British. Equally important was their prestige in the Middle East, to say nothing of the fact that the British government owned a controlling interest in the Canal.[5] The French were also upset because Egypt was supporting the Algerian national liberation front in its battle for independence. The British and the French, accordingly, began to plan ways to retake the Canal. Their displeasure with Nasser now coincided with that of Israel.

In August of 1956 the French Interior Minister Maurice Bourgès–Maunoury sent for Shimon Peres, then an assistant to Prime Minister Ben–Gurion, and asked: "If we make war on Egypt, would Israel be prepared to fight alongside us?"[6] The message was conveyed to the Israeli Cabinet, which discussed the matter with great care. Ben–Gurion was worried about the reactions of other nations, particularly the United States, the Soviet Union, and influential non–aligned countries like India.[7]

On October 24, 1956, when Egypt, Jordan, and Syria announced the creation of a joint military command,[8] Israel's decision was made much easier. On October 29 a combined Israeli, French, and British military force seized control of the Suez Canal, along with the Gaza strip and the entire Sinai peninsula. The United Nations, the United States, and the Soviet Union all criticized the action, with the United Nations General Assembly passing an immediate ceasefire resolution demanding Israeli withdrawal to the 1949 armistice line. On November 6th Britain and France announced that they would comply with the UN resolution, and on November 8th a United Nations Emergency Force was created to help maintain peace in the area. In March, 1957, following promises from Egypt that it would cease all maritime blockades, and guarantees from American President Dwight Eisenhower that the United States would help see that Egypt kept its word,[9] Israel returned to Egypt all of the captured territory. Egypt's promises, as it turned out, were not kept. Neither were the promises of the United States to be the guarantor of Egyptian commitments.

By June, 1967, Israel again found itself in a precarious position.[10] Both Egypt and Syria had begun a massive program of military mobilization and it became increasingly clear to Israeli intelligence analysts that they were preparing for another attack. Egypt ordered the United Nations Peacekeeping Forces out of the Sinai, where they had been maintaining a demilitarized zone,[11] moved its own forces toward the Israeli border, and again closed the Straits of Tiran to all Israeli shipping. When Israel sought American support based upon Eisenhower's 1957 promises, President Lyndon Johnson—at this time involved in an unpopular and unsuccessful war in Vietnam—responded that the United States was "not the policeman of the world" and that Israel would have to take care of its own problems.

And so the Israelis did. On June 5, 1967, their Air Force launched a preemptive strike that destroyed virtually the entire Egyptian Air Force on the ground.[12] At the outset the Jordanians stayed out of the fighting. Israel assured Amman that it had no expansionist motives and indicated that if Jordan remained neutral Israel would take no action along its eastern border.[13] However, after the overwhelming Israeli successes against Egypt and Syria on the first day of the war, Nasser began to exert a great deal of pressure on King Hussein, arguing that if Israel were forced to fight a three–front war the Arab governments would ultimately prevail. Indeed, Nasser is reported to have told Hussein that three–quarters of Israel's air force had been wiped out by the Egyptian forces at the outset of the fighting, "and that Egyptian armored units were fighting deep inside Israeli territory." Hussein himself later admitted that "we were misinformed about what had happened . . ."[14] By then, of course, it was too late. Confounding the expectations of Nasser, six days later Israel had captured the entire Sinai desert to the south, the Golan Heights to the north, and the West Bank of the Jordan River to the east.[15] (See Map 9.2)

After the war, Israel made several offers to exchange the captured territories for peace treaties, not renewed armistices. But at the August 29–September 1, 1967, Arab Summit held in Khartoum, Sudan, the Arab governments announced their "three no" doctrine: "No recognition. No negotiation. No peace."[16] Between the spring of 1969 and the summer of 1970, Israel had to endure the so–called "War of Attrition," during which time Egypt regularly fired across the Suez cease–fire lines.[17] In August, 1970, another Egyptian–Israeli cease–fire was negotiated, and a temporary peace again came to the region. But it was also not to last.

Although the period from 1970 to 1973 did not see outright war in the Middle East, neither was it a time of peace. Israel was expending considerable effort rearming itself and maintaining its post–1967 frontiers. Egypt and Syria continued to import arms from the Soviet Union, deny Israel's right to exist, and issue various threats related to Israeli security. Tensions waxed and waned, but were never far below the surface.

In October, 1973, the country was to face its most severe challenge to date.[18] Israeli intelligence once again notified the political leadership

MAP 9.2
Borders of Israel After the 1967 War

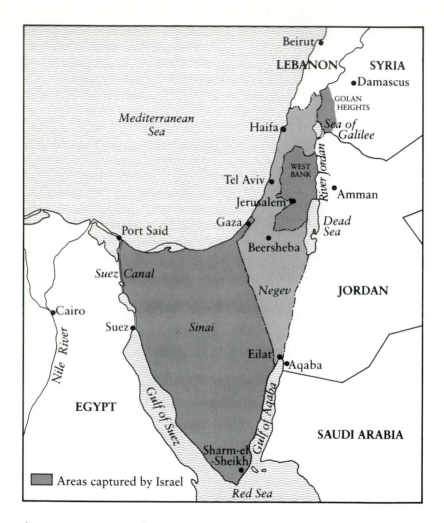

that it now possessed clear evidence of an impending joint Egyptian–Syrian attack. Meanwhile, President Anwar Sadat (who had replaced Nasser after his death in 1970) was taking the public position that Egypt could no longer tolerate a continued Israeli presence in the Sinai. In response, some in the Israeli leadership advocated another preemptive strike, arguing that if they were to wait for an Egyptian–Syrian attack the materiel and human costs to Israel would be prohibitively high. Golda Meir, the Prime Minister at the time, contacted American President Richard Nixon regarding the impending crisis. Nixon, like Johnson in 1967, urged restraint and cautioned against preemption. Even if Israel was correct that an invasion was imminent, he argued, she could not afford to be labelled by the Arab powers as the "aggressor," as had been the case in 1967. Nixon promised that if Israel would wait, it could count on American assistance should an attack occur.

Coming from the country's principal ally and supplier, Nixon's advice carried great weight. The Israeli Government's position was also influenced by the fact that Yom Kippur, the holiest day of the Jewish year, was fast approaching. The Government was loathe to split up virtually every Israeli family by mobilizing the armed forces without it being absolutely necessary. The Cabinet decided, finally, not to mobilize the Israel Defense Forces (IDF) and adjourned from its meeting on October 5.

Early on the morning of Yom Kippur, October 6, 1973, the armed forces of Egypt and Syria launched their "surprise" attack.[19] The IDF suffered extraordinarily heavy losses, but managed to hold, and then repel, the invading armies on both fronts.[20] When Prime Minister Meir telephoned Nixon to inform him of the invasion and request American assistance, he indicated he would begin the arrangements, but it was literally days before any American supplies reached Israel, despite persistent and even frantic telephone calls from Meir. Nixon's response was that it was necessary to follow established procedures, to inform Congress, and that Israel should "be patient" and help would come.[21] Eventually American aid did begin to arrive, although the delay once again reminded Israel of its vulnerability. A new cease–fire agreement was subsequently arranged, sponsored by the United States, after more than two weeks of fighting.

Following the 1973 war, a period of profound reassessment emerged in Israeli politics. The self–confidence which had followed the Six Day War was now severely shaken. In the first three days of the two–week war there had been some real doubt—not hysterical but sincere, objective, self–confidence–shattering doubt—about the conflict's outcome.[22] One consequence was that there were a number of political casualties. Long–time political leaders, including Meir and Defense Minister Moshe Dayan, resigned over strategic decisions made in relation to the non–mobilization. Israel was increasingly sensitive to its vulnerability and the need for continuing to be well–armed.

The most recent major military action involving Israeli troops occurred in June of 1982 when the Government undertook a highly controversial military action in Lebanon. Called "Operation Peace for Galilee," the IDF entered the southern part of the country to search out and destroy Palestine Liberation Organization (PLO) terrorist bases which had long used the area to launch artillery and rocket attacks against settlements in northern Israel. This also became the first military action in Israel's history in which significant portions of the population expressed vocal criticism of the Government's military policy. Indeed, many referred to involvement in Lebanon as "Israel's Vietnam." When the army finally withdrew in 1988, many Israelis breathed a deep sigh of relief.[23]

More recently, Israel has been sorely troubled by the "intifada"— the "uprising" on the West Bank sparked not by the PLO but rather by the residents of the Occupied Territories themselves. For over a year this "uprising" has been a constant source of anxiety for Israeli authorities in several respects. First, the authorities were largely unprepared for the massive demonstrations that have occurred. Soldiers and police were untrained in how to respond to crowds throwing rocks. Even though the military forces have changed from "conventional" ammunition to rubber bullets, literally hundreds of Palestinians have been killed by the IDF for doing nothing more than throwing rocks.

In addition, the "uprising" has caught the attention of the world in a far more sympathetic fashion than any of the past actions of the PLO. Scenes of women and children throwing rocks at armed Israeli troops have been terribly effective in convincing many around the world— including many in Israel itself—that the occupation of the West Bank simply *cannot* continue indefinitely. The level of the Palestinian casualties has become an effective propaganda weapon supporting their argument that they are being oppressed in the Occupied Territories.

Finally, it has been difficult for many in Israel to see how the "uprising" might be brought to an end. The Palestinian leadership has vowed to continue as long as Israel refuses to negotiate directly with the PLO. Although Israel has expressed its willingness to negotiate with moderate Palestinian leaders, it has steadfastly refused to have anything to do with PLO chief Yasser Arafat and his representatives. Thus, for many in Israel there is no "light at the end of the tunnel."

On the whole, then, what the preceding discussion has sought to demonstrate is that the legacy of warfare in the Middle East is significant for its duration, intensity, and policy implications. This is true in at least three important dimensions. First, the entire context of Israeli foreign policy decision—making has been shaped by evaluating virtually every situation from a national security perspective since the country has been forced to engage in a struggle for national survival throughout its entire existence. This has had the effect of graphically and periodically reminding all Israelis of their vulnerability in the sense that their neighbors (with the exception of Egypt) do not want them to be there, and of the reality that many others (such as the PLO) have the ability to affect their lives through acts of terrorism and warfare.

A second legacy of warfare has conditioned Israel's relations with her neighbors. Apart from Egypt, which we shall discuss further in the next chapter, relations with Arab nations have been uniformly hostile. The country is *still* technically at war with its neighbors—and has been since 1948. Although the last full–scale regional conflict was 1973, the IDF has been heavily involved in southern Lebanon for several years, as well as maintaining a constant state of alert along the remaining frontiers. In brief, with the exception of Israeli-Egyptian relations very little progress has been made on a bilateral basis in the Middle East.

The third legacy involves Israel's relations with the superpowers. Although the country has recently voiced hopes of reestablishing "official" diplomatic relations with the Soviet Union, there is no doubt that since the early 1950's Moscow has been a prominent sponsor and supporter of the Arab camp in Middle East conflict.[24] On several occasions over the past forty years the two superpowers have been extremely active in the Middle East. At times their involvement has escalated dangerously close to direct confrontation. During the 1973 Yom Kippur War, for instance, Soviet Communist Party General Secretary Leonid Brezhnev called Nixon on the Moscow–Washington "hot line" to warn that if the United States could not convince Israel to release an Egyptian division surrounded in the Sinai Desert, the Kremlin would be forced to send in its own troops to help the Egyptians. At that point the fear that had been articulated for years—namely, that the Middle East held the potential to start a war between the superpowers—was alarmingly clear. President Nixon was able to convince the Israelis to release the Egyptians, the Soviets did not intervene more directly than providing arms for the Egyptians, and the superpowers successfully avoided direct conflict.

Strategic Considerations

In his definitive study of Israeli foreign policy, Michael Brecher suggests that the system is divided into three component parts: "Input," "Process," and "Output." The "Input" segment is in turn made up of three sub-elements: the "operational environment," "communication," and the "psychological environment." The "Process" segment deals with the formulation of strategic and tactical decisions, along with the way these decisions are implemented by various governmental structures. Lastly, the "Output" segment pertains to the substance of decisions and actions by the government. Each of these parts deserves individual comment, for each makes its separate contribution to our understanding of the entire scheme.[25]

The "External Environment" suggested by Brecher includes a general consideration of global politics, or, as he puts it, the "total web of relationships among all actors within the international system (states, blocs, organizations)."[26] All of these relationships can affect the manner in which Israel acts in any given situation. Regional relationships, or what the author terms "subordinate systems," focus primarily upon the Middle East, for obviously this environment has the most direct bearing upon foreign policy decisions. Other bilateral relationships, especially those with the superpowers (the US and the USSR), must also be factored into the formulation of Israeli foreign policy.[27]

The "Internal Environment" is composed of the domestic forces which can influence foreign policy. Among them would be included: military capability, economic strength and resources, the current political environment, and the overall context within which decisions are made (i.e., public opinion, government coalitions, and short—term domestic political considerations). Interest group involvement in the political system and the degree of popular consensus or discord over foreign policy options also provide significant clues to identifying who the competing elites are, as well as ascertaining their respective political strengths.

The views or "inputs" of these various factors in the international and domestic environments are communicated to decision—making elites through a variety of communications outlets, including the mass media, press, radio, television, and the bureaucracy. These decision—making elites, then, become what Brecher refers to as the "core decision—making group" of the foreign policy system, consisting of the Head of Government, the Foreign Minister, and a relatively narrow range of other political actors.[28]

As this "core decision—making group" tries to make foreign policy decisions, its individual members must operate within their own "psychological environments." Each decision—maker brings with him or her a set of attitudes about the world, other nations in the foreign policy setting, ideology, tradition, and the desirability of various policy options. Decision—makers also bring in their psychological predispositions a set of images of the environment and their perceptions of reality

FIGURE 9.1
The Foreign Policy System of Israel

```
I. Inputs

The Operational Environment
External (Global Politics, Regional Issues, Bilateral — — — — →┐
      Issues)                                                    │
Internal (Military, Economic, Political, Interest Groups, — — →┤
      Competing Elites)                                          │
                                          is communicated by the ↓
                                          media, bureaucracy, etc.

The Psychological Environment                                    │
Attitudes of Political Elites — — — — — — — — — — — — — →┐
Elites' Images of the Environment — — — — — — — — — →┤

II. Process                                                      │

Formulation — — — — — — — — — — — — — — — →┐
Implementation — — — — — — — — — — — — →┤

III. Outputs                                                     │

Acts and Decisions of Government — — — — — — — →Policy
```

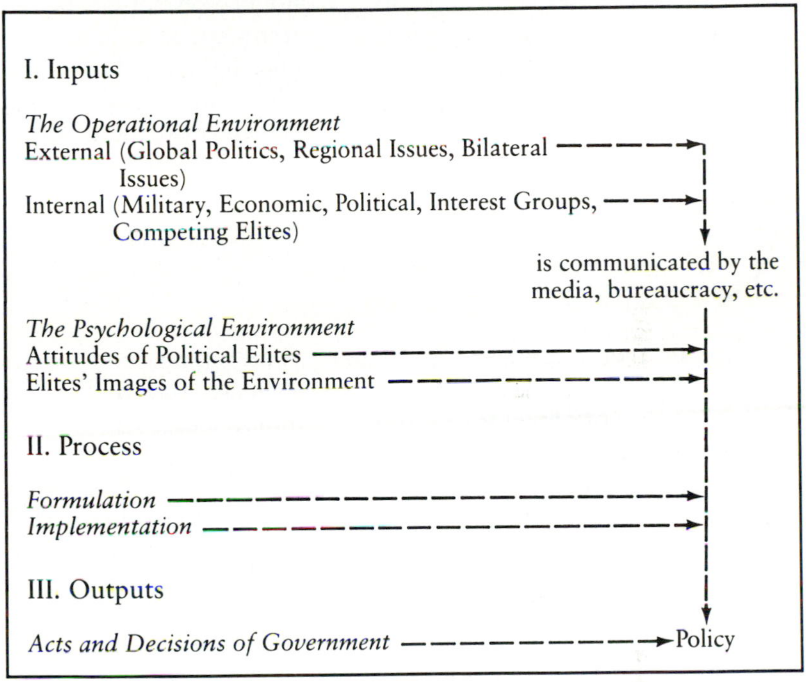

Source: Based upon Michael Brecher, The Foreign Policy System of Israel: Setting, Images, Process (New Haven: Yale University Press, 1972), p. 4

in the political world. These images may be more or less realistic, more or less flexible, and can color the information they receive from the respective operational environments.

After the elements making up the operational environment have been communicated to the elite and then filtered through the psychological screens of individual decision–makers, the policy–making process itself helps to determine what option is chosen and how that policy is implemented. Factored in here would be the number of individuals involved in the decision–making process, the chain of command or power relationships among them, whether or not a given policy decision is seen as "political," the degree to which it must be openly debated and discussed, and a variety of other factors unique to the Israeli political world.[29]

Brecher furthermore suggests[30] that there are four identifiable issue areas in Israeli foreign policy: "military–security"—such as violence, warfare, or national security; "political–diplomatic"—involving relations with other international actors; "economic–developmental"— which pertain to trade, aid, or foreign investment; and "cultural– status"—which focus on educational, scientific, and related concerns. Each "cluster" of issues is handled differently by the overall foreign policy system from other "clusters" and, consequently, the different clusters must be analyzed and studied with an awareness that each is distinct from the others.

Military–Security

A crucial aspect of Israeli foreign policy is the military one, for the status, structure, and operation of the Israeli Defense Force (IDF) is not the same as that of armed forces in other nations. This is true for two reasons. First, relations between civilians and the military are different in Israel from relations one finds in other settings. Second, the underlying doctrine of Israel's military establishment differs from other armies. The fact that only a small proportion of the army is "called up" at any given time has strategic implications for Israeli foreign policy considerations.

The concept of defense, in the words of one analyst, "has been a central issue in [Jewish] society ever since the beginning of the Zionist Movement in Central and Eastern Europe at the turn of the century."[31] If for no other reason, defense and the military would be significant in Israel because of the proportion of national resources they consume.[32] As a percentage of the total national budget, defense spending, at its lowest point (1961) consumed 19 percent. At its peak (1973) it consumed almost 50 percent![33]

The military is also very visible in Israeli society.[34] From one perspective this is so because it is a virtually universal phenomenon. Since 1974 the IDF has drafted over 90 percent of all Israeli males. Indeed, the average Israeli man will serve 36 months in active service and close to 30 additional months in the reserves prior to his 54th birthday, assuming no extra service in times of war. This is a rather obvious reason why the military is so significant in most Israeli lives.[35]

One direct consequence for foreign policy is the above–mentioned call–up pattern. Only a small proportion of the military is on "active duty" at any given time. It is officially calculated that the IDF needs 72 hours to reach fully mobilized status, although some estimates suggest a considerably shorter period than this. One study, for example, has indicated that partial—mobilization time can range from four to eighteen hours and full mobilization within 16 to 48 hours, considerably less than the official figure of 72.[36]

Whatever the time involved, when decision—makers have had to decide whether to launch a preemptive attack (as was the case in 1967), or to wait (as happened in 1973), they know that their decision will have real consequences. The IDF suffered especially high casualties in 1973 during the first 72 hours, until it reached full strength, and post—war analysis was very explicit in its criticism of Golda Meir and her government. Among other factors, critics noted that many of these casualties could have been avoided if the IDF had been fully mobilized prior to Yom Kippur, even if she had *not* ordered a preemptive strike.

Another issue of military—security concerns in foreign affairs is the nuclear.[37] Although Israel has continued to insist that it does not possess nuclear weapons, many observers feel that even if it is literally true that the country does not have *intact* nuclear weapons, it is the case that Israel possesses the ability to *assemble* such weapons in relatively short order. A nuclear capability would permit the IDF to offset an enemy with much greater numerical strength. Israel has also stated publicly on several occasions that she will not stand by while her Arab neighbors develop their own nuclear capability. This policy was demonstrated in 1979 when Iraq was constructing a nuclear reactor ostensibly for the production of electricity. Israeli bombers attacked and destroyed the facility, with the justification being that such a facility could too readily be diverted to military as well as commercial uses.

Finally, military—security concerns involve what Israelis commonly refer to as the "defensible borders" issue. We noted in Chapter Three that one of the central goals of "classical" Zionism was a secure Jewish population in a secure Jewish state. This has been translated in more modern times into a call for "secure and defensible borders."[38] The quest for stability and national security has been a continual, and as yet unrealized, goal in Israeli foreign policy.

The problem, of course, is that except for Egypt *all* of Israel's neighbors are still technically in a "state of war" with Israel. The cease—fires signed in 1949, 1956, 1967, and 1973 are *not* peace treaties. Thus the common description of Israeli foreign policy, as we have already remarked, as "one long war."[39]

This quest for "secure and defensible borders" has become the *sine qua non* of Israeli foreign policy since 1948, and has been the subject of a great deal of debate and scholarship. Israel has contended that it has a *right* to secure boundaries,[40] and that the only way to maintain secure boundaries is to make them as easily defensible as possible. This means, in the case of policy towards Jordan, Syria, or Lebanon (to say nothing of Egypt), that geopolitical factors must constantly be taken into consideration.

When Israel occupied the entire Sinai Peninsula following the 1967 War it obtained a degree of security that it had not previously possessed. With military observation stations at the southern tip of the Sinai, Israel would have a twenty–minute warning period between its first detection of hostile Egyptian aircraft taking off from Cairo and their arrival time on the outskirts of Tel Aviv. When the Sinai was returned to Egypt in 1982, this advance warning time was decreased from twenty to two minutes, if Israel had to rely only on the usual sources of intelligence.[41]

Similarly, the occupation and eventual annexation of part of the Golan Heights was undertaken for strategic reasons. Given the topography of northern Israel, a hostile Syria controlling all of the territory of the Golan Heights for years meant that entire cohorts of children living in kibbutzim and urban settlements frequently had to seek underground shelters because of the constant fear and periodic reality of Syrian sniping and attack. Once this territory was captured in 1973, the quest for "secure and defensible borders" meant that Israel would not return high ground to a nation with which it was still at war.

The search for national security motivates all states in their foreign policy. It is only reasonable to expect that states that have never known *real* security will be even more desirous of obtaining it. Israel has concluded that the only way it can have real security is through military preparedness, since most of her neighbors are committed to her destruction. Any long–term peace in the Middle East must therefore require that all her neighbors acknowledge Israel's right to exist within mutually recognized and secure borders before the parties involved can begin to look beyond their own immediate security needs to an examination of what they can all do to de–escalate the tensions and perceived threats which exist in this part of the world.[42]

Political–Diplomatic

On a more global level, one of Israel's major concerns since independence has simply been to "be accepted" by the community of nations. This has not been an easy task, for Israel still has not even "arrived" as an accepted member of the United Nations. Although the function of the UN is to play the role of "disinterested third party" capable of being neutral in any political crisis, it has not been perceived in this light by Israel.[43] Israel's view instead is that since 1967 it has never been able to get a "fair hearing" in the General Assembly, that the combination of the Soviet Union's influence among Eastern Bloc and Third World nations and the Arab world's own influence in the Third World (through "oil politics" in general, as well as regional groupings like the Organization of African Unity), has resulted in an "automatic" anti–Israeli majority in both the General Assembly and most of the UN's specialized agencies. As the Israeli government has put it:

> The Arab states and their Communist allies commanded an automatic majority—and they did not wish to have the UN involved. Instead they preferred to continue to use the world organization and its specialized agencies as platforms for often totally irrational attacks on Israel.[44]

Under its Charter, for example, UN Peacekeeping Forces can only be stationed in an area if they are requested by all parties concerned. Such forces, as is well–known, were stationed in various Middle East locales between 1956 and 1967. But when President Nasser ordered them to leave the Sinai in 1967, they had no choice but to comply.[45] This, according to Israel, is one of the weaknesses of the UN—that it has no real "power" of its own to play a more active role. In situations in which the opportunity has presented itself, Israel has accordingly favored using independent multinational peacekeeping contingents rather than UN Forces to guarantee disengagement agreements.

Because of Israel's view that the United Nations cannot be objective in the Israeli–Arab conflict and because of its recognition of and grant-ing "Observer Status" to the PLO, the United Nations has lost virtually all of its potential to act as a credible mediator in the Middle East. In-stead, Israel has appeared to favor using other parties, primarily the United States, to help it negotiate with its Arab neighbors.

Outside the confines of the UN, Israel has had inconsistent relations with the Europeans. For a time France was a strong supporter, and it was during the period of Franco–Israeli harmony that Israel is reported to have acquired its nuclear capability.[46] In recent years, as the French have taken decidedly more pro–Palestinian and pro-Arab stands, relations between Jerusalem and Paris have suffered accordingly. Brit-ain has never had a particularly close relationship with Israel, a fact most Israelis attribute to the "unpleasant" events leading up to inde-pendence. Relations with West Germany were greatly affected at the outset by the issue of "reparations" to be paid by the West German Government for the Holocaust.[47] Over time, however, their ties for the most part have been stable.[48]

Israel's greatest foreign policy successes in the early years were with the Third World. Prior to the Six Day War, in fact, Israel had extremely good relations with most Third World countries. From Independence through the 1956 Suez War in particular, Israel was seen by many African and Latin American states as another small nation grappling with the same kinds of development problems they faced. Israel developed a number of very popular aid programs with states in Sub–Saharan Africa,[49] Asia,[50] and Latin America.[51] Through the mid–1970's, over 5,500 Israeli experts had been sent as scientific, educational, and agricultural advisers overseas, while over 20,000 citizens of Africa, Asia, and Latin America had travelled to Israel for training.[52]

It was the Six Day War that significantly changed Israel's status, most prominently in Africa. Egypt, especially, used the Organization of African Unity to isolate Israel, claiming that she had been the aggressor and that pan–African solidarity required all member states to cut ties with Israel. In fact, virtually all of them did, except for South Africa. Israel has worked at improving relations with Sub–Saharan Africa since then, but only in recent years has significant progress been made in re–establishing links.[53] Otherwise, much of Israel's dealings with the Third World has involved arms transactions.[54] The country is a major arms supplier to various Third World states, and many in Latin America, for example, have maintained diplomatic ties and continued diplomatic support as a direct *quid pro quo* for Israel's ongoing arms sales to them.

Clearly Israel's most important political–diplomatic concerns, though, involve relations with the United States and the Soviet Union. Although Washington was the first to recognize Israel as an independent state,[55] the Soviet Union was in fact Israel's strongest supporter during the early years.[56] By the time of the 1956 Suez War, however, it was clear that Moscow had opted to back the Arab powers in the Middle East while Israel was moving towards closer relations with the West. In recent years, of course, Israel's most intimate political and diplomatic ties have been with the United States.

The subject of United States–Israeli relations is simply far too large and significant in the context of Israeli foreign policy to be adequately handled in the space available here. The United States is Israel's largest supplier of aid, both civilian and military, Israel's guarantor of energy,[57] largest trading partner, and most consistent defender in a variety of international diplomatic arenas.[58] The role of the United States as a mediator in the Middle East, from Secretary of State Henry Kissinger's "shuttle diplomacy"[59] through President Jimmy Carter and Camp David, clearly illustrates this. Although events in recent years have created occasional tensions in the bilateral relationship,[60] overall the two have been important to each other and good allies.[61] Israel has functioned as a source of military intelligence in a strategically important geopolitical setting and, equally important, as a stable democracy in a part of the world where stable democracies are not all that common.

Economic–Developmental

The third of Brecher's four general issue areas involves economic and developmental considerations. Israel's economic development has not progressed as smoothly or as rapidly as many had hoped.[62] For this, foreign policy has played a direct as well as frequently disruptive role.

Because Israel is forced to spend so much of its budget on military and defense–related activities, it has continued to have a severe balance–of–payments problem.[63] After the 1973 Yom Kippur War, and owing to other international factors,[64] the economy slowed considerably, with growth rates of 5.0 percent in 1978–79, 3.2 percent in 1980–81, 1.2 percent in 1982–83, and 1.8 percent in 1983–84.[65] This slowdown has resulted in serious domestic economic problems, with inflation at one point running close to 1000 percent annually.[66] Israel's balance–of–payments deficit, which in 1970 was 644.3 million dollars, was 2.24 billion dollars by 1980. As a result of severe and painful domestic policy decisions, by 1986 it had improved slightly, shrinking to 1.98 billion.[67] The foreign loan picture has not improved, however. Total loans to Israel outstanding at the end of the year have continued to grow, totalling $22.1 billion in 1980, $29.8 billion in 1983, and $31.5 billion in 1986.[68]

In short, Israel is economically tied to the Western world despite its geographical setting in the Middle East. More than half of the country's imports come from the European Economic Community (Common Market), while almost half of her exports go there. In fact, in 1977 Israel signed an agreement with the Common Market creating a "special association" status that essentially provides for lower tariff barriers than most non–Common Market countries would have to face.[69]

Cultural–Status

Educational, scientific, and cultural concerns also appear in the formulation of Israeli foreign policy. As indicated above, since 1948 Israel has sought acceptance and legitimacy in the international community. In many cases this desire for acceptance, or put another way, the rejection of Israel by other nations of the world, has extended from the political to the cultural realm. A number of efforts have been made by Arab nations to defeat Israel not on the battlefield but in the cultural arena. Israel must always be prepared, in other words, to "do battle" in the halls of the United Nations where attempts are regularly made to expel her from one or another of the United Nations' many bodies, such as UNESCO (the United Nations Educational, Scientific, and Cultural Organization).

Israel participates wherever opportunities present themselves, although efforts at involvement more often than not result in rejection. When the Israeli delegation rose to speak at the International Women's Year conference in Mexico City, for instance, a prearranged bloc of African and Third World delegates rose and left the hall. Culturally, as well, then, Israel has continued to be closely linked to the West, often participating in artistic, cinematic, athletic, and musical events.

The Foreign Policy Setting: A Recapitulation

When studying the political context within which public policy is made it is important, indeed crucial, to understand not only those factors in the domestic, or "internal," environment and how they might influence policy, but to understand as well those in the "external" domain. It is clear from even this admittedly cursory examination of Israeli foreign policy that there are a variety of factors which influence both the formulation and the execution of policy decisions.

Overall, Brecher contends that there are eight "key components" of Israel's foreign policy "system." These are as follow:

1. Israel is a self–conscious Jewish state whose historical legacy and *raison d'être* link her indissolubly to Jewish communities everywhere.
2. Israel is dependent upon one or more super and great power(s) for military and economic assistance and diplomatic support.
3. The combined voting strength of the Arab, Soviet, and non–aligned groups at the UN has made a pro–Israel resolution in the General Assembly or the Security Council impossible since the early 1960s.
4. Israel is totally isolated within the Core of the Middle East system and is confronted with a permanent challenge to her security; that

condition, and her geographic position, have imposed a persistent quest for military aid.

5. Israel is vastly outnumbered by the Arab states, thereby creating a continuous demand for immigrants to augment her military and economic manpower.

6. Coalition government is a fixed element of Israel's political system, causing restraints on foreign policy choices.

7. 'Ein breirah' (no alternative) is the linchpin of Israel's political thought and behaviour.

8. Historical legacy and Arab enmity have created the necessity for activism and militancy in Israeli behavior.[70]

The legacy of war and the pattern of tension that exists is clearly the most important single factor in Israeli foreign policy. There is no legacy of goodwill, trust, faith, or confidence existing between Israel and her neighbors. While it is true that Israel and Egypt have been "at peace" now for almost a decade, the "peace" has run "hot" and "cold" and has not been perceived as being sufficiently secure for Israelis to feel that they no longer need to be concerned about their southern border. All of Israel's other neighbors are still technically in a state of war, which does little to alleviate short–range concerns there, as well as long–range anxieties about demands for the creation of an independent Palestinian state, a topic to which we shall turn our attention in the next chapter.

There are likewise important strategic considerations which need to be kept in mind. Israel must be aware of the separate environments within which policy must operate, ranging from the domestic (internal), to the regional (Middle Eastern) and international (global) levels. Psychological perceptions of leaders, their attitudes, beliefs, and values, and how these can affect policymaking must also be accounted for. These factors, to say nothing of the actual policymaking process itself, all make up the strategic environment in which foreign policy decisions are made.

Equally important is the military dimension to foreign policy. The size, organizational nature, and needs of the Israel Defense Force must be constantly evaluated when political leaders make policy decisions that can have military consequences. The time needed to fully mobilize the Israeli armed forces, the effect of such a mobilization on the economy, and similar factors, all must be considered in the development of foreign policy. The issues of national security and defensible borders form an important part of this agenda. Because Israel is small and her larger and more populous neighbors are overwhelmingly hostile, the concept of defensible borders becomes even more salient than it might be for the United States and Canada, two nations with the longest open and unarmed border in the world.

Israel has existed as an independent nation now for over four decades, but Israel has not yet known a moment's peace. One of the elements that will contribute in a very significant way to the realization of a state of peace in the foreseeable future is the role of the Palestinians and the status of the West Bank, the Gaza Strip, and the city of Jerusalem. It is to an examination of these questions that we turn our attention.

NOTES

1. The discussion that follows is partially based upon *Facts About Israel* (Jerusalem: Ministry of Foreign Affairs, 1985), pp. 39–40.

2. Some good general military histories of this period include work by Lynn Banks, *Torn Country: An Oral History of the Israeli War of Independence* (New York: Watts, 1982); Jon Kimche and David Kimche, *A Clash of Destinies: The Arab–Jewish War and the Founding of the State of Israel* (New York: Praeger, 1960); Dan Kurzman, *Genesis 1948: The First Arab–Israeli War* (New York: World, 1970); Netanel Lorch, *Israel's War of Independence: 1947–1949* (Hartford: Hartford House, 1968); and Edgar O'Ballance, *The Arab–Israeli War, 1948* (New York: Praeger, 1957).

3. Some reference material for this event would include Moshe Dayan, *Diary of the Sinai Campaign* (Jerusalem: Steimatzky's Agency, 1966); or Robert Henriques, *A Hundred Hours to Suez: An Account of Israel's Campaign in the Sinai Peninsula* (New York: Viking, 1957).

4. See, for example, B. Andrews, "Suez Canal Controversy," *Albany Law Review* 21:1 (1957): 14–33; or Simcha Dinitz, "The Legal Aspects of the Egyptian Blockade of the Suez Canal," *Georgetown Law Journal* 45:2 (1957): 166–99.

5. Howard Sachar, *A History of Israel: From the Rise of Zionism to Our Time* (New York: Alfred A. Knopf, 1981), p. 486.

6. Ibid., p. 489.

7. Ibid., p. 494.

8. Alfred Katz, *Government and Politics in Contemporary Israel, 1948–Present* (Washington, D.C.: University Press of America, 1980), p. 155.

9. Gideon Rafael, *Destination Peace: Three Decades of Israeli Foreign Policy. A Personal Memoir* (New York: Stein and Day, 1981), p. 64.

10. There is a very good and detailed discussion of this in Rafael, *Destination Peace*, pp. 153–90. One of the best analyses of the decision–making process involved here is Michael Brecher's *Decisions in Israel's Foreign Policy* (New Haven: Yale University Press, 1975), pp. 318–453.

11. On this subject, see Indar Rikhye, *The Sinai Blunder: Withdrawal of the United Nations Emergency Force Leading to the Six Day War of June, 1967* (Totowa, N.J.: Frank Cass, 1980).

12. A fascinating discussion of the value of pre–emption is found in Robert Harkavy, *Pre–emption and Two Front Conventional Warfare* (Jerusalem: Hebrew University Press, 1977).

13. On this subject see David Ben–Gurion, *Israel: A Personal History* (New York: Funk and Wagnalls, 1971), pp. 774–86.

14. Sachar, *A History of Israel*, p. 643.

15. On the Six–Day War in general, see David Kimche, *The Sandstorm: The Arab–Israeli War of 1967* (New York: Stein and Day, 1968); Michael Brecher, *Decisions in Crisis: Israel, 1967 and 1973* (Berkeley: University of California Press, 1980); and Randolph Churchill, *The Six Day War* (Boston:

Houghton, Mifflin, 1967). Yehoshafat Harkabi offered an interesting analysis of the outcome in his "Basic Factors in the Arab Collapse During the Six Day War." *Orbis* 2:3 (1967): 677–91.

16. *Facts About Israel*, p. 39.

17. On this war see Yaacov Bar–Simon Tov, *The Israeli–Egyptian War of Attrition, 1969–1970* (New York: Columbia University Press, 1980).

18. Rafael, *Destination Peace*, pp. 281–303.

19. Michael Handel, *Perception, Deception, and Surprise: The Case of the Yom Kippur War* (Jerusalem: Hebrew University Press, 1975).

20. There is a significant literature on the 1973 war. Examples of analyses that have been published would include: Avraham Adnan, *On the Banks of the Suez: An Israeli General's Personal Account of the Yom Kippur War* (San Rafael, Ca.: Presidio Press, 1980); Peter Allen, *The Yom Kippur War* (New York: Scribner, 1982); Riad Ashkar, "The Syrian and Egyptian Campaign," *Journal of Palestine Studies* 3:2 (1974): pp. 15–33; Michael Brecher, *Decisions in Crisis: Israel, 1967 and 1973* (Berkeley: University of California Press, 1980); E. Monroe, *The Arab–Israeli War, 1973* (London: International Institute for Strategic Studies, 1974); and Zeev Schiff, *October Earthquake: Yom Kippur, 1973* (Tel Aviv: University Publishing Projects, 1974).

21. Edmund Ghareeb, "The U.S. Arms Supply to Israel During the October War," *Journal of Palestine Studies* 3:2 (1974): pp. 114–21.

22. Alon Ben–Meir, "Israel in the War's Long Aftermath," *Current History* 80:462 (1981): 23–26; Harold Hart, *Yom Kippur Plus 100 Days* (New York: Har Publications, 1974).

23. For a very dramatic example of this, Jacobo Timmerman, *The Longest War: Israel in Lebanon* (New York: Knopf, 1982). Another interesting study is that of Yohanan Ramati, "Strategic Effects of Israel's Campaign in Lebanon," *Midstream* 28:7 (1982): 3–4.

24. For a discussion of why the Soviet Union turned increasingly hostile to Israel during the 1949–1953 period, see Sachar, *A History of Israel*, pp. 461–63. Studies of the role of the Soviets in the 1973 War include Galia Golan, *The Soviet Union and the Arab–Israeli War of October, 1973* (Jerusalem: Hebrew University Press, 1974); Galia Golan, *Yom Kippur and After: The Soviet Union and the Middle East* (New York: Cambridge University Press, 1977); and Foy Kohler, *The Soviet Union and the October 1973 Middle East War* (Coral Gables, Fl.: University of Miami Press, 1974).

25. Michael Brecher, *The Foreign Policy System of Israel: Setting, Images, Process* (New Haven: Yale University Press, 1972). Another excellent general study of Israeli foreign policy strategy is that by Yoav Ben–Horin and Barry Posen, *Israel's Strategic Doctrine* (Santa Monica, Ca.: Rand Corporation, 1981).

26. Brecher, *The Foreign Policy System*, p. 5.

27. Examples of research in this area would include Arnold Krammer, *The Forgotten Friendship: Israel and the Soviet Bloc, 1947–1953* (Urbana, Il.: University of Illinois Press, 1974); Galia Golan, *Yom Kippur and After*; Robert

Drinan, *Honor the Promise: America's Commitment to Israel* (Garden City: Doubleday, 1977); Avigdor Dagan, *Moscow and Jerusalem: Twenty Years of Relations Between Israel and the Soviet Union* (New York: Abelard–Shuman, 1970); and M. Confino and S. Shamir (eds.), *The U.S.S.R. and the Middle East* (New York: Wiley, 1973).

28. Brecher, *The Foreign Policy System*, p. 11.

29. A very good analysis of the kinds of decisions that are made and the operation of the policy–making process, especially in military decisions, can be found in Yoram Peri, *Between Battles and Ballots: Israeli Military in Politics* (Cambridge: Cambridge University Press, 1983), pp. 156–74.

30. Brecher, *The Foreign Policy System*, p. 13.

31. Peri, *Between Battles and Ballots*, p. 20.

32. See Paul Rivlin, "The Burden of Israel's Defence," *Survival* 20:4 (1978): 146–54.

33. Peri, *Between Battles and Ballots*, p. 21.

34. Major studies of the Israeli army include Yigal Allon, *The Making of Israel's Army* (New York: Universe Books, 1970); Edward Luttwak and Dan Horwitz, *The Israeli Army* (New York: Harper and Row, 1975); and Gunther Rothenberg, *The Anatomy of the Israeli Army: The Israel Defense Force, 1948–1978* (New York: Hippocrene Books, 1979).

35. Peri, *Between Battles and Ballots*, p. 22.

36. John E. Mroz, *Beyond Security: Private Perceptions Among Arabs and Israelis* (New York: Pergamon Press, 1980), p. 47.

37. On this subject see J.B. Bell, "Israel's Nuclear Option," *Middle East Journal* 26 (1972): 372–88; Alan Dowty, "Nuclear Proliferation: The Israeli Case," *International Studies Quarterly* 22:1 (1978): 79–120; Yair Evron, "Israel and the Atom: The Uses and Misuses of Ambiguity, 1957–1967," *Orbis* 17:4 (1974): 1326–43; Shai Feldman, *Israeli Nuclear Deterrence: A Strategy for the 1980's* (New York: Columbia University Press, 1982); or Robert Harkavy, *Spectre of a Middle Eastern Holocaust: The Strategic and Diplomatic Implications of the Israeli Nuclear Weapons Program* (Denver: University of Denver Press, 1977).

38. For discussions of this concept, see Yigal Allon, "Israel: The Case for Defensible Borders," *Foreign Affairs* 55 (1976): 38–53; and Dan Horowitz, *Israel's Concept of Defensible Borders* (Jerusalem: Institute for International Relations, 1975).

39. Indeed, one of the classic works of military history in Israel is the volume of the same title by Netanel Lorch, *One Long War: Arab Versus Jew Since 1920* (Jerusalem: Keter Publishing, 1976). The volume traces the history of wars in Israel from the pre–state period, but beginning in detail with the 1948 War of Independence, through the 1973 Yom Kippur War.

40. One of the classic references is the study by Yehuda Z. Blum, *Secure Boundaries and Middle East Peace* (Jerusalem: Faculty of Law, Hebrew University, 1971), especially Part II: "On Israel's Right to Secure Boundaries," pp. 61–110.

41. In September, 1988, Israel launched its own "spy satellite," designed to observe troop movements and military activities in the Middle East from space. This factor, Israel has claimed, would help to make up for relatively small geo-political area of the State, and would help to provide some of the advanced warning security Israel had given up with its peace negotiations with Egypt.

42. Mroz, *Beyond Security*.

43. Michael Curtis, "The United Nations and the Middle East Conflict, 1967–1975," *Middle East Review* 3 (1975): 18–22.

44. *Facts About Israel* (1977), p. 192.

45. Katz, *Government and Politics*, p. 155.

46. Raymond Aron, *DeGaulle, Israel, and the Jews* (New York: Praeger, 1969); and Sylvia Crosbie, *A Tacit Alliance* (Princeton: Princeton University Press, 1974).

47. Michael Brecher, "Images, Process, and Feedback in Foreign Policy: Israel's Decisions on German Reparations," *American Political Science Review* 67:1 (1973): 73–102.

48. Nicholas Balabkins, *West German Reparations to Israel* (New Brunswick: Rutgers University Press, 1971); Inge Deutschkron, *Bonn and Jeru-salem* (Philadelphia: Clinton Books, 1970); Nicholas Balabkins, "The Course of West German–Israeli Relations," *Orbis* 14:3 (1970): 776–818.

49. For example, see Adefuye, Ade, "Nigeria and Israel," *International Studies* 18:4 (1979): 629–40; Y. Kohn, "Israel and the New Nation–States of Asia and Africa," *Annals of the American Academy of Political and Social Science* 324 (1959): 96–102; Mordechai Kreinin, *Israel and Africa: A Study in Technical Cooperation* (New York: Praeger, 1964); or A. Rivkin, "Israel and the Afro–Asian World," *Foreign Affairs* 37:3 (1959): 486–95.

50. Michael Curtis and Susan Gitelson, *Israel in the Third World* (New Brunswick, N.J.: Transaction Books, 1976); or R. Kozicki, "India and Israel: A Problem in Asian Politics," *Middle Eastern Affairs* 9:5 (1958): 162–71.

51. Curtis and Gitelson, *Israel in the Third World*; Edy Kaufman, *Israeli–Latin American Relations* (New Brunswick, N.J.: Transaction Press, 1979); or Y. Shapira, "Israel's International Cooperation Program with Latin America," *Inter–American Economic Affairs* 30:2 (1976): 3–32.

52. *Facts About Israel* (1977), p. 195.

53. See H. S. Chabra, "The Competition of Israel and the Arab States for the Friendship with the African States," *India Quarterly* 31:4 (1976): 362–70; Susan Gitelson, *Israel's African Setback in Perspective* (Jerusalem: Hebrew University Press, 1974); Ethan Nadelmann, "Israel and Black Africa: A Rap-prochement?" *Journal of Modern African Studies* 19:2 (1981): 183–220; or Frank Sankari, "The Costs and Gains of Israel's Pursuit of Influence in Africa," *Middle Eastern Studies* 15 (1979): 270–79.

54. See Abel Jacob, "Israel's Military Aid to Africa, 1960–1966," *The Journal of Modern African Studies* 9:2 (1971): 165–88.

55. See John Snetsinger, *Truman, the Jewish Vote, and the Creation of Israel* (Palo Alto, Ca.: Stanford University Press, 1974); and Evan Wilson, *Deci-

sion on Palestine: How the U.S. Came to Recognize Israel (Stanford: Hoover Institution Press, 1979).

56. Krammer, *The Forgotten Friendship*; Yaacov Ro'i, *Soviet Decision–Making in Practice, the USSR and Israel, 1947–1954* (New Brunswick: Transaction Press, 1980); Dagan, *Moscow and Jerusalem*; R. Khan, "Israel and the Soviet Union: A Review of Postwar Relations," *Orbis* 9:4 (1966): 999–1012.

57. Martin Feinrider, "America's Oil Pledges to Israel: Illegal but Binding Executive Agreements," *New York University Journal of International Law and Politics* 13:3 (1981): 525–70; Bishara Bahbah, "The United States and Israel's Energy Security," *Journal of Palestine Studies* 11:2 (1982): 113–31.

58. Michla Pomerance, *American Guarantees to Israel and the Law of American Foreign Relations* (Jerusalem: Hebrew University of Jerusalem Press, 1974); Joseph Shattan, "Israel, the United States, and the United Nations," *World Affairs* 143:4 (1981): 335–45.

59. Gil C. AlRoy, *The Kissinger Experience: American Policy in the Middle East* (New York: Horizon Press, 1975).

60. See George Gruen's essay "Israeli–United States Relations in the Post–Begin Era," in Gregory Mahler, (ed.), *Israel in the Post–Begin Era* (Albany: State University of New York Press, forthcoming). An example of a more specific study would be that by James Ennes, *Assault on the Liberty: The True Story of the Israeli Attack on an American Intelligence Ship* (New York: Random House, 1979). Critical studies of the relation between American Jewish supporters of Israel and American political institutions would include Ghassan Bishara, "Israel's Power in the U.S. Senate," *Journal of Palestine Studies* 10 (1980): 58–79; and Odah Abu–Redeneh, "The Jewish Factor in U.S. Politics," *Journal of Palestine Studies* 1:4 (1972): 92–107.

61. Shlomo Slonim, *United States–Israel Relations, 1967–1973* (Jerusalem: Hebrew University Press, 1974). See also "Israel and the United States: The Special Relationship Reexamined," by Bernard Reich, in Steven Heydemann, (ed.), *Issues in Contemporary Israel: The Begin Era* (Boulder, Co.: Westview, 1984), pp. 1–20.

62. A good overall analysis of Israel's first two decades can be found in Nadav Halevi and Ruth Klinow–Malul's volume *The Economic Development of Israel* (New York: Praeger, 1968). See also David Horowitz, *The Enigma of Economic Growth: A Case Study of Israel* (New York: Praeger, 1972).

63. Marion Mushkat, "The Socio–Economic Malaise of Developing Countries as a Function of Military Expenditures: The Case of Egypt and Israel." *Co–Existence* 15:2 (1978): 135–45.

64. Edi Karni, "The Israeli Economy, 1973–1976," *Economic Development and Cultural Change* 28:1 (1979): 63–76.

65. *Facts About Israel* (1985), p. 64; Michael Wolffsohn, *Israel: Polity, Society, and Economy, 1882–1986* (Atlantic Highlands, NJ: Humanities Press, International, 1987), p. 223.

66. For an excellent analysis of the economic problems of the first Begin government and the 1977–1984 economic policy of the Israeli government, see

Yakir Plessner, "Israel's Economy in the Post–Begin Era," in Gregory Mahler, (ed.), *Israel in the Post–Begin Era*. See also Donald Losman, "Inflation in Israel: The Failure of Wage and Price Controls," *Journal of Social and Political Studies* 3:1 (1978): 41–62.

67. Wolffsohn, *Israel*, p. 258; *Statistical Abstract of Israel* (Jerusalem: Central Bureau of Statistics, 1987), pp. 216–17.

68. *Statistical Abstract of Israel, 1987*, pp. 206–207.

69. See *Facts About Israel* (1977), p. 194.

70. Brecher, *The Foreign Policy System*, p. 555.

Chapter 10

THE WEST BANK, THE PALESTINIANS, AND JERUSALEM: THE PROSPECTS FOR PEACE

Introduction

Who should control the lands called the Occupied Territories, presently administered by the State of Israel? This is one of the most simple and yet most complex questions to be addressed in this volume, for it touches upon some of the most fundamental and enduring points of contention in the Middle East debate. In this chapter we shall begin by reviewing some of the historical claims of the parties involved, then direct our attention to the Palestinians as a people, to their attitudes, values, and patterns of behavior. Linked is the issue of the West Bank and Gaza Strip, the major components of the Occupied Territories. Why are they so important to Israelis and Palestinians? The same holds true for the city of Jerusalem and the role that it plays in the modern history of three world religions. Finally, we shall examine the progress that has been made toward peace in the Middle East, the Camp David Agreement, and prospects for the future. Although we do not claim that this type of systematic examination will suggest *answers* to all of the problems and tensions to be found in this part of the world, our goal is an increased *understanding* of these tensions, a greater *sensitivity* to the issues involved, and a greater *awareness* of the feelings of political actors on both sides of the dilemma.

History

The term "West Bank" is rooted in history.[1] Prior to the British partition of 1922, in which the boundaries of Transjordan were created, the term "Palestine" was used very broadly and "generally denoted the southern third of Ottoman Syria," according to the *Encyclopedia Britannica* of 1911.[2] Eventually, the territory on the East Bank of the Jordan River became Transjordan (today called Jordan), while the area on the West Bank became known as Palestine. Transjordan itself comprised 78.2 percent of the British Mandate. It has been within the other 21.8 percent of pre–1922 Palestine that the turbulence of subsequent decades has been most acutely experienced. Transjordan was considered a *fait accompli* and not a subject for further discussion or negotiation.

During the inter–war period, as we have seen in Chapter One, several Royal Commissions were created to deal with outbreaks of violence and questions of competing nationalisms. The Peel Report, issued in 1937, concluded that the Jewish and Arab communities would not be able to live together in peace and recommended partition, recognizing that "it would be difficult to draw lines that would satisfy either party and that major population displacements might ensue."[3] Under the partition proposed by Peel, none of what is referred to today as the West Bank would have been in the Jewish state. A subsequent study by the Woodhead Commission produced another partition recommendation, with the Jewish state in this plan substantially smaller than the one envisioned in the Peel Report. In Chapter One we further noted how the British had, in fact, made contradictory promises to the two major groups involved, the Zionists and the Arabs, and how they themselves could not decide which position to favor in relation to the demands of the Zionists. Ultimately, of course, the British simply gave up and passed the issue on to the fledgling United Nations.

In 1947, when Britain turned the "Palestine Question" over to the United Nations for resolution, it did so to a great degree because awareness of the Holocaust had shifted world public opinion strongly in favor of the Zionists and against the Arab community. In November the United Nations Special Committee on Palestine issued yet another in the chain of recommendations for partition, proposing the creation of two sovereign states, one Jewish and the other Palestinian. As one author paraphrased its essence:

> The country was to be divided into a Jewish state consisting of the coastal plain, eastern Galilee, and most of the southern Negev. Its 32 percent of Palestine's population would receive about 55 percent of the land. The Arabs would retain central Galilee, the mountain district (most of which was later to become the West Bank), the southern coast (some of which was later called the Gaza Strip), and the city of Jaffa. Jerusalem and its environs would become an international enclave under U.N. Trusteeship.[4]

As we already know, the Zionists supported this proposal and the Arabs were opposed. (See Map 1.4, page 22)

As a result of the War of Independence and the Israeli–Jordanian Armistice of 1949, the area known today as the West Bank was occupied by Jordan. (See Map 1.5, page 24) On April 1, 1949, King Abdallah proceeded to formally annex it.[5] The following April (1950) both chambers of a newly elected Jordanian Parliament (including representatives from the West Bank) passed legislation sealing this status and supporting "unity between the two sides of the Jordan and their union into one state, which is the Hashemite Kingdom of Jordan, at whose head reigns King Abdullah Ibn al Husain, on a basis of constitutional representative government and equality of rights and duties of all citizens."[6] This act was *not* universally endorsed by the local Palestinian population. Indeed, in addition to the leaders of the Arab League, many Palestinians themselves felt that their social and political institutions were "far more advanced than those of the indigenous bedouin inhabitants of the East."[7] Many also saw annexation as inconsistent with their ultimate goal of Palestinian nationalism. Little more was actually done, however, for the next decade and a half.

In 1964 the Arab League endorsed the establishment of the Palestine Liberation Organization, whose first congress was held in East Jerusalem (Jordan) that May. Thus would begin a long and arduous relationship between it and Jordan. Although Amman originally supported the creation and objectives of the PLO, the fact that the PLO's goals "threatened Jordan's effort to make Jordanians of the Palestinians," provoked tensions between the PLO delegation in Jerusalem and Jordanian government officials.[8] For the next quarter century this relationship would vacillate between cooperation and confrontation, for any future Palestinian state, after all, would encompass both Israeli and Jordanian Territory. In June, 1967, Israel launched her preemptive attack on Egypt, Syria, and Iraq. Succumbing to pressure from her Arab allies, Jordan entered the War, despite assurances from Israel that no hostilities along their border would be forthcoming if Amman remained neutral. Once Jordan became involved, Israeli forces launched a crushing campaign. Within a matter of days Israel had captured the entire West Bank to the Jordan River, along with the Sinai Desert (subsequently returned to Egypt), the Gaza Strip, and part of the Golan Heights (Syrian territory which was later formally annexed).

The important points to re–emphasize in discussing the historical context at this point are that: (a) the territory which is today known as the West Bank was not originally part of Jordan; (b) in all of the proposed partition plans which referred to what was called "Palestine," there was the intention to create a Jewish State *and* a Palestinian State—a Palestinian State independent from an already–established Transjordan; and, (c) a "Palestinian Nationalist" movement existed in this area *before* 1967 which opposed the annexation of the West Bank by King Hussein as well as *before* it opposed the prospect of similar annexation by Israel. Its goal was sovereignty and independence from *any* external control, be it Israeli or Jordanian.

The Palestinians

Palestine as a whole has been part of the map of the Middle East for nearly two thousand years, a name that first appeared during the Roman occupation of the area and lasted until 1949 when the Israeli War of Independence left the land that was to be called the State of Palestine occupied by both Jordan and Israel. The people who lived on that land were historically referred to as Palestinians.

Perhaps the central claim of the Palestinians has been most eloquently expressed by Edward Said when he wrote:

> We were on the land called Palestine; were our dispossession and our effacement, by which almost a million of us were made to leave Palestine and our society made nonexistent, justified even to save the remnant of European Jews that had survived Nazism? By what moral or political standard are we expected to lay aside our claims to our national existence, our land, our human rights?[9]

The idea of a Palestinian nation and the quest for an independent state, as noted earlier, predated the most recent tensions of the Palestinian–Israeli conflict, since there was a Palestinian nationalism prior to the creation of the State of Israel.[10] This claim to nationalism has survived the years and is the basis of unrest today in the Occupied Territories.[11] When Abdallah of Jordan annexed the West Bank in 1949 the Arab League, after a period of objection, agreed to its "temporary administration" by Jordan, but continued to express its sympathy for the desire of the indigenous Palestinians for a nation of their own.[12] In 1957 King Hussein (who inherited the throne after the assassination of Abdallah) moved against the leadership of the Palestinian nationalist movement in the Jordanian Parliament, arresting thousands of Palestinians, especially those living on the West Bank. Ensuing demonstrations against Hussein's actions were suppressed by the King's army, thus establishing a "pattern of control which was to characterize Jordanian policy toward the West Bank up until the Israeli occupation."[13]

Historically, the relationship between King Hussein and the Palestinians has not been an especially warm one. From the time of his ascension to the throne he was suspicious of the Palestinians and feared their questioning of the legitimacy of *his* monarchy. Until the Israeli occupation in 1967, West Bank inhabitants were characterized as "second class citizens" within the Jordanian Kingdom, "discriminated against politically and economically."[14] In a final wave of arrests following demonstrations against him in 1966 virtually the entire leadership of the West Bank opposition was again imprisoned.[15] In September 1970, three years after the Israeli occupation, the Jordanian army massacred a large number of Palestinians in refugee camps inside Jordan itself; the goal being to crush those Palestinian organizations opposed to the Jordanian King. Hussein's actions have since come to be known as "Black September."[16]

Despite this history of enmity between Jordan and the Palestinians, many continue to believe that Jordan will eventually play a significant role in the resolution of the Palestinian problem.[17] Some suggest further that Hussein himself has, in recent years, sought to play a more positive and substantive role.[18] This is so because some see essentially three types of Arab Palestinians in the world today: (a) those inside pre–1967 Israel who did not flee during the War of Independence and who are, consequently, Israeli citizens with full civil and political rights; (b) those in the Occupied Territories who have always lived in the villages, towns, and camps in which they are presently found or who fled during fighting in 1948–49 and became refugees in the Jordanian–controlled West Bank from 1949 until 1967; and, (c) those who live outside of the former Palestine (many now in Jordan itself).[19] Geopolitics and demographics, therefore, encourage if not mandate Jordanian involvement in a solution to the problem.

The major desire of many Palestinians today is the establishment of a Palestinian state. Many claim, in fact, that they already have a well–defined sense of "nationhood," but simply lack a state to complete the development of their sense of Palestinian identity.[20] It is ironic, in fact, that one of the best historical parallels to the contemporary Palestinian situation was that of the early Zionists when they, too, were developing a strong sense of national identity but lacked a state of their own. As Said has written:

> There *is* a Palestinian people, there *is* an Israeli occupation of Palestinian lands, there *are* Palestinians under Israeli military occupation, there *are* Palestinians—650,000 of them—who are Israeli citizens and who constitute 15 percent of the population of Israel, there is a large Palestinian population in exile: these are actualities which the United States and most of the world have directly or indirectly acknowledged, which Israel too has acknowledged, if only in the form of denial, rejection, threats of war, and punishment . . . Short of complete obliteration, the Palestinians will continue to exist and they will continue to have their own ideas about who represents them, where they want to settle, what they want to do with their national and political future.[21]

Along with cultivating a better sense of Palestinian identity, many refugees also demand the right to return to the property from which they fled in 1948–49 or 1967, or they at least want compensation from Israel for the loss of that property.[22] Israel's reply has consistently been that since the Palestinians left voluntarily and at the behest of other Arab states in 1948, Israel has no legal or moral obligation to allow their return or to compensate them for lost property.

Many Palestinians respond that they were *coerced* from their land. In any case, they say, whatever the cause of their departure a variety of United Nations resolutions plus the International Covenant on Civil and Political Rights (1966) guarantees them the right to return. They argue that fleeing the fighting in 1948 did not constitute a permanent rejection of their property rights and, consequently, that Article 12 of the International Covenant, officially adopted by the United Nations in 1976, applies when it notes that "No one shall be arbitrarily deprived of the right to enter his own country."[23] Following the 1967 war tens of thousands of Palestinians moved out of the West Bank. One estimate suggests that the Arab population decreased by over 200,000 between the last Jordanian census and an Israeli one taken after the fighting ceased.[24]

One by–product of Palestinian nationalism, as previously mentioned, has been the Palestine Liberation Organization (PLO).[25] Its organization, historical evolution, and behavior are beyond the scope of our discussion here.[26] Basically, the PLO is an "umbrella" organization of many different groups, including *Fateh*, the *Democratic Front for the Liberation of Palestine*, the *Popular Front for the Liberation of Palestine*, *Saiqa*, and several others, who both compete and cooperate with each other. Despite the fact that there has never been a referendum taken among the Palestinian population, the PLO claims that it is the only organization with the capacity to represent all of the Palestinians scattered throughout the world, as well as in the Middle East.

The PLO has a National Congress and a constitution, called the *Palestinian National Charter.*[27] It has "Observer" Status at the United Nations,[28] and has established formal diplomatic relations with a number of countries. Its relations with Arab nations have been in flux. At times Egypt and Jordan, for example, have supported the PLO and its goals, while on other occasions each has together and separately criticized and cut off any communications with it.[29]

Originally the PLO called for the "total liberation of all occupied Palestine." At its Twelfth National Council in Cairo in 1974, however, it changed this goal, seeking instead to establish "a national authority in every part of Palestinian territory that is liberated . . ."[30] This position was vigorously debated by the major factions in the PLO, but ultimately the view of the "pragmatists" carried the day. Much like Herzl 70 years earlier, realism and some territory was seen as preferable to purism and no territory.

The PLO suffered a great loss of dignity, to say nothing of military influence, when it was driven out of its bases in Lebanon by Israeli forces in 1982. The view that the world received of PLO troops being put on ships and sent out of Beirut harbor robbed it of much of its self–proclaimed record of victory and effectiveness. Although the PLO did not honor its commitment to stay out of Lebanon and is now back in Beirut, its standing in Arab eyes suffered from these events.[31] Another, more recent, loss of standing for the PLO has been the "intifada," (or "uprising") on the West Bank, which was organized not by the PLO, but rather by Palestinians living in the Occupied Territories who felt that the PLO was not doing enough to "keep the pressure on Israel." That groups of essentially disorganized and untrained West Bank Palestinians could in a few months bring the world's attention to their situation far more effectively than the PLO had managed to do after more than two decades served to lower the PLO in the eyes of many Palestinians. In any event, many scholars claim that whatever the status of the PLO, there can be no overall peace in the Middle East until the "Palestinian Question" is resolved.[32]

The West Bank and Gaza

According to the Israeli Government, until such time as peace is achieved in the Middle East, official policy in Judea and Samaria (the Biblical terms for what is today most of the West Bank of the Jordan River) and Gaza is based on the Camp David Accords (1979). These accords, as we shall later see, called for establishing autonomy for the local population while simultaneously guaranteeing the security needs of Israel.[33] In recent years Israel has sought to encourage the emergence of a moderate Palestinian Arab leadership. But attempted and sometimes successful assassinations of moderate Arab leaders have made such individuals hesitant to step forward into public leadership roles.

Israel's "Open Bridges" policy has permitted Palestinians living in the Occupied Territories a remarkable degree of continued economic and social contact with Jordan.[34] Transit points across the Jordan River are open and individuals can cross from one side to the other along with their commercial goods.[35] This does not imply that crossing the border is always effortless or without challenge. But it does mean that a degree of commerce and travel has been permitted to continue between Israel and Jordan virtually unprecedented between two countries still technically "at war" with each other.

Since becoming the Occupying Power in 1967 Israel has been responsible for fundamental social services to the West Bank and Gaza populations.[36] The Government provides twelve years of free schooling, nine of them mandatory, following the curricula set in Jordan and

Egypt prior to 1967.[37] There are also a number of universities in the Occupied Territories, although many of them have been closed on numerous occasions by Israeli authorities in response to acts of civil disobedience.

Most recently, as intimated above, the "intifada" has been the most prominent manifestation of the underlying tension between Israel and the West Bank Palestinians. The "uprising" was begun in 1987 and has successfully—from the point of view of its organizers—continued to exert pressure on Israel to remove itself from the Occupied Territories. The point of the "intifada" has not been armed resistance but rather continued mass demonstrations requiring Israeli military attention. These demonstrations have "played" effectively on television, with scenes of Israeli troops firing on crowds of civilians having proven to be quite instrumental in mobilizing public opinion around the world against Israel's presence in the West Bank and its policies there. This attention has not been achieved without cost, however, for literally hundreds of Palestinians had been killed in the demonstrations through the middle of 1989, virtually all shot by Israeli troops.

Ephraim Sneh, the former head of the civil administration of the West Bank, wrote in a *Ha'aretz* editorial that an analysis of the "intifada" yielded both costs and benefits for the Palestinians. The costs include hundreds killed and thousands wounded—or "about 20 times the order of magnitude of the annual casualties during the previous years of the occupation." Despite the fact that most of the Israeli forces involved have since changed from "conventional ammunition" to "rubber bullets" (deemed more appropriate for "crowd control" situations), the casualty rate on the West Bank is still significant. Among the additional costs is the fact that the economy of the occupied territories has been virtually destroyed and the normal balance of society upset, with schools periodically shut down, a perception of anarchy existing, and gaps between social classes widening.

As for benefits, Sneh found that the "intifada" has succeeded in placing the Palestinian problem "on the international agenda." As well, "Israeli public opinion has been rocked." To wit:

> Israelis who had become used to the fact that the cost of ruling over one– and–a–half million Palestinians was limited to an easy and far–off security burden, have now been confronted with the realization that it will be impossible to continue with the status quo in the territories for much longer.[38]

The "intifada" has been responsible for two other remarkable phenomena: A significant increase in the Israeli population now advocating withdrawal from the Occupied Territories; and, public discussions by soldiers claiming that they are not adequately trained for, nor want to be involved in, the types of military activities demanded on the West Bank today.

The period from 1967 to the present, in short, has been a continuing source of anguish for both Israelis and Palestinians.[39] Israel has often been criticized in the international community for many of the policies it has undertaken in the Occupied Territories.[40] These criticisms and accusations[41] have included charges that Jerusalem has engaged in illegal acquisition of Palestinian land,[42] forced resettlement of parts of the Palestinian population, refusal to permit Palestinian refugees from the 1967 War to return to their homes and property, forcible expulsion and deportation of Arab residents of the West Bank to Lebanon or Jordan,[43] restrictions on local political, educational, and medical institutions from openly operating, prohibitions on political activity, demolition of buildings and residences, unreasonable curfews, administrative detention without judicial hearings,[44] unacceptable conditions of detention and interrogation (including charges of torture and prisoner abuse), censorship of publications, closed universities, and, in general, a wide range of other violations of human rights.[45]

Israel's response to many of these charges has been that domestic security concerns militate some of these actions. The fact of the matter is that there *is* concern about terrorism because there *are* terrorist incidents; bombs *are* placed on Israeli buses, in apartment houses, markets, and other public places; arms and explosives *are* smuggled into Israel; and public demonstrations that turn violent *do* occur in the Occupied Territories. Israel's position has been that until the question of the future of the Occupied Territories is determined, it has an obligation to its own citizens to insure a safe and secure existence.[46] Whether this necessitates continuation of the *status quo*, some form of association with Jordan, eventual independence, or outright Israeli annexation akin to what Abdullah did in 1949 has long been one of the most contentious and partisan issues in the Israeli political system.

Finally, Israel contends that compared to the period of Jordanian rule, West Bank and Gaza Arabs have benefitted from Israeli control. For example, many Arabs from the Occupied Territories work in Israel proper during the day. According to government figures, one–third of the total West Bank and Gaza labor force is employed in Israel: 14 percent in agriculture, 21 percent in industry, 47 percent in construction, and 18 percent in other economic activities. Accordingly, for much of the period of Occupation the Israeli Government has claimed that there has been virtually no unemployment in Judea, Samaria, or Gaza.[47]

Jerusalem

The city of Jerusalem itself carries with it an importance far out-weighing any strategic or "conventional" geopolitical significance. Its historical, emotional, and international complexities make it truly unique, and suggest a set of problems to be resolved that go far beyond issues of "mutually agreed—upon boundaries."[48] As one scholar has indicated:

> . . . no other city in the world has been subject to such intense competition for control as Jerusalem during its 4,000 years of recorded history. The religious interests of the three world faiths for whom Jerusalem is so paramount can be fulfilled without their having to hold territorial control of the city. But territorial control is an overriding issue for the two nationalisms, Arab and Jewish, whose governments are in contention for the city. In the struggle of nationalisms sovereign space cannot be shared, although some sharing of political power is possible.[49]

Jerusalem's symbolic role in the Arab—Israeli struggle and, consequently, the dispute over "to whom it belongs," is a profoundly emotional and intensely personal issue. David Ben-Gurion once stated that "the struggle for Jerusalem will determine the fate not only of the country, but of the Jewish people." Jordanian King Abdallah's view was that Jerusalem "holds a special position for every Muslim nation because of the Arab, Kurdish, Circassion, and Turkish blood which has been shed on its behalf throughout the history of Islam."[50] In short, *neither* side is inclined to compromise on the issue.

A major point of contention, then, is often simply *which* religious group has the stronger claim. It is clear that the three religious traditions, Jewish, Christian, and Islamic, each have links to Jerusalem and desire to exercise control over its future. Many argue, however, that "Jerusalem has a far more powerful corporate meaning for Judaism than for Christianity and Islam."[51] The most commonly—articulated sequence is that Christians have Rome, Moslems have Mecca and Medina, but Jews have only Jerusalem.[52] Although there may be some degree of logic to this argument, it carries little persuasive power for the Christian and Moslem communities.

As Cohen notes,[53] during most of Jerusalem's history it was territorially united under the rule of whichever nation dominated the politics of the region. The city's division in 1949 was an unusual situation and one which convinced *both* sides in the dispute that it could not be permitted to happen again. Long—time Mayor of Jerusalem Teddy Kollek concurs:

The Jerusalem question cannot be decided by drawing a line. The future of Jerusalem cannot be resolved by division. This does not mean that Jerusalem is an insoluble problem. It means that Jerusalem's people of differing faiths, cultures, and aspirations must find peaceful ways to live together other than by drawing a line in the sand with a stick. It is no solution to rebuild concrete walls and barbed wire through the middle of the city.[54]

The actual process of partition occurred as a strictly military consequence. There were several stages in the eventual division of the territory of Palestine as a whole, beginning with the 1922 British White Paper delimiting Palestine and Transjordan, followed by the Peel (1936) and the Woodhead (1939) Commissions, and culminating in the United Nations Special Committee on Palestine (UNSCOP) of 1947. Yet, none ever advocated the partition of Jerusalem itself. Indeed, all proposed leaving the city intact, either under mandatory or international authority.[55] It was rather the 1949 Armistice between Israel and Jordan that left Jerusalem divided, with Jordan controlling all of the Holy Places in the city's eastern sector.

Between 1949 and 1967 Jerusalem continued to be very significant for an Israeli Government which never abandoned hope of eventually reunifying the city and securing access to Jewish Holy Places. In fact, during this period of time Jerusalem functioned as the capital of Israel. Virtually all major national governmental institutions were moved from Tel Aviv, albeit to the Western part of the city, as a symbolic gesture of Israel's commitment to have Jerusalem eventually reunited.

When reunification came in 1967, the Israeli Government in effect announced that:

the June 5th map [1967, the date of the beginning of the Six Day War] of the region had been "destroyed irrevocably," but that Israel was prepared to negotiate new frontiers with its Arab neighbors. Jerusalem was an exception, not subject to negotiation. Within a month after the cease–fire the city was incorporated into the Israeli West Jerusalem municipality.[56]

Although Israel was willing to negotiate with its Arab neighbors over a variety of territorial questions, the issue of Jerusalem was settled: The city would never again be divided. This unification and annexation by Knesset legislation had some curious legal consequences as the Government made a number of efforts to facilitate adaptation to the anomalies of this new situation. For example, once the Jordanian part of the city had been incorporated, under international law the Arab population automatically became inhabitants of the State of Israel while simultaneously retaining Jordanian citizenship, since Jordan continued to claim jurisdiction over the territory.[57]

Some have suggested, emotions apart, that there are "geopolitical imperatives" which explain why Jerusalem must remain unified, "irrespective of whatever internal geopolitical structural changes may take place."[58] Reasons offered for a united Jerusalem include:

1. Historical struggles to continue ties to territories, such as those fought by the Jews through the years, create strong "national values." This is especially true when the struggles have been carried out with little assistance from other national actors.
2. Jerusalem's geopolitical location in Israel makes the city and the "Jerusalem corridor" especially significant for Israel's development.
3. Jerusalem is a unique city, and part of its uniqueness comes from its several and varied neighborhoods. Although the whole may be greater than the sum of its parts, it is clear that the loss of some would diminish the character of the whole.
4. Jerusalem has a strategic and economic significance for Arab Palestine, and consequently is strategically valuable to Israel, independent of any other reasons.
5. The rapid growth of the city makes it a second "political core" in Israel, along with Tel Aviv. Israel could not permit its second "political core" to be divided.

It is precisely the "special" status of the city and its extremely heterogeneous nature that makes the Jerusalem issue so difficult to resolve.[59] The heterogeneity of Jerusalem represents a microcosm of Israel itself, and the question of what kind of government Jerusalem should have, the administrative roles of the various ethnic groups, the relationship between religious and political questions, and other fundamental and emotional issues, all serve to make the question of Jerusalem's future even more complex than it would be if it had to resolve *only* the question of which national actor would exercise sovereignty over it.[60]

Israeli Attitudes, Intentions, and Policies

Long Term Plans

Israeli policy in the West Bank, then, can be seen as a function of a number of different factors, including ideological, historical, security, as well as short–term demands of contemporary political groups.

These factors, and many others, influence the attitudes and values of government leaders, and correspondingly influence the policies promulgated by the Israeli government.

The question of Israel's precise long term intentions and plans for the Occupied Territories is one that has generated much disagreement inside the country.[61] From the outset of occupation in 1967 to the present, one of the sources of policy inconsistency has been the fact that Israeli politicians have debated repeatedly and inconclusively the status of the Occupied Territories.[62] There have been those who firmly believe that the West Bank (excluding Gaza) is the same as Biblical "Judea and Samaria," and as such constitutes a part of what some religious Zionists believe is Greater Israel. Their solution, therefore, is annexation without further debate. Others, conversely, have argued that Israel should use the West Bank and Gaza as strategic buffer zones and bargaining chips for negotiation, being willing, in effect, to trade territory for peace. Still others have taken the position that Israel has no right to keep territories captured through warfare. The territory must eventually be returned to either the Palestinians, who desire it as their state, or the Jordanians, from whom it was captured.[63]

The official Labor Government position in the years following the 1967 War was that the territories were occupied "for security considerations." In reality, there was a great deal of disagreement within the Government over what its policy actually should be. Its policy positions suggested four central principles:

1. Maintenance of the status quo, with emphasis on security, under conservative local leadership supervised by Israel;
2. Economic integration of the West Bank . . . through the use of Arab labor, the marketing of Israeli products in the West Bank and of noncompetitive West Bank primary products in Israel, and the linking of West Bank infrastructure with Israel;
3. Using the West Bank as an opening wedge to the Arab world, through Dayan's "Open Bridges" policy, facilitating visits from Arab countries of "trustworthy" visitors and through export of products from Israel across the bridges to Jordan, and from Jordan to other Arab countries;
4. Establishment of Jewish settlements in selected areas as security outposts.[64]

Although it is possible to discuss underlying principles of the Labor Governments during the ten years they controlled the West Bank, they proved unable to reach an accord with Jordan or the Palestinians. With the rise to power of the Likud in 1977, a change in direction could be perceived. Prime Minister Menachem Begin supported the policy of creating West Bank settlement "facts" and advocating establishing so many "facts" that what was done could never be undone.[65] The number of settlements on the West Bank, and the rate of establishment of these settlements, was increased dramatically.

Settlements

Some political geographers have seen the pattern of settlements established by Israel after 1977 as a new set of "walls" designed to insure a continued presence in the Occupied Territories, as well as a strategy to protect already–existing Israeli settlements there. They suggest that the West Bank settlement process is an example of the "basically political nature of planning," and argue that the settlements show that "value–free planning is actually impossible."[66] Saul Cohen's "geopolitical" study of the Jerusalem area refers to new settlement patterns as a "third wall," despite being some distance removed, around Jerusalem.[67] It is clear, however, that the future of the Jewish communities already built in the Occupied Territories, to say nothing of future developmental plans for more communities, "largely depends on Israel's internal politics and international developments."[68] Critics of this approach have argued that the building of settlements in occupied territory is patently illegal under international law.[69] Others have suggested that the legality of the situation is basically ambiguous, but could be resolved with some action by the Israeli government.[70] (See Map 10.1)

As far back as 1969 (Labor) Defense Minister Moshe Dayan proposed a "new facts" doctrine, under which Israel would gradually establish new settlements and a continued presence in the Occupied Territories, arguing that Israel was in the West Bank "of right and not on sufferance."[71] Dayan proposed expanded settlement, along with increased roads, trade, commerce, and general infrastructure in the Territories. Others in the Labor leadership opposed this view, for both philosophical and pragmatic reasons. For example, Finance Minister Pinhas Sapir argued that the Israeli economy would become dependent upon less–expensive Arab labor; Sapir warned that "to preserve Israel as the Jewish state . . . it would be necessary to not only maintain political separation, but to sever the economic bonds that were rapidly binding the two peoples together."[72]

One recent study has indicated that two major phases may be distinguished in the establishment of settlements in the Occupied Territories, one corresponding with the Alignment (Labor) Government's term

MAP 10.1
Israeli Settlements on the West Bank

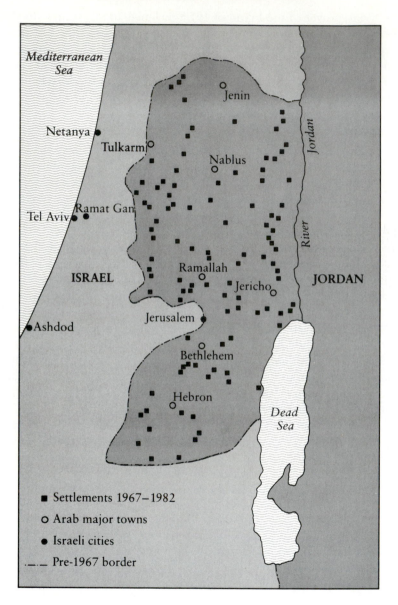

in office from 1968 to 1977, and the other corresponding with the Likud's term in office, 1977 to 1984. Under the Alignment, the average rate of new settlers in the Territories was about 770 per year; under the Likud, through 1984, the average rate was almost 5,400 per year. Indeed, during 1984, "for the first time, the growth exceeded 10,000 settlers a year."[73] (See Figure 10.1)

This difference in party policies, with Labor being more moderate, more conciliatory, and less extreme than Likud, is a theme that regularly has been highly visible in Israel's relations with her neighbors. This should come as no surprise, since foreign policy is one of the two major issue areas over which the major Israeli parties strongly disagree (the other being domestic economics). Labor's strategy has historically been more pragmatic, more supportive (in principle) of negotiations with Arab neighbors, and more opposed to significant expansion of Israeli settlements in the Occupied Territories, with the articulated goal of eventually exchanging land for peace. Likud, on the other hand, has been seen as far less "pragmatic," and far more ideologically committed to the policy of expanding settlements, supporting the "Greater Israel Movement," demonstrating less flexibility with Arab neighbors, and maintaining greater suspicion of negotiations. These general party tendencies, Labor's moderate, pragmatic style versus Likud's ideological, rigid style, have been regularly demonstrated in actual Israeli foreign policy even as recently as negotiations with Egypt over the Taba settlement, a point to be discussed later in this Chapter.

Regardless of viewpoint, the pattern of settlement building has long–term implications.[74] One of the major justifications offered by Menachem Begin was that of "establishing facts,"[75] not unlike the proposal of Moshe Dayan almost a decade earlier. What he meant by "facts" was, in fact, the geographical pattern of settlements that would provide a security perimeter for the bulk of the Israeli population. When enough settlers were established in the West Bank, a "critical mass" would be established that would be impossible to reverse.[76]

As for the settlers themselves, scholars have suggested that there are two general types of motives behind their behavior: "ideological" and "self–interest."[77] For many advocates of expanded settlement building, the justification is a religious one: "Eretz Israel" is a concept having religious significance. The creation of more and more settlements on the Occupied Territories—or Judea and Samaria—can be seen as fulfilling a Biblical commandment.[78] The *Gush Emunim* is a group representing this point of view which has been very active in promoting more and more settlements on the West Bank,[79] although it must be noted

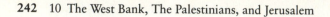

FIGURE 10.1
Jewish Population in the West Bank

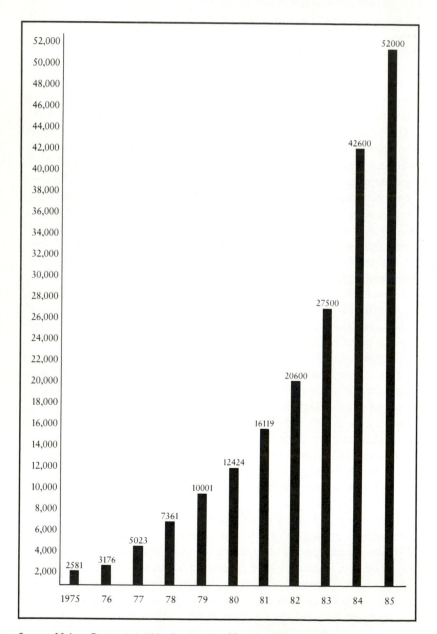

Source: Meiron Benvenisti, 1986 Report (Boulder, Co.: Westview, 1986), p. 46.

that "Jewish settlement in the West Bank did not start with *Gush Em-unim*, nor has it ended with them."[80]

Groups that settle out of self–interest tend to be less visible precisely because they are not there out of ideological motives. Many are attracted for purely financial reasons—the Government has built villages, encouraged industry, and offered apartments for sale (often at attractive financial terms) at prices considerably lower than could be found in other areas. It is thus an entirely pragmatic decision on the part of many young couples. They can now afford to purchase an apartment in a settlement on the West Bank with guaranteed security and transportation to Jerusalem, while they cannot afford a comparable apartment anywhere else. Settling on the West Bank is clearly secondary to owning their own apartment. Recently–published data show quite clearly that new settlements in the West Bank are far more popular than new settlements in either the Galilee or the Negev. The percentage of unsold apartments in the West Bank by mid–1985 was 34.2 percent, compared to nearly 75 percent in Galilee and over 60 percent in the Negev. The study concluded that the higher demand for West Bank apartments was at least partially caused by the Government's more generous financial incentives for settlements there, including both prices and mortgage rates. Indeed, the difference in financial incentives between high Government priority settlements and low Government priority settlements may be as much as 50 percent.[81]

Military Government

Among the major sources of tension to be expected in any military occupation is the fact of the occupation itself. In this regard the period from 1967 to the present has been a continuing source of anguish for both Israelis and Palestinians.[82] Israel has been criticized by many in the international community over policies it has undertaken in the Occupied Territories, including dismissal of mayors of large West Bank cities, forcible expulsion of Arab residents to Lebanon or Jordan, curfews, demolition of houses, censorship of publications, closing of universities, and a wide range of human rights violations, as was discussed in the earlier section on the West Bank.[83]

It is also the case, as noted earlier, that the "intifada" has brought the military government into much more public a role than it would prefer. Its high–profile approach to dealing with the mass public demonstrations has resulted not only in the deaths of many Palestinians, but also in a great deal of domestic division within Israel over the tactics of the military government and the overall propriety of Israel's presence on the West Bank.

Demographics

One of the most important questions derived from Israeli occupation of the territories has been the status of its Arab residents. Should Israel annex the territories and the residents thus become Israeli citizens (something that may happen when a territory is annexed), there would be significant implications for the continued existence of a Jewish majority in Israel.[84] In 1967 the total estimated population of the area called "Judea and Samaria" by the Government of Israel was 585,900. By 1985 this had grown to 813,400. In 1967 the population of Israel was 2,776,300, of which 2,383,600 was Jewish. If the (non–Jewish) population of the West Bank had been added to Israel's population at the time, Jews would have constituted 2,383,600 out of 3,362,200, or 70.9 percent of the total. In 1985 the total estimated population of the West Bank was 813,400 and the total Jewish population of Israel was 3,517,200 out of a total of 4,266,200. If the (non–Jewish) population of the West Bank had been added to Israel's population at the time, Jews would have constituted 66 percent of the total population.[85] This drop of almost five percent of projected "national" population illustrates very effectively the concerns of political parties such as *Kach*, adding impetus to their belief that it will only be a matter of time before Jews constitute less than 50 percent of Israel's population. Simple demographics, then, can have profound implications which further complicate the situation.

Camp David and the Peace Process

Surely the most celebrated and controversial step toward resolution of the Middle East dilemma came in March, 1979, when Israel signed her first peace treaty with an Arab state since independence in 1948. The process leading up to this watershed event was both extraordinarily rapid and excruciatingly slow. It was rapid in the sense that once Egyptian President Anwar Sadat expressed a willingness to go to Jerusalem and meet with Israeli leaders progress was made (in the historical context of the last six decades) remarkably quickly. On the other hand, it was slow in that the negotiations were constantly being frustrated and bogged down by a seemingly endless stream of issues and details. In the end it would take 18 months of extraordinary effort to complete the treaty–making process.

That process had of course commenced with the stunning announcement by Sadat that he was prepared to be received in Jerusalem by Israeli leaders to discuss prospects for peace between the two nations.[86]

This was the first public summit of an Israeli and an Arab head of state, and everyone involved recognized its significance. (It should be noted that "secret summits" had taken place between King Hussein and Israeli leaders from time to time prior to this, although they failed to produce any tangible result.) Sadat made it very clear from the outset that he was not seeking a peace treaty between Israel and Egypt separate from other issues in the region. He sought an overall framework for peace in the Middle East, including progress on the question of the Palestinians and their rights. In Sadat's words, "there could be no peace without the Palestinians."[87] The major issues to be negotiated were apparent to all: Peace and diplomatic recognition between Israel and Egypt in exchange for return of the Egyptian territories occupied by Israel and progress on the Palestinian question.

After Sadat and Begin's initial negotiations in Jerusalem, they met a month later in Ismailia, Egypt (Christmas Day, 1977) to discuss Israel's counter–proposal. Sadat rejected the Begin plan because its "autonomy" arrangement for the Palestinians fell significantly short of Cairo's definition of progress. It was at this point that the United States began to play a more active role in the proceedings.[88]

Washington's expanding involvement reflected the fact that after a series of meetings between Israeli and Egyptian delegations during the early part of 1978, several problems persisted. First, the Begin government continued to argue that it had the right to develop settlements in the Occupied Territories. This view was strongly supported by significant segments of the Israeli electorate and especially by Ariel Sharon, Begin's Minister of Agriculture and a contender for leadership of Begin's Likud party. The position of the Egyptians and other Arab powers, shared by the United States, was that these settlements were not permitted under international law and thus should not be established or continued. Second was the question of the future of the West Bank and the Gaza Strip. Begin and Likud were willing to consider some form of limited self–rule or autonomy with a final decision to be decided upon later, while Egypt demanded total Israeli military withdrawal. Third, there was concern over the "linkage" between Israel's returning the Sinai and the establishment of direct diplomatic relations between Jerusalem and Cairo, with Egypt preferring full and immediate Israeli withdrawal and phased diplomatic recognition versus Israel's goal of immediate full diplomatic recognition and phased withdrawal from the Sinai. Fourth, President Sadat continued to insist that foremost on the Israeli–Egyptian agenda had to be the "Palestinian Question," while Prime Minister Begin wanted the Israeli–Egyptian peace treaty to be the centerpiece. Last, but by no means least important, the issue of Jerusalem appeared irreconcilable, with Israel insisting on continued complete sovereignty (although it would permit Arab control of Islamic holy places) and Egypt insisting on Israeli withdrawal from East Jerusalem, thereby reestablishing the *status quo ante* 1967, but this time with guaranteed Israeli access to Jewish holy places.

Although American presidents Nixon and Ford had devoted great energy to the quest for peace, it was President Jimmy Carter who was able to provide the setting and the momentum for the process to develop. In hindsight, this was to be the highlight of the Carter presidency. President Carter played an active role as "broker" between Israel and Egypt at the Camp David summit in September, 1978, and worked hard between then and the final treaty–signing ceremony the following March to keep the movement towards peace from being halted by one group or another. Although America had supported a comprehensive Geneva peace conference as the preferred mechanism for the development of peace treaties in the Middle East,[89] once the Begin–Sadat opening was made, President Carter supported that vehicle.

During a thirteen–day period, from September 5 to 17, 1978, Prime Minister Begin, and Presidents Sadat and Carter met at Camp David, Maryland. Carter felt that an informal setting would be more conducive than negotiations conducted in the glare of international publicity. Reflecting his position as "facilitator" and sense of the personalities involved, Carter was convinced that progress toward peace could only come if both Begin and Sadat had the chance once again to meet and talk face–to–face.[90] Over those two weeks at Camp David he held a series of one–on–one discussions with both Begin and Sadat, "shuttling" back and forth between their cabins, arranging sessions with their respective advisors, then conducting direct negotiations when the prospects of gain were more favorable.

The agreement on the exchange of the Sinai for peace and diplomatic recognition was achieved in fairly short order. The difficult issue was Sadat's predictable insistence that he would only sign a peace treaty if it were linked in some way to broader progress toward peace in the Middle East and on the Palestinian issue. It would take all of their skills and powers of persuasion to bridge, however imperfectly, the distance dividing them.

Eventually two agreements were reached.[91]. The first, a "Framework for Peace in the Middle East," dealt with the question of the West Bank and Gaza. It established a five–year transitional regime for the Occupied Territories, suggested that freely elected local authorities would gradually assume power, outlined the redeployment of Israeli

armed forces into less visible positions, and set the st
tiations to determine the status of the West Bank, (
Jordanian relations. It did not specifically mention t.

The second part was a "Framework for the Con
Treaty Between Egypt and Israel." This document ca
of the Sinai to Egypt, limitations on the number of Egyptian forces that
could be stationed there, a timetable for the withdrawal of Israeli forces
tied to the signing of an Egyptian–Israeli peace treaty, the establishment of diplomatic relations between the two countries, a date by
which a total Israeli withdrawal from the Sinai was to be completed, a
permanent stationing of U.N. troops in the Sinai which could not be
removed on the sole authority of either of the two parties,[92] and a
guarantee of free passage of Israeli ships through the Suez Canal and
the Straits of Tiran.

The Arab world was not pleased with the outcome of the Camp
David talks.[93] Although Sadat had insisted that any bilateral peace
treaty be linked to progress on the overall Palestinian issue, other Arab
nations claimed that not enough progress on this score had been made,
due largely to Israeli intransigence.[94] Arab criticism of Sadat increased
when Israel later permitted more settlements on the West Bank. In the
end the question of linkage was finessed by an agreement between Begin and Sadat providing for a specific timetable for negotiations on the
West Bank and Gaza. To date, these follow–up negotiations have not
taken place.

On March 26, 1979, the two treaties conceived at Camp David
were finally signed in Washington, formally ending the state of war
between Israel and Egypt.[95] In April, 1982, under the terms of the Peace
Treaty, Israel completed its staged withdrawal from the Sinai, returning
this vast buffer zone to Egypt in exchange for peace. In fact, to the
surprise of many, the Israeli–Egyptian peace treaty was implemented
remarkably smoothly. Israel pulled out of the Sinai in distinct phases,
returning portions on May 25, July 25, September 25, November 15,
and November 25, 1979, January 25, 1980, and the final installment on
April 25, 1982.[96] Egypt, correspondingly, initiated and upgraded its
level of diplomatic contact with Israel, eventually establishing "open
borders" and beginning scientific and cultural exchanges. (See Map
10.2) Although the peace between Israel and Egypt has run "hot" and
"cold" over the last ten years, primarily as a result of Israeli policies in
Lebanon and the West Bank, the peace has continued to hold.

The last—almost symbolic—source of tension between Israel and
Egypt involved a border dispute over 250 acres of land at Taba, just

MAP 10.2
Israeli Borders Today

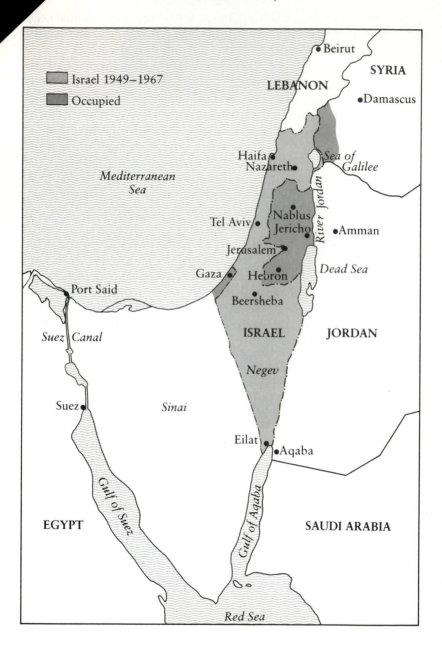

south of the city of Eilat. The area was occupied by Israel after the 1967 war, and the dispute became complicated by the fact that a beach resort was then built. When Israel returned its final installment of the Sinai in April of 1982, it maintained that Taba was exempt, using a map from 1906 which placed the disputed beachfront strip inside of Israel. After much negotiation within the Israeli Cabinet (favored by Labor's Peres, opposed by Likud's Shamir), Israel agreed in 1986 to an Egyptian proposal to accept binding arbitration from a five–member international tribunal. In September, 1988, the panel ruled that Taba belonged to Egypt.[97] From September 30, 1988, through February, 1989, Israel and Egypt negotiated over the financial settlement Israel would accept for the hotel that had been built on the land. Finally, in March, 1989, the Israeli flag was lowered from the front of the Sonesta Beach Hotel and the Egyptian flag was raised, signalling the end of the final chapter of Israeli–Egyptian disputes over their precise boundary.

The issue of the legitimacy of the Palestinian claim to statehood and by extension the legitimacy of Israeli jurisdiction over territories in the West Bank and Gaza (the other half of the Camp David agenda), has been a central issue, perhaps *the* central issue, in the quest for peace in the region since then. As Edward Said has said, there *is* a Palestinian people. No party to the debate disputes that. The dispute, rather, is over what to *do* about the Palestinian people and their claim to land and nationhood. Do these people have claim to the West Bank? Do they have claim to what today is Jordan? Or do they have claim to no territory of their own and instead must be content with assimilation into Israel, Jordan, Lebanon, Syria, and/or Egypt.

We have demonstrated here that there are many different responses to these questions, intensely held and articulated, and generally not subject to change through debate and discussion. Yet, one thing remains clear: Without a resolution of the "Palestinian Question" there can be no stability and long–term peace in the Middle East.

NOTES

1. An expanded discussion of this material can also be found in Chapter One.

2. Don Peretz, *The West Bank: History, Politics, Society, and Economy* (Boulder, Co.: Westview, 1986), p. 4. Much of what follows is based upon the substantially greater and more detailed analysis found in Peretz, pp. 13–42.

3. Ibid., p. 26.

4. Ibid., p. 29. See also the publication by the United Nations, Special Unit on Palestinian Rights. *The Origins and Evolution of the Palestine Problem* (New York: United Nations Press, 1967).

5. Jan Metzger, Martin Orth, and Christian Sterzing, *This Land is Our Land* (London: Zed Press, 1983), p. 133.

6. Peretz, *The West Bank*, p. 32.

7. Ibid., p. 36.

8. Ibid., p. 40.

9. Edward Said, *The Question of Palestine* (New York: Vintage Books, 1980), pp. xvi–xvii.

10. W. F. Abboushi, "The Road to Rebellion: Arab Palestine in the 1930's," *Journal of Palestine Studies* 6:3 (1977); 23–46.

11. See the historical analysis by William B. Quandt, "Political and Military Dimensions of Contemporary Palestinian Nationalism," in Quandt, Fuad Jabber, and Ann M. Lesch, *The Politics of Palestinian Nationalism* (Berkeley: University of California Press, 1973), especially pp. 45–52, "The Eclipse of Palestinian Nationalism, 1947–1967."

12. Metzger, Orth, and Sterzing, *This Land*, p. 133.

13. Ibid., p. 134.

14. Saul Mishal, *West Bank East Bank: The Palestinians in Jordan, 1949–1967* (New Haven: Yale University Press, 1976).

15. Metzger, Orth, and Sterzing, *This Land*, p. 135.

16. See Russell Stetler (ed.), *Palestine: The Arab–Israeli Conflict* (San Francisco: Ramparts Press, 1972), especially Part III: "Black September," pp. 223–89.

17. Clinton Bailey, "Changing Attitudes Toward Jordan in the West Bank," *Middle East Journal* 32:2 (1978); 155–66.

18. See Arthur Day, *East Bank/West Bank: Jordan and the Prospects for Peace* (New York: Council on Foreign Relations, 1986), especially Chapter 6, "Jordan's Future and the Palestinian Question."

19. Said, *The Question of Palestine*, p. 46.

20. For examples of this body of literature, see Issa Al–Shuaibi, "The Development of a Palestinian Entity–Consciousness, Part I," *Journal of Palestine Studies* 9:1 (1979); 67–84; "Part II," 9:2 (1980); 50–70; 9:3 (1980); 99–124; Tawfic Farah, "Political Socialization of Palestinian Children in Kuwait," *Journal of Palestine Studies* 6:4 (1977); 90–102; Hanan Ashrawi, "The Contemporary Palestinian Poetry of Occupation," *Journal of Palestine Studies* 7:3

(1978); 77–101; or Ibrahim Abu–Lughod, "Educating a Community in Exile: The Palestinian Experience," *Journal of Palestine Studies* 2:3 (1973); 94–111.

21. Said, *The Question of Palestine*, p. 51.

22. David Gilmour, *Dispossessed: The Ordeal of the Palestinians: 1917–1980* (London: Sidgwick and Jackson, 1980).

23. Said, *The Question of Palestine*, pp. 47–48. See also Regina Sharif, "The United Nations and Palestinian Rights, 1974–1979," *Journal of Palestine Studies* 9:1 (1979); 21–45; and W. Thomas Mallison, and Sally V. Mallison, *The Palestine Problem in International Law and World Order* (London: Longman, 1986).

24. Peretz, *The West Bank*, pp. 89–90.

25. Rashid Hamid, "What is the PLO?" *Journal of Palestine Studies* 4:4 (1975); 90–109; and Naveed Ahmad, "The Palestine Liberation Organization," *Pakistan Horizon* 28:4 (1975); 81–115.

26. See Helena Cobban, *The Palestinian Liberation Organization: People, Power, and Politics* (New York: Cambridge University Press, 1984), for a thorough study of the development of the movement, the internal relations of its many factions and its external ties with the Arab powers, other nations, and international organizations, such as the United Nations.

27. Ibid., pp. 267–70. A more critical examination of the Covenant can be found in Yehoshafat Harkabi, *The Palestinian Covenant and Its Meaning* (London: Vallentine Mitchell, 1979).

28. William Korey, "The PLO's Conquest of the U.N.," *Midstream* 25:9 (1979); 10–15; and Hazem Nusibeh, *Palestine and the United Nations* (New York: Quartet Books, 1982).

29. For a historical approach to this topic, see "The Palestinian Resistance and Inter–Arab Politics," by Fuad Jabber, in Quandt, Jabber, and Lesch, *The Politics of Palestinian Nationalism*, pp. 155–216. See also Aaron David Miller, *The Arab States and the Palestine Question: Between Ideology and Self–Interest* (New York: Praeger, 1986).

30. Metzger, Orth, Sterling, *This Land*, p. 244.

31. Emile Sahliyeh, *The Lebanon War: Implications for the PLO* (Boulder, Co.: Westview Press, 1985).

32. Michael Akehurst, "The Place of the Palestinians in an Arab–Israeli Peace Settlement," *The Round Table* (October, 1980), pp. 443–50.

33. *Facts About Israel* (Jerusalem: Ministry of Foreign Affairs, 1985), p. 43.

34. Arie Bregman, *The Economy of the Administered Areas, 1968–1973* (Jerusalem: Bank of Israel, 1975).

35. *Facts About Israel*, pp. 44–45.

36. See essays by Sasson Levi, "Local Government in the Administered Territories," and by Avraham Lavine, "Social Services in the Administered Territories," in Daniel J. Elazar (ed.), *Judea, Samaria, and Gaza: Views on the Present and Future* (Washington, D.C.: American Enterprise Institute for Public Policy Research, 1982).

37. *Facts About Israel*, p. 45.

38. Ephraim Sneh, as quoted in Gary Wolf (ed.), *Israel Press Highlights* (New York: Institute of Human Relations, American Jewish Committee, December 12, 1988), pp. 1–2.

39. One of the best studies of recent Israeli policy and the nature of Arab life there is that by Ian Lustick, *Arabs in the Jewish State* (Austin: University of Texas Press, 1980).

40. One of the most frequently–cited sources in this area is the Report of the National Lawyers Guild 1977 Middle East Delegation, *Treatment of Palestinians in Israeli–Occupied West Bank and Gaza* (New York: National Lawyers Guild, 1978).

41. See for instance Michael Adams, "Israel's Treatment of the Arabs in the Occupied Territories," *Journal of Palestine Studies* 6:2 (1977); 19–40.

42. See Sabri Jiryis, "The Legal Structure for the Expropriation and Absorption of Arab Lands in Israel," *Journal of Palestine Studies* 2:4 (1973); 82–104.

43. Ann Lesch, "Israeli Deportation of Palestinians from the West Bank and the Gaza Strip, 1967–1978," *Journal of Palestine Studies* 8:3 (1979); 81–107.

44. "Document: Amnesty International: Administrative Detention in Israeli Occupied Territories," *Middle East Journal* 32:3 (1978); 337–40.

45. See, for example, the full text of the United Nations Security Council Resolution on Israeli Actions in the Occupied Territories passed December 29, 1987 by a vote of 14 in favor, none against, with the U.S abstaining. This is published in *American–Arab Affairs* 23 (1987–1988), pp. 145–47. See also Ghayth Armanazi, "The Rights of Palestinians: The International Definition," *Journal of Palestine Studies* 3:3 (1974); 88–96; Ghassan Bishara, "The Human Rights Case Against Israel," *Journal of Palestine Studies* 8:4 (1979); 3–30; and Esther Cohen, *Human Rights in the Israeli–Occupied Territories, 1967–1982* (Manchester: Manchester University Press, 1986).

46. See Rephael Vardi, "The Administered Territories and the Internal Security of Israel," in Elazar, *Judea, Samaria, and Gaza*, pp. 171–90.

47. *Facts About Israel*, p. 45.

48. Teddy Kollek, "Introduction: Jerusalem—Today and Tomorrow," in *Jerusalem: Problems and Prospects*, Joel Kraemer (ed.), (New York: Praeger, 1980), p. 1.

49. Saul B. Cohen, *Jerusalem—Bridging the Four Walls: A Geopolitical Perspective* (New York: Herzl Press, 1977), p. 11.

50. Ibid.

51. Colin Williams, *Jerusalem: A Universal Cultural and Historical Resource* (New York: Aspen Institute for Humanistic Studies), as cited in Cohen, *Jerusalem—Bridging the Four Walls*, p. 23.

52. See Joel Kraemer, "The Jerusalem Question," in Kraemer (ed.), *Jerusalem: Problems and Prospects*, especially pp. 24–35.

53. Cohen, *Jerusalem*, p. 12.

54. Kollek, "Introduction," p. 1.

55. See the discussion of this in Alisa Ginio, "Plans for the Solution of the Jerusalem Problem," in Kraemer, *Jerusalem: Problems and Prospects*, pp. 41–71.

56. Peretz, *The West Bank*, p. 45.

57. Uzi Benziman, "Israeli Policy in East Jerusalem After Reunification," in Kraemer (ed.), *Jerusalem: Problems and Prospects*, p. 101. Benziman discusses a wide range of actions by the Israeli government in response to the needs of the Arab population in the annexed area, in such policy areas as education, culture, language, the press, consulates, the United Nations, tax law, the economic system, and religious autonomy.

58. Cohen, *Jerusalem—Bridging the Four Walls*, p. 33; the five "geopolitical imperatives" which follow, are derived from more detailed discussion by Cohen, pp. 33–34.

59. A full discussion of the kinds of issues that surface in this context can be found in the essay by Emanuel Gutmann and Claude Klein, "The Institutional Structure of Heterogeneous Cities: Brussels, Montreal, and Belfast," in Kraemer (ed.), *Jerusalem: Problems and Prospects*, pp. 178–207. At the end of their comparative essay they discuss the lessons that the political leadership of Jerusalem can learn from the experiences of these three cities.

60. A good essay addressing many of these questions is Daniel Elazar, "Local Government for Heterogeneous Populations: Some Options for Jerusalem," in Kraemer (ed.), *Jerusalem: Problems and Prospects*, pp. 208–28.

61. For examples of this kind of study and criticism, see Abdul–Illah Abu–Ayyash, "Israeli Regional Planning Policy in the Occupied Arab Territories," *Journal of Palestine Studies* 5 (1976); 83–108; Abdul–Illah Abu–Ayyash, "Israeli Planning Policy in the Occupied Arab Territories," *Journal of Palestine Studies* 11:1 (1981); 111–23; and, Bakir Abu–Kishk, "Arab Land and Israeli Policy," *Journal of Palestine Studies* 11:1 (1981); 124–35.

62. See, for example, Avner Yaniv and Fabian Pascal, "Doves, Hawks, and Other Birds of a Feather: The Distribution of Israel Parliamentary Opinion on the Future of the Occupied Territories, 1967–1977," *British Journal of Political Science* 10:3 (1980); 260–66.

63. The problem with this position is that recently King Hussein has announced that he is giving up any claim to the Occupied Territories and supporting the Palestine Liberation Organization. See "Jordan's West Bank Move Upsetting Daily Life," *New York Times* (Tuesday, October 18, 1988), p. 1.

64. Peretz, *The West Bank*, pp. 50–51. A lengthy discussion of the bureaucratic processes governing these settlements, how they are established, plans for future settlements, and domestic Israeli opposition to these settlements, can be found in Chapter 5: Jewish Settlement in the West Bank, pp. 59–77.

65. See Ian Lustick, "Israel and the West Bank After Elon Moreh: The Mechanics of De Facto Annexation," *Middle East Journal* 35:4 (1981); 557–77.

66. See Efraim Ben–Zadok, "The Limits to the Politics of Planning," in *The Impact of Gush Emunim: Politics and Settlement in the West Bank*, David Newman (ed.), (New York: St. Martin's Press, 1985), p. 141.

67. Cohen, *Jerusalem—Bridging the Four Walls*, pp. 109–70.

68. Ben–Zadok, "Limits to the Politics of Planning," p. 150.

69. For examples of this kind of criticism see Abu–Ayyash, "Israeli Regional Planning Policy"; Salah El–Din Amer, "The Problem of Settlements in Occupied Territories," *Revue Egyptienne de Droit Internationale* 35 (1979); 11–44; and Ann Lesch, "Israeli Settlements in the Occupied Territories," *Journal of Palestine Studies* 8:1 (1978); 100–20.

70. Moshe Drori, "The Israeli Settlements in Judea and Samaria: Legal Aspects," in Elazar, *Judea, Samaria, and Gaza*, pp. 44–80.

71. Peretz, *The West Bank*, p. 46.

72. Ibid., p. 47.

73. Meron Benvenisti, with Ziad Abu–Zayad and Danny Rubenstein. *The West Bank Data Base Project 1986: Demographic, Economic, Legal, Social, and Political Developments in the West Bank* (Boulder, Co.: Westview Press, 1986), p. 46.

74. See Avner Yaniv and Yael Yishai, "Israeli Settlements in the West Bank: The Politics of Intransigence," *Journal of Politics* 43:4 (1981); 1105–28; William Harris, *Taking Root: Israeli Settlement in the West Bank, the Golan, and Gaza–Sinai, 1967–1980* (New York: Research Studies Press, 1980); and Ann Lesch, "Israeli Settlements in the Occupied Territories."

75. Author's interview with Menachem Begin, May 30, 1980, in the Knesset in Jerusalem.

76. For discussion of this philosophy, and its empirical validity, see Benvenisti, *The West Bank*. See also Seth Tillman, "The West Bank Hearings: Israel's Colonization of Occupied Territory," *Journal of Palestine Studies* 7 (1978); 71–87.

77. David Weisburd and Elin Waring, "Settlement Motivations in the Gush Emunim Movement: Comparing Bonds of Altruism and Self Interest," in *The Impact of Gush Emunim*, Newman (ed.), pp. 183–99.

78. One recent fascinating study of this phenomenon is by Ian Lustick, *The Land and the Lord: Jewish Fundamentalism in Israel* (New York: Council on Foreign Relations, 1988). The book is a study of Jewish fundamentalism, tracing its evolution and impact, focusing upon Gush Emunim, contemporary Israeli policy, and the issue of settlements in the Occupied Territories.

79. See the essay "Interpretation and Misinterpretation of Jewish Territorialism," by Yosseph Shilhav, in *The Impact of Gush Emunim: Politics and Settlement in the West Bank*, pp. 111–24.

80. Gershon Shafir, "Institutional and Spontaneous Settlement Drives: Did Gush Emunim Make a Difference?" in Ibid., p. 153.

81. Benvenisti, *The West Bank*, pp. 46–7, 53.

82. One of the best discussions of this is to be found in Abraham Becker, *Israel and the Palestinian Occupied Territories: Military–Political Issues in the Debate* (Santa Monica, Ca.: Rand, 1971).

83. A discussion of the mechanics of the military government administration can be found in Peretz, *The West Bank*, pp. 79–87.

84. Ibid., p. 45.

85. *Statistical Abstract of Israel* (Jerusalem: Central Bureau of Statistics, 1986), p. 26.

86. There has been much discussion over what happened that caused Sadat to undertake this momentous journey. One interesting account is to be found in Uri Dan and Sidney Zion, "Untold Story of Mideast Talks," *New York Times Magazine* (January 21, 1979, pp. 20–22; January 28, 1979, pp. 32–38, 42–43).

87. C. Paul Bradley, *The Camp David Peace Process: A Study of Carter Administration Policies (1977–1980)* (Grantham, N.H.: Tompson and Rutter, 1981), 19.

88. Analyses of the long–term peace process can be found in, *inter alia* Melvin Friedlander, *Sadat and Begin: The Domestic Politics of Peacemaking* (Boulder, Co.: Westview Press, 1983); and Lester Sobel, (ed.), *Peace–Making in the Middle East* (New York: Facts on File, 1980).

89. Bradley, *The Camp David Peace Process*, pp. 4–17.

90. For some interesting perspectives on the personal dynamics of this period, see Ezer Weizman, *The Battle for Peace* (New York: Bantam Books, 1981), especially chapter 25 "Of Squirrels and Presidents"; and Moshe Dayan's *Breakthrough: A Personal Account of the Egypt–Israel Peace Negotiations* (New York: Knopf, 1981), pp. 152–59; and William Quandt's *Camp David: Peacemaking and Politics* (Washington, D.C.: Brookings Institution, 1986), pp. 168–259.

91. For the text of the agreements, see "A Framework for Peace in the Middle East Agreed at Camp David," and "Framework for the Conclusion of a Peace Treaty Between Egypt and Israel," *Middle East Journal* 32:4 (1978); 471–94.

92. This was an important issue. See "Egypt–Israel: Protocol Establishing the Sinai Multinational Forces and Observers," *International Legal Materials* 20:5 (1981); 1190–97.

93. An example of such a reaction can be found in "Egyptian–Israeli Treaty: An Appraisal," *Pakistan Horizon* 32:3 (1979); 15–29.

94. Typical of this literature is the contribution of Fayez Sayegh, "The Camp David Agreement and the Palestine Problem," *Journal of Palestine Studies* 8:2 (1979); 3–54.

95. For a detailed chronology of the progress made in the period between Camp David and the eventual signing of the Treaties, see Clete Hinton's book *Camp David Accords* (Los Alamitos, Ca.: Hwong Publishing, 1980).

96. An analysis of stages of the return of Sinai to Egypt appeared in the *New York Times*, April 26, 1982, p. 1.

97. *The New York Times*, Friday, September 30, 1988, p. 1.

EPILOGUE

Israel is a study in contrasts. It can be described as a Western democracy in a non-Western setting, as a stable regime (despite a basically tumultuous political style) in a region in which stable democracies are rare. It is a maturing state that still faces many of the problems characteristic of developing nations and yet, at the same time, has many of the problems of industrialized and developed states. It has a well-developed system of government, yet lacks a fully written constitution and is a polity in which many of the most basic principles of the regime have yet to be fully resolved. It is a country in which debates over the role of religion in the political process continue to take place, yet is a society in which citizens openly question whether Zionism has any role in public policy. It is a culture in which immigrants share a common religious and even cultural ancestry, yet is a society where, unlike those in which it is possible to talk about a political culture and political values that are passed from one generation to the next, the chronological and geographical pattern of immigration makes it difficult to isolate a uniform political belief system.

It was suggested at the outset of this volume that the study of the history of any country is a prerequisite for an understanding and appreciation of how and why its political system has come to be the way it is, and that this statement is nowhere more true than in Israel. We noted that the country's very existence was challenged from the moment of independence, and that this challenge has been continued by most of her neighbors to the present day. Our purpose at the outset was to highlight some of the major issues necessary for a basic understanding of the historical context from which modern Israel emerged. The development of the concept of Zionism was, as we have seen, crucial to Israel's evolution. From a political movement in 19th century Europe through the British Mandate period, the Holocaust, and finally the establishment of the State of Israel in 1948, we witnessed the continual interplay of global, regional, national, and individual forces shaping the political context within which Israel would operate. Yet, the achievement of independence, in retrospect, merely ushered in a new chapter in the already eventful history of the Jewish people. The new state, born of such an ancient lineage, has experienced many of the same rites of passage which states and nations of more recent vintage must also endure.

Although this is first and foremost a study of the Israeli *political* system, an understanding and an awareness of the cultural and economic, along with the purely historical, dimensions of Israeli society becomes a prerequisite for a more complete appreciation of contemporary politics. After all, social, cultural, and economic factors can be directly translated into political variables. Concepts of ethnicity and immigration serve as vivid reminders of this. Being a Jewish immigrant from Yemen or from France *can* and *does* make a difference in the political world. The fact that Israel's population is heterogeneous, that not all Israelis are Jewish, and that not all Jewish Israelis come from the same ethnic, geographic, or religious background, has implications for society and consequently for politics.

Narrowing our focus of inquiry to politics necessarily highlights the significance of the Jewish character of Israel, for it is the central unifying thread of an overwhelming majority of the population. In Israel, unlike most democratic states, religious questions have often become politicized and are, therefore, relevant to political analysis. Differences between and among sub-groups of the Jewish population further remind us that although outsiders might *a priori* suppose that Israeli Jews would be politically different from Israeli non-Jews, one must also be aware of the fact that some Israeli Jews are different from other Israeli Jews. Politics constantly intrudes in relations between Ashkenazim and Sephardim, and among the Orthodox, Conservative, and Reform strands of Judaism.

All of the above is still merely a prelude to describing the legal principles and major structural components of the actual political system, be it the constitution or the role of the courts in the creation of Israel's constitutional regime. Nonetheless, it is in the institution of the political party that all these underlying factors and contradictions most clearly coalesce. Most of the contemporary Israeli political parties in fact have direct links to the past through their roots in prestate political organizations. Encouraged by a process that fragments rather than unifies, the act of governance becomes less a science than an artform. An electoral system which promotes the splintering of even established political parties on the one hand, yet demands strict party discipline and close control of individual legislators on the other, further personifies the myriad contrasts that comprise modern Israel. Why should we be surprised, then, when calls for reform of the electoral system have been intensely opposed by major existing political parties?

A final major dimension of contrast came in the study of Israeli foreign policy. An immigrant nation with vivid memories of discrimination must now bear the uncomfortable stigma of "occupier." A people who once peered into the abyss of annihilation now apparently possess weapons of mass destruction. A culture aware and proud of its tradition now struggles for acceptance and legitimacy. And a country determined to stand on its own must accept that a substantial degree of its security largely relies in the final analysis on the largess of its super-power patron.

Our study concluded with the observation that although this type of examination may not suggest answers to some or all of the problems found in this part of the world today, an increased understanding of and sensitivity to the issues involved, as well as a greater awareness of the feelings of political actors on both sides of the dilemma, is a goal to which we all can subscribe. Some readers may feel that they now have a clear perception of what a "correct" policy outcome should be regard-ing the Middle East; others may be less sure. What *is* certain is that one individual's correct policy can also be another's injustice.

And what of the future? Is it safe to predict that Israeli politics will continue to be highly contentious, with divisive issues promoting the kind of issue—oriented politics that we have seen characteristic of the past? Is that the price a political system pays for democracy? Many Israelis in fact would reply that it is a burden that should willingly be accepted, given the alternatives. Israel *is*, after all, a heterogeneous soci-ety, and we should expect that a truly representative political system in such a society will display a contentious political style, with issue—oriented politics and vigorous, even fierce, debate over important ques-tions of the day. Political parties will continue to come and go, new domestic alliances will be created, and the same basic issues will con-tinue to generate reexaminations of the most fundamental questions long on the public and political agenda: What is the best way to address ethnic and cultural pluralism in society? What is an appropriate current interpretation of the term "Zionism"? How much interaction should there be between religion and politics? What is the "best" degree of representation of minority parties in a political system? Should the pre-sent electoral system remain as it is, or should it be modified to decrease representation for smaller parties and make the process of coalition formation easier?

All of these questions, and indeed many more, are important in the Israeli political world. They are important not only because they serve as proof of a pluralistic Israeli democracy, they are important because they help to keep Israeli society vigorous. A society that is vigorous and continuously reexamining its most fundamental beliefs is not a society that will become complacent and "drift" into stagnation. This does not mean, of course, that all governmental policy will be popular or that all Israelis (or all non-Israelis) will agree with all decisions. Many in Israel today feel very strongly that current government policy on the West Bank is wrong and are prepared to demonstrate to that effect. What it does mean is that government will not adopt unpopular policies as a result of popular apathy or inactivity. The long–term hope is that an open society with enough debate and discussion can eventually determine the "correct" policy, and that reason will prevail. There are, of course, no guarantees of this, for history books are replete with examples of "majority tyranny." However, given the choice of an open, pluralistic (and possible contentious and divisive) society or its alternative, there really is no choice: Whatever inconveniences the system may generate, it is far better than its antithesis.

While societies may applaud themselves for their willingness to tolerate pluralism and fervent debate in their domestic political arenas, this is often riskier to encourage in foreign policy. Open disagreement here can project to outside audiences images of indecision, irresolution, and weakness. For a state as geographically vulnerable as Israel the costs of others acting on the basis of such impressions could be dire indeed. Yet even here the parameters of debate are surprisingly wide. Policy towards the Occupied Territories is merely the latest case in point. The future of the West Bank and Gaza has split both the electorate and the political establishment. When survival is at stake political differences are naturally quickly set aside. Otherwise, so it seems, even foreign affairs is not immune from partisanship.

The outcome of the regional disputes in the Middle East today is not likely to be a sudden "discovery" of a comprehensive peace settlement acceptable to all parties involved. What is more likely, instead, is that gradually the arena of peace will expand—first Egypt and Israel, then Jordan and Israel, and so on—or contract (as happened with the "cold peace" between Israel and Egypt during the War in Lebanon), depending upon pressing issues of the day. Although no breakthroughs appear imminent at the time of this writing, we should never forget that before Egyptian President Anwar Sadat announced his willingness to go to Jerusalem to discuss peace in the Middle East with the Israelis, few would have predicted such an action. And yet, once that step was taken, a peace treaty was signed within two years.

We therefore close as we began, noting the inescapable contrasts that appear before us. Israel is both Western and Middle Eastern, unified and divided, secular and theocratic, and politically institutionalized and still developing. We could say, in fact, that in a number of very important respects Israel has not yet permanently established its identity, much as we might say of a individual who is no longer a child yet not fully mature. Just as we would do with any individual, we must watch and wait in order to observe what forms and behavior a "maturing" polity like Israel eventually takes.

BIBLIOGRAPHY

Abboushi, W. F. "The Road to Rebellion: Arab Palestine in the 1930's." *Journal of Palestine Studies* 6:3 (1977): 23–46.

Abella, Irving, and Harold Troper. *None is Too Many: Canada and the Jews of Europe, 1933–1948*. Toronto: Lester and Orpen Dennys, 1982.

Abramov, Sheva. *Perpetual Dilemma: Jewish Religion in the Jewish State*. Rutherford, N.J.: Associated University Presses, 1975.

Abu-Ayyash, Abdul-Illah. "Israeli Planning Policy in the Occupied Arab Territories." *Journal of Palestine Studies* 11:1 (1981): 111–23.

Abu-Ayyash, Abdul-Illah. "Israeli Regional Planning Policy in the Occupied Arab Territories." *Journal of Palestine Studies* 5 (1976): 83–108.

Abu-Kishk, Bakir. "Arab Land and Israeli Policy." *Journal of Palestine Studies* 11:1 (1981): 124–35.

Abu-Lughod, Ibrahim. "Educating a Community in Exile: The Palestinian Experience." *Journal of Palestine Studies* 2:3 (1973): 94–111.

Abu-Redeneh, Odah. "The Jewish Factor in U.S. Politics." *Journal of Palestine Studies* 1:4 (1972): 92–107.

Adams, Michael. "Israel's Treatment of the Arabs in the Occupied Territories." *Journal of Palestine Studies* 6:2 (1977): 19–40.

Adefuye, Ade. "Nigeria and Israel." *International Studies* 18:4 (1979): 629–40.

Adnan, Avraham. *On the Banks of the Suez: An Israeli General's Personal Account of the Yom Kippur War*. San Rafael, Ca.: Presidio Press, 1980.

Ahmad, Naveed. "The Palestine Liberation Organization." *Pakistan Horizon* 28:4 (1975): 81–115.

Akehurst, Michael. "The Place of the Palestinians in an Arab-Israeli Peace Settlement." *The Round Table* (October, 1980): 443–50.

Akzin, Benjamin. "The Role of Parties in Israeli Democracy." *Journal of Politics* 17 (1955): 507–45.

Akzin, Benjamin. "Israel's Knesset." *Ariel* 15 (1966): 5–11.

Akzin, Benjamin. "Who is a Jew? A Hard Case." *Israel Law Review* 5:2 (1970): 259–63.

Akzin, Benjamin, and Y. Dror. *Israel: High Pressure Planning*. Syracuse: Syracuse University Press, 1966.

Al-Qazzaz, Ayad. "Army and Society in Israel." *Pacific Sociology Review* 16:2 (1973): 143–66.

Al-Shuaibi, Issa. "The Development of a Palestinian Entity-Consciousness, Part I." *Journal of Palestine Studies* 9:1 (1979): 67–84; "Part II," 9:2 (1980): 50–70; "Part III," 9:3 (1980): 99–124.

Alexander, Ernest. "The Development of an Entitlement Formula for Capital Budget Allocations to Local Government in Israel." *Planning and Administration* 7:2 (1980): 13–25.

Allen, Peter. *The Yom Kippur War*. New York: Scribner, 1982.

Allon, Yigal. *Shield of David: The Story of Israel's Armed Forces*. New York: Random House, 1970.

Allon, Yigal. *The Making of Israel's Army*. New York: Universe Books, 1970.

Allon, Yigal. "Israel: The Case for Defensible Borders." *Foreign Affairs 55* (1976): 38–53.

Almond, Gabriel, and Powell, G. Bingham Jr. *Comparative Politics: A Developmental Approach*. Boston: Little, Brown, and Company, 1966.

Alroy, Gil C. *The Kissinger Experience: American Policy in the Middle East*. New York: Horizon Press, 1975.

Amer, Salah El-din. "The Problem of Settlements in Occupied Territories." *Revue Egyptienne de Droit Internationale* 35 (1979): 11–44.

Amir, Shimon. *Israel's Development Cooperation with Africa, Asia and Latin America*. New York: Praeger, 1974.

Amnesty International. "Administrative Detention in Israeli Occupied Territories." *Middle East Journal* 32:3 (1978): 337–40.

Andrews, B. "Suez Canal Controversy." *Albany Law Review* 21:1 (1957): 14–33.

Arian, Asher. *The Elections in Israel—1969*. Jerusalem: Jerusalem Academic Press, 1972.

Arian, Asher. *The Elections in Israel—1973*. Jerusalem: Jerusalem Academic Press, 1975.

Arian, Alan. "Were the 1973 Elections in Israel Critical?" *Comparative Politics* 8 (1975):152–65.

Arian, Asher, ed. *The Elections in Israel—1977*. Jerusalem: Jerusalem Academic Press, 1980.

Arian, Alan. "Health Care in Israel: Political and Administrative Aspects." *International Political Science Review* 2:1 (1981): 43–56.

Arian, Asher. *The Elections in Israel—1981*. Tel Aviv: Ramon Publishing Co., 1983.

Arian, Asher. *Politics in Israel: The Second Generation*. Chatham, N.J.: Chatham House, 1985.

Arian, Alan and Weiss, Shevah. "Split Ticket Voting in Israel." *Western Political Quarterly* 22 (1969):375–89.

Armanazi, Ghayth. "The Rights of Palestinians: The International Definition." *Journal of Palestine Studies* 3:3 (1974): 88–96.

Aron, Raymond. *De Gaulle, Israel, and the Jews*. New York: Praeger, 1969.

Aronoff, Myron. "Political Change in Israel: The Case of a New Town." *Political Science Quarterly* 89:3 (1974): 613–26.

Aronoff, Myron. *Power and Ritual in the Israeli Labor Party: A Study in Political Anthropology*. Assen, Amsterdam: Van Gorcum, 1977.

Aronoff, Myron, ed. *Cross-Currents in Israeli Culture and Politics*. New Brunswick: Transaction, 1984.

Aronson, Geoffrey, "Israel's Policy of Military Occupation." *Journal of Palestine Studies* 7:4 (1978): 79–98.

Ashkar, Riad. "The Syrian and Egyptian Campaign." *Journal of Palestine Studies* 3:2 (1974): 15–23.

Ashrawi, Hanan. "The Contemporary Palestinian Poetry of Occupation." *Journal of Palestine Studies* 7:3 (1978): 77–101.

Avnery, Shlomo. *The Making of Modern Zionism: The Intellectual Origins of the Jewish State.* New York: Basic Books, 1981.

Avnery, Uri. *Israel Without Zionism: A Plan for Peace in the Middle East.* New York: Collier Books, 1971.

Azarya, Victor, and Kimmerling, Baruch. "New Immigrants in the Israeli Armed Forces." *Armed Forces and Society* 6:3 (1980): 455–82.

Azmon, Yael. "The 1981 Elections and the Changing Fortunes of the Israeli Labour Party." *Government and Opposition* 16:4 (1981): 432–46.

Bahbah, Bishara. "The United States and Israel's Energy Security." *Journal of Palestine Studies* 11:2 (1982): 113–31.

Bailey, Clinton. "Changing Attitudes Toward Jordan in the West Bank." *Middle East Journal* 32:2 (1978): 155–66.

Baker, Henry. *The Legal System of Israel.* Jerusalem: Israel University Press, 1968.

Balabkins, Nicholas. "The Course of West German-Israeli Relations." *Orbis* 14:3 (1970): 776–818.

Balabkins, Nicholas. *West German Reparations to Israel.* New Brunswick: Rutgers University Press, 1971.

Banks, Lynne. *Torn Country: An Oral History of the Israeli War of Independence.* New York: Watts, 1982.

Bar-Simon Tov, Yaacov. *The Israeli-Egyptian War of Attrition, 1969–1970.* New York: Columbia University Press, 1980.

Becker, Abraham. *Israel and the Palestinian Occupied Territories: Military-Political Issues in the Debate.* Santa Monica, Ca.: Rand, 1971.

Begin, Menachem. *The Revolt.* New York: Nash Publishing, 1977.

Bell, J. B. "Israel's Nuclear Option." *Middle East Journal* 26 (1972): 372–88.

Bell, J. B. *Terror Out of Zion: Lehi and the Palestine Underground, 1929–1949.* New York: St. Martin's Press, 1977.

Ben-Gurion, David. *Israel: A Personal History.* New York: Funk and Wagnalls, 1971.

Ben-Horin, Yoav, and Posen, Barry. *Israel's Strategic Doctrine.* Santa Monica, Ca.: Rand Corporation, 1981.

Ben-Meir, Alon. "Israel in the War's Long Aftermath." *Current History* 80:462 (1981): 23–6.

Ben-Sira, Zeev. "The Image of Political Parties and the Structure of a Political Map." *European Journal of Political Research* 6:3 (1978): 259–84.

Benvenisti, Meron. *The West Bank Data Project: A Survey of Israel's Policies.* Washington, D.C.: American Enterprise Institute, 1984.

Benvenisti, Meron. *The West Bank Data Base Project 1986: Demographic, Economic, Legal, Social, and Political Developments in the West Bank.* Boulder, Co.: Westview Press, 1986.

Bernstein, Marver. "Israel's Ninth General Election." *International Studies* 17 (1978): 27–50.

Bilski, Raphaella, ed. *Can Planning Replace Politics? The Israeli Experience.* Boston: Martinus Nijhoff, 1980.

Bin-Nun, Ariel. "The Borders of Justiciability." *Israel Law Review* 5 (1980): 569–79.

Birnbaum, Ervin. *The Politics of Compromise: State and Religion in Israel.* Rutherford, N.J.: Fairleigh Dickinson University Press, 1970.

Bishara, Ghassan. "Israel's Power in the U.S. Senate." *Journal of Palestine Studies* 10 (1980): 58–79.

Bishara, Ghassan. "The Human Rights Case Against Israel." *Journal of Palestine Studies* 8:4 (1979): 3–30.

Blum, Yehuda. *Secure Boundaries and Middle East Peace.* Jerusalem: Faculty of Law, Hebrew University, 1971.

Bradley, C. Paul. *The Camp David Peace Process: A Study of Carter Administration Policies (1977–1980).* Grantham, N.H.: Tompson and Rutter, 1981.

Bradley, C. Paul. *Parliamentary Elections in Israel: Three Case Studies.* Grantham, N.H.: Thompson and Rutter, 1985.

Brecher, Michael. "Images, Process, and Feedback in Foreign Policy: Israel's Decisions on German Reparations." *American Political Science Review* 67:1 (1973): 73–102.

Brecher, Michael. *The Foreign Policy System of Israel: Setting, Images, Process.* New Haven: Yale University Press, 1972.

Brecher, Michael. *Decisions in Israel's Foreign Policy.* New Haven: Yale University Press, 1975.

Brecher, Michael. *Decisions in Crisis: Israel, 1967 and 1973.* Berkeley: University of California Press, 1980.

Bregman, Arie. *The Economy of the Administered Areas, 1968–1973.* Jerusalem: Bank of Israel, 1975.

Browne, Eric. "Testing Theories of Coalition Formation in the European Context." *Comparative Political Studies* 3 (1971): 391–412.

Browne, Eric, and Franklin, Mark. "Editors' Introduction: New Directions in Coalition Research." *Legislative Studies Quarterly* 11:4 (1986), 469–8´

Brownstein, Lewis. "Decision-making in Israeli Foreign Policy: An Unplanned Process." *Political Science Quarterly* 92:2 (1977): 259–79.

Burstein, Moshe. *Self Government of the Jews in Palestine Since 1900.* New Haven: Hyperion Press, 1934.

Burstein, Paul. "Political Patronage and Party Choice Among Israeli Voters." *Journal of Politics* 38 (1976): 1024–32.

Burstein, Paul. "Social Cleavages and Party Choice in Israel: A Log-Linear Analysis." *American Political Science Review* 72 (1978): 96–109.

Butler, David, Penniman, Howard, and Ranney, Austin, eds. *Democracy at the Polls.* Washington: American Enterprise Institute, 1981.

Caiden, Gerald. *Israel's Administrative Culture.* Berkeley: Institute of Government Studies, University of California, 1970.

Caspi, Dan, Diskin, A., and Gutmann, E., eds. *The Roots of Begin's Success: The 1981 Israeli Elections*. New York: St. Martin's Press, 1983.

Chabra, H. S. "The Competition of Israel and the Arab States for the Friendship with the African States." *India Quarterly* 31:4 (1976): 362–70.

Chertoff, Mordechai, ed. *Zionism: A Basic Reader*. New York: Herzl Press, 1975.

Chiger, M. "The Rabbinical Courts in the State of Israel." *Israel Law Review* 2:2 (1967):147–81.

Churchill, Randolph. *The Six Day War*. Boston: Houghton, Mifflin, 1967.

Cobban, Helena. *The Palestinian Liberation Organization: People, Power, and Politics*. New York: Cambridge University Press, 1984.

Cohen, Boaz. *Law and Tradition in Judaism*. New York: Jewish Theological Seminary of America, 1959.

Cohen, Esther. *Human Rights in the Israeli-Occupied Territories, 1967–1982*. Manchester: Manchester University Press, 1986.

Cohen, Israel. *A Short History of Zionism*. London: F. Muller, 1951.

Cohen, Michael. *Palestine, Retreat from the Mandate: The Making of British Policy, 1936–1945*. New York: Holmes and Meier, 1978.

Cohen, Saul B. *Jerusalem—Bridging the Four Walls: A Geopolitical Perspective*. New York: Herzl Press, 1977.

Cohen, Stuart. "Israel Zangwill's Plan for Jewish Colonization in Mesopotamia." *Middle Eastern Studies* 16:3 (1980): 200–8.

Comay, Yochanan, and Kirschenbaum, Alan. "The Israeli New Town: An Experiment at Population Redistribution." *Economic Development and Cultural Change* 22:1 (1973): 124–34.

Confino, M., and Shamir, S., eds. *The U.S.S.R. and the Middle East*. New York: Wiley, 1973.

Crosbie, Sylvia. *A Tacit Alliance: France and Israel, From Suez to the Six Day War*. Princeton: Princeton University Press, 1974.

Curtis, Michael. "The United Nations and the Middle East Conflict, 1967–1975." *Middle East Review* 3 (1975): 18–22.

Curtis, Michael, and Gitelson, Susan. *Israel in the Third World*. New Brunswick, N.J.: Transaction Books, 1976.

Czudnowski, Moshe. "Legislative Recruitment Under Proportional Representation in Israel: A Model and a Case Study." *Midwest Journal of Political Science* 14 (1970): 216–48.

Czudnowski, Moshe. "Sociocultural Variables and Legislative Recruitment." *Comparative Politics* 4 (1972): 561–587.

Czudnowski, Moshe, and Landau, Jacob. *The Israeli Communist Party and the Elections for the Fifth Knesset, 1961*. Stanford, Ca.: Hoover Institution, 1965.

Dagan, Avigdor. *Moscow and Jerusalem: Twenty Years of Relations Between Israel and the Soviet Union*. New York: Abelard-Shuman, 1970.

Danet, Brenda. "The Language of Persuasion in Bureaucracy: 'Modern' and 'Traditional' Appeals to the Israel Customs Authorities." *American Sociology Review* 36:5 (1971): 847–49.

Danet, Brenda, and Hartman, Harriet. "Coping with Bureaucracy: The Israeli Case." *Social Forces* 51:1 (1972): 7–22.

Davis, W. D. *The Territorial Dimension of Judaism*. Berkeley: University of California Press, 1982.

Day, Arthur. *East Bank/West Bank: Jordan and the Prospects for Peace*. New York: Council on Foreign Relations, 1986.

Dayan, Moshe. *Diary of the Sinai Campaign*. Jerusalem: Steimatzky's Agency, 1966.

Dayan, Moshe. *Breakthrough: A Personal Account of the Egypt-Israel Peace Negotiations*. New York: Knopf, 1981.

Deutschkron, Inge. *Bonn and Jerusalem*. Philadelphia: Clinton Books, 1970.

Dinitz, Simcha. "The Legal Aspects of the Egyptian Blockade of the Suez Canal." *Georgetown Law Journal* 45:2 (1957): 166–99.

Divine, Donna. "The Modernization of Israeli Administration." *International Journal of Middle Eastern Studies* 5 (1974): 295–313.

Don-Yehiya, Eliezer. "Origins and Developments of the Agudah and Mafdal Parties." *The Jerusalem Quarterly* Summer, 1981, pp. 49–64.

Donin, Haim. *To Be a Jew: A Guide to Jewish Observance in Contemporary Life*. New York: Basic Books, 1972.

Dowty, Alan. "Nuclear Proliferation: The Israeli Case." *International Studies Quarterly* 22:1 (1978), 79–120.

Drinan, Robert. *Honor the Promise: America's Commitment to Israel*. Garden City: Doubleday, 1977.

Dror, Yehezkel. "A Guide Through the Perplexities of Israeli Politics After Begin." *Political Quarterly* 55:1 (1984): 38–47.

Duchacek, Ivo. *Power Maps: Comparative Politics of Constitutions*. Santa Barbara, Calif.: Clio Press, 1973.

Dulter, Lee. "Eastern and Western Jews: Ethnic Divisions in Israeli Society." *Middle East Journal* 31 (1977): 451–68.

Duverger, Maurice. *Political Parties*. New York: John Wiley, 1963.

Eban, Abba. *My People: The Story of the Jews*. New York: Random House, 1968.

Edelman, Martin. "Politics and Constitution in Israel." *State Government* 53:3 (1980): 171–82.

Edelman, Martin. "The Rabbinical Courts in the Evolving Political Culture of Israel." *Middle Eastern Studies* 16 (1980). 145–66.

Eisenstadt, S. N. *The Transformation of Israeli Society*. Boulder, Co.: Westview Press, 1985.

Elarby, N. "Some Legal Implications of the 1947 Partition Resolution and the 1949 Armistice Agreement." *Law and Contemporary Problems* 33:1 (1968): 97–109.

Elazar, Daniel J., ed. *Judea, Samaria, and Gaza: Views on the Present and Future*. Washington, D.C.: American Enterprise Institute for Public Policy Research, 1982.

Elazar, Daniel. *Israel: Building a New Society*. Bloomington, Ind.: Indiana University Press, 1986.

Eliav, Arie. *The Voyage of the Ulua*. New York: Funk and Wagnalls, 1969.

Elon, Amos. *The Israelis: Founders and Sons*. New York: Bantam, 1971.

Elon, Amos. *Herzl*. New York: Holt, Rinehart, Winston, 1975.

England, Izhak. "The Law of Torts in Israel: The Problems of Common Law Codification in a Mixed Legal System." *American Journal of Comparative Law* 22:2 (1974): 302–29.

Ennes, James. *Assault on the Liberty: The True Story of the Israeli Attack on an American Intelligence Ship*. New York: Random House, 1979.

Etzioni, Amitai. "Agrarianism in Israel's Party System." *Canadian Journal of Economics and Political Science* 23:3 (1957): 363–75.

Etzioni-Halevi, Eva, and Shapira, Rina. *Political Culture in Israel: Cleavage and Interaction Among Israeli Jews*. New York: Praeger, 1977.

Evron, Yair. "Israel and the Atom: The Uses and Misuses of Ambiguity, 1957–1967." *Orbis* 17:4 (1974): 1326–43.

Eytan, Walter. *The First Ten Years: A Diplomatic History of Israel*. New York: Simon and Schuster, 1958.

Facts About Israel. Jerusalem: Israel Information Centre, 1985.

Facts About Israel. Jerusalem: Israel Information Centre, 1977.

Falk, Gloria. "Israeli Public Opinion: Looking Toward a Palestinian Solution." *Middle East Journal* 39:3 (1985): 247–69.

Farah, Tawfic. "Political Socialization of Palestinian Children in Kuwait." *Journal of Palestine Studies* 6:4 (1977): 90–102.

Fein, Leonard. *Israel: Politics and People*. Boston: Little, Brown and Company, 1966.

Feinrider, Martin. "America's Oil Pledges to Israel: Illegal but Binding Executive Agreements." *New York University Journal of International Law and Politics* 13:3 (1981): 525–70.

Feldman, Lily G. *The Special Relationship Between West Germany and Israel*. Boston: Allen and Unwin, 1984.

Feldman, Shai. *Israeli Nuclear Deterrence: A Strategy for the 1980's*. New York: Columbia University Press, 1982.

Felsenthal, Dan. "Aspects of Coalition Payoffs: The Case of Israel." *Comparative Political Studies* 12 (1979): 151–68.

Freedman, Robert O., ed. *Israel in the Begin Era*. New York: Praeger, 1982.

Freudenheim, Yehoshua. *Government in Israel*. Dobbs Ferry, N.Y.: Oceana Publications, 1967.

Friedlander, Dov, and Goldscheider, Calvin. *The Population of Israel*. New York: Columbia University Press, 1978.

Friedlander, Melvin. *Sadat and Begin: The Domestic Politics of Peacemaking*. Boulder, Co: Westview Press, 1983.

Freidman, Daniel. "Independent Development of Israeli Law." *Israel Law Review* 10:4 (1975): 515–65.

Friedman, Daniel. "Infusion of the Common Law into the Legal System of Israel." *Israel Law Review* 10:3 (1975): 324–77.

Friedman, Daniel. "The Effect of Foreign Law on the Law of Israel." *Israel Law Review* 10:2 (1975):192–206.

Friedman, Isaiah "The McMahon-Hussein Correspondence and the Question of Palestine." *Journal of Contemporary History* 5:2 (1970): 83–122.

Gerber, Israel. *Heritage Seekers: American Blacks in Search of Jewish Identities.* New York: Jonathan David Publishing, 1977.

Ghareeb, Edmund. "The U.S. Arms Supply to Israel During the October War." *Journal of Palestine Studies* 3:2 (1974): 114–21.

Gillon, D. J. "The Antecedents of the Balfour Declaration." *Middle Eastern Studies* 5:2 (1969): 225–37.

Gilmour, David. *Dispossessed: The Ordeal of the Palestinians: 1917–1980.* London: Sidgwick and Jackson, 1980.

Gitelman, Zvi. *Becoming Israelis: Political Resocialization of Soviet and American Immigrants.* New York: Praeger, 1982.

Gitelson, Susan. *Israel's African Setback in Perspective.* Jerusalem: Hebrew University Press, 1974.

Globerson, Arye. "A Profile of the Bureaucratic Elite in Israel." *Public Personnel Management* 2:1 (1973): 9–15.

Golan, Galia. *The Soviet Union and the Arab–Israeli War of October, 1973.* Jerusalem: Hebrew University Press, 1974.

Golan, Galia. *Yom Kippur and After: The Soviet Union and the Middle East.* New York: Cambridge University Press, 1977.

Goldweber, Max. "Israel's Judicial System." *Queen's Bar Bulletin* (April, 1960), p. 200–12.

Goodland, Thomas. "A Mathematical Presentation of Israel's Political Parties." *British Journal of Sociology* 8 (1957): 263–66.

Greilsammer, Alain. "Communism in Israel: 13 Years After the Split." *Survey* 23 (1977–78): 172–92.

Gutmann, Emanuel. "Israel." *Journal of Politics* 25 (1963): 703–17.

Halevi, Nadav, and Klinow-Malul, Ruth. *The Economic Development of Israel.* New York: Praeger, 1968.

Hamid, Rashid. "What is the PLO?" *Journal of Palestine Studies* 4:4 (1975): 90–109.

Handel, Michael. *Perception, Deception, and Surprise: The Case of the Yom Kippur War.* Jerusalem: Hebrew University Press, 1975.

Harkabi, Yehoshafat. "Basic Factors in the Arab Collapse During the Six Day War." *Orbis* 2:3 (1967): 677–691.

Harkabi, Yehoshafat. *The Palestinian Covenant and Its Meaning.* London: Vallentine Mitchell, 1979.

Harkavy, Robert. *Pre-emption and Two Front Conventional Warfare.* Jerusalem: Hebrew University Press, 1977.

Harkavy, Robert. *Spectre of a Middle Eastern Holocaust: The Strategic and Diplomatic Implications of the Israeli Nuclear Weapons Program.* Denver: University of Denver Press, 1977.

Haron, Miriam. "The British Decision to Give the Palestine Question to the United Nations." *Middle Eastern Studies* 17:2 (1981): 241–48.

Harris, William. *Taking Root: Israeli Settlement in the West Bank, the Golan, and Gaza-Sinai, 1967–1980.* New York: Research Studies Press, 1980.

Hart, Harold. *Yom Kippur Plus 100 Days*. New York: Har Publications, 1974.

Hausner, Gideon. *Justice in Jerusalem*. New York: Holocaust Library, 1966.

Henriques, Robert. *A Hundred Hours to Suez: An Account of Israel's Campaign in the Sinai Peninsula*. New York: Viking, 1957.

Herman, Valerie, and Pope, John. "Minority Governments in Western Democracies." *British Journal of Political Science* 3 (1973): 191–212.

Herzl, Theodor. *Complete Diaries*. New York: Herzl Press, 1960.

Herzl, Theodor. *The Jewish State*. New York: Scopus Publishing Company, 1943.

Heydemann, Steve, ed. *The Begin Era: Issues in Contemporary Israel*. Boulder: Westview Press, 1984.

Hilberg, Raul. *The Destruction of the European Jews: Revised and Definitive Edition*. New York: Holmes and Meier, 1985.

Hinton, Clete. *Camp David Accords*. Los Alamitos, Ca.: Hwong Publishing, 1980.

History Until 1880. Jerusalem: Keter Publishing, 1973.

Hoffman, Steven. "Candidate Selection in Israel's Parliament: The Realities of Change." *Middle East Journal* 34 (1980): 285–301.

Horowitz, Dan. *Israel's Concept of Defensible Borders*. Jerusalem: Institute for International Relations, 1975.

Horowitz, Dan, and Lissak, Moshe. *Origins of the Israeli Polity: Palestine Under the Mandate*. Chicago: University of Chicago Press, 1978.

Horowitz, David. *The Enigma of Economic Growth: A Case Study of Israel*. New York: Praeger, 1972.

Hurewitz, J. S. *The Struggle for Palestine*. New York: Norton, 1950.

Isaac, Rael. *Israel Divided: Ideological Politics in the Jewish State*. Baltimore: Johns Hopkins University Press, 1976.

Isaac, Rael. *Party and Politics in Israel: Three Visions of a Jewish State*. New York: Longman, 1981.

Jacob, Abel. "Israel's Military Aid to Africa, 1960–1966." *The Journal of Modern African Studies* 9:2 (1971): 165–88.

Jiryis, Sabri. "The Legal Structure for the Expropriation and Absorption of Arab Lands in Israel." *Journal of Palestine Studies* 2:4 (1973): 82–104.

Johnston, Scott. "Party Politics and Coalition Cabinets in the Knesset." *Middle Eastern Affairs* 13 (1962): 130–8.

Johnston, Scott. "Politics of the Right in Israel." *Social Science* 40 (1965): 104–13.

Kanovsky, Eliyahu. *The Economy of the Israeli Kibbutz*. Cambridge: Harvard University Press, 1966.

Kanovsky, Eliyahu. *The Economic Impact of the Six Day War*. New York: Praeger, 1970.

Kark, Ruth. "Jewish Frontier Settlement in the Negev, 1880–1948." *Middle Eastern Studies* 17:3 (1981): 334–56.

Karni, Edi. "The Israeli Economy, 1973–1976." *Economic Development and Cultural Change* 28:1 (1979): 63–76.

Katz, Alfred. *Government and Politics in Contemporary Israel, 1948–Present.* Washington, D.C.: University Press of America, 1980.

Katz, Daniel, and Golomb, Naphtali. "Integration, Effectiveness, and Adaptation in Social Systems: A Comparative Analysis of Kibbutzim Communities." *Administration and Society* 6:4 (1975): 389–422.

Kaufman, Edy. *Israeli-Latin American Relations.* New Brunswick, N.J.: Transaction Press, 1979.

Kedourie, Elie. "Sir Herbert Samuel and the Government of Palestine." *Middle Eastern Studies* 5:1 (1969): 44–68.

Khan, R. "Israel and the Soviet Union: A Review of Postwar Relations." *Orbis* 9:4 (1966):999–1012.

Kimche, David. *The Sandstorm: TheArab—Israeli War of 1967.* New York: Stein and Day, 1968.

Kimche, Jon, and Kimche, David. *A Clash of Destinies: The Arab-Jewish War and the Founding of the State of Israel.* New York: Praeger, 1960.

Kirschenbaum, Alan, and Comay, Yochanan. "Dynamics of Population Attraction to New Towns: The Case of Israel." *Socio-Economic Planning Sciences* 7:6 (1973): 687–96.

Klein, Claude. "A New Era in Israel's Constitutional Law." *Israel Law Review* 6 (1971): 376–97.

Knox, D. Edward. *The Making of a New Eastern Question: British Palestine Policy and the Origins of Israel, 1917–1925.* Washington, D.C.: Catholic University Press, 1981.

Kohler, Foy. *The Soviet Union and the October 1973 Middle East War.* Coral Gables, Fl.: University of Miami Press, 1974.

Kohn, Y. "Israel and the New Nation-States of Asia and Africa." *Annals of the American Academy of Political and Social Science* 324 (1959): 96–102.

Korey, William. "The PLO's Conquest of the U.N." *Midstream* 25:9 (1979): 10–15.

Kozicki, R. "India and Israel: A Problem in Asian Politics." *Middle Eastern Affairs* 9:5 (1958): 162–71.

Kraemer, Joel, ed. *Jerusalem: Problems and Prospects.* New York: Praeger, 1980.

Kraines, Oscar. *Government and Politics in Israel.* Boston: Houghton Mifflin, 1961.

Kraines, Oscar. *The Impossible Dilemma: Who is a Jew in the State of Israel.* New York: Block, 1976.

Krammer, Arnold. "Soviet Motives in the Partition of Palestine, 1947–1948." *Journal of Palestine Studies* 2:2 (1973): 102–19.

Krammer, Arnold. *The Forgotten Friendship: Israel and the Soviet Bloc, 1947–1953.* Urbana, Il.: University of Illinois Press, 1974.

Kreinin, Mordechai. *Israel and Africa: A Study in Technical Cooperation.* New York: Praeger, 1964.

Kurzman, Dan. *Genesis 1948: The First Arab-Israeli War.* New York: World, 1970.

Landau, Asher Felix. *Selected Judgments of the Supreme Court of Israel.* Jerusalem: Ministry of Justice, 1971.

Landau, Asher Felix. "The Woman and the Religious Council." *Jerusalem Post* Monday, June 6, 1988, p. 5.

LaPalombara, Joseph. *Politics Within Nations.* Englewood Cliffs, N.J.: Prentice-Hall, 1974.

Laqueur, Walter. *A History of Zionism.* New York: Holt, Rinehart, and Winston, 1972.

Laufer, Joseph. "Israel's Supreme Court: The First Decade." *Journal of Legal Education* 17 (1964): 40–57.

Lesch, Ann. "Israeli Deportation of Palestinians from the West Bank and the Gaza Strip, 1967–1978." *Journal of Palestine Studies* 8:3 (1979):81–107.

Lesch, Ann. "Israeli Settlements in the Occupied Territories." *Journal of Palestine Studies* 8:1 (1978): 100–20.

Leslie, Clement. *The Rift in Israel: Religious Authority and Secular Democracy.* New York: Schocken, 1971.

Levin, Norman. *The Zionist Movement in Palestine and World Politics, 1880–1918.* Lexington, Ma.: D.C. Heath, 1974.

Lewis, Arnold. *Power, Poverty, and Education.* Ramat Gan: Turtledove Publishing, 1979.

Liebman, Charles. *Pressure Without Sanctions: The Influence of World Jewry on Israeli Policy.* Rutherford, N.J.: Fairleigh Dickinson University Press, 1977.

Liebman, Charles, and Don-Yehiya, Eleizer. *Civil Religion in Israel: Traditional Judaism and Political Culture in the Jewish State.* Los Angeles: University of California Press, 1983.

Liebman, Charles, and Don-Yehiya, Eleizer. *Religion and Politics in Israel.* Bloomington, In.: Indiana University Press, 1984.

Likhovski, Eliahu. "The Courts and the Legislative Supremacy of the Knesset." *Israel Law Review* 3:3 (1968):345–67.

Loewenberg, Gerhard. *Modern Parliaments: Change or Decline?* Chicago: Atherton, 1971.

Lorch, Netanel. *One Long War: Arab Versus Jew Since 1920.* Jerusalem: Keter Publishing, 1976.

Lorch, Netanel. *Israel's War of Independence: 1947–1949.* Hartford: Hartford House, 1968.

Losman, Donald. "Inflation in Israel: The Failure of Wage and Price Controls." *Journal of Social and Political Studies* 3:1 (1978): 41–62.

Lustick, Ian. *Arabs in the Jewish State.* Austin: University of Texas Press, 1980.

Lustick, Ian. "Israel and the West Bank After Elon Moreh: The Mechanics of De Facto Annexation." *Middle East Journal* 35:4 (1981): 557–77.

Lustick, Ian. *For the Land and the Lord: Jewish Fundamentalism in Israel.* New York: Council on Foreign Relations, 1988.

Luttwak, Edward, and Horowitz, Dan. *The Israeli Army.* New York: Harper and Row, 1975.

Mahler, Gregory. "The Effects of Electoral Systems Upon the Behavior of Members of a National Legislature: The Israeli Knesset Case Study." *Journal of Constitutional and Parliamentary Studies* 14:4 (1980): 305–18.

Mahler, Gregory. *The Knesset: Parliament in the Israeli Political System.* Rutherford: Fairleigh Dickinson University Press, 1981.

Mahler, Gregory. *Comparative Politics: An Institutional and Cross-National Approach.* Cambridge, Ma.: Schenkman Publishing, 1983.

Mahler, Gregory, ed. *Israel in the Post-Begin Era.* Albany: State University of New York Press, forthcoming.

Mahler, Gregory, and Trilling, Richard. "Coalition Behavior and Cabinet Formation: The Case of Israel." *Comparative Political Studies* 8 (1975): 200–233.

Mallison, W. Thomas, and Mallison, Sally V. *The Palestine Problem in International Law and World Order.* London: Longman, 1986.

Mansour, Antoine. "Monetary Dualism: The Case of the West Bank Under Occupation." *Journal of Palestine Studies* 11:3 (1982): 103–16.

McTague, John. "The British Military Administration in Palestine, 1917–1920." *Journal of Palestine Studies* 7:3 (1978): 55–76.

Medding, Peter. *Mapai in Israel: Political Organization and Government in a New Society.* Cambridge: Cambridge University Press, 1972.

Meir, Golda. *My Life.* New York: Putnam, 1975.

Merhav, Peretz. *The Israeli Left, History, Problems, Documents.* New York: Barnes and Co., 1980.

Metzger, Jan, Orth, Martin, and Sterzing, Christian. *This Land is Our Land.* London: Zed Press, 1983.

Miller, Aaron David. *The Arab States and the Palestine Question: Between Ideology and Self-Interest.* New York: Praeger, 1986.

Mishal, Saul. *West Bank East Bank: The Palestinians in Jordan, 1949–1967.* New Haven: Yale University Press, 1976.

Monroe, E. *The Arab–Israeli War, 1973.* London: International Institute for Strategic Studies, 1974.

Morris, Benny. *The Birth of the Palestine Refugee Problem, 1947–1949.* New York: Cambridge University Press, 1987.

Mroz, John E. *Beyond Security: Private Perceptions Among Arabs and Israelis.* New York: Pergamon Press, 1980.

Muassasat al-Dirasat al-Filastiniyah (PLO in Arabic), *The Arab–Israeli Armistice Agreements, February–July, 1949. U.N. Texts and Annexes.* Beirut: Institute for Palestine Studies, 1967.

Mushkat, Marion. "The Socio-Economic Malaise of Developing Countries as a Function of Military Expenditures: The Case of Egypt and Israel." *Coexistence* 15:2 (1978): 135–45.

Mushkag, Miron, Jr. "Transferring Administrative Skills from the Military to the Civilian Sector in the Process of Development." *Il Politico* 46:3 (1981): 427–442.

Machmias, David. "A Note on Coalition Payoffs in a Dominant Party System: Israel." *Political Studies* 21:3 (1973): 301–5.

Nachmias, David. "Coalition Politics in Israel." *Comparative Political Studies* 7 (1974): 316–33.

Nachmias, David. "The Right Wing Opposition in Israel." *Political Studies* 24 (1976): 268–80.

Nachmias, David, and Rosenbloom, David. *Bureaucratic Culture: Citizens and Administrators in Israel*. New York: St. Martin's Press, 1978.

Nadelmann, Ethan. "Israel and Black Africa: A Rapprochement?" *Journal of Modern African Studies* 19:2 (1981): 183–220.

Nahas, Dunia. *The Israeli Communist Party*. New York: St. Martin's Press, 1976.

National Lawyers Guild 1977 Middle East Delegation. *Treatment of Palestinians in Israeli-Occupied West Bank and Gaza*. New York: National Lawyers Guild, 1978.

Newman, David, ed. *The Impact of Gush Emunim: Politics and Settlement in the West Bank*. New York: St. Martin's Press, 1985.

Nimmer, Melville. "The Uses of Judicial Review in Israel's Quest for a Constitution." *Columbia Law Review* 70 (1970): 1217–61.

Nusibeh, Hazem. *Palestine and the United Nations*. New York: Quartet Books, 1982.

O'Ballance, Edgar. *The Arab-Israeli War, 1948*. New York: Praeger, 1957.

Oke, Mim Kemal. "The Ottoman Empire, Zionism, and the Question of Palestine, 1890–1908." *International Journal of Middle East Studies* 14:3 (1982): 329–42.

Oren, Stephen. "Continuity and Change in Israel's Religious Parties." *Middle East Journal* 27 (1973): 36–54.

Paltiel, K. Z. "The Israeli Coalition System," *Government and Opposition* 10 (1975): 396–414.

Penniman, Howard, ed. *Israel at the Polls: The Knesset Elections of 1977*. Washington, D.C.: American Enterprise Institute, 1979.

Penniman, Howard, ed. *Israel at the Polls, 1981: A Study of the Knesset Elections*. Washington, D.C.: American Enterprise Institute, 1986.

Peres, Yochanan. "Ethnic Relations in Israel." *American Journal of Sociology* 76:6 (1971): 1021–47.

Peretz, Don. "Israel's 1969 Election Issues—The Visible and the Invisible." *Middle East Journal* 24:1 (1970): 31–71.

Peretz, Don. "The War Election and Israel's Eighth Knesset." *Middle East Journal* 28 (1974): 111–125.

Peretz, Don. *The Government and Politics of Israel*. Boulder, Co.: Westview Press, 1979.

Peretz, Don. *The West Bank: History, Politics, Society, and Economy*. Boulder, Co.: Westview, 1986.

Peretz, Don and Smooha, Sammy. "Israel's Tenth Knesset Elections: Ethnic Upsurgence and Decline of Ideology." *Middle East Journal* 35 (1981): 506–526.

Peri, Yoram. *Between Battles and Ballots, Israeli Military in Politics*. Cambridge: Cambridge University Press, 1983.

Perlmutter, Amos. "The Israeli Army in Politics." *World Politics* 20:4 (1968): 606–43.

Perlmutter, Amos. *Military and Politics in Israel*. New York, Praeger, 1969.

Perlmutter, Amos. *Politics and the Military in Israel: 1967–1977*. London: F. Cass, 1978.

Pomerance, Michla. *American Guarantees to Israel and the Law of American Foreign Relations*. Jerusalem: Hebrew University of Jerusalem Press, 1974.

Quandt, William, Jabber, Fuad, and Lesch, Ann M. *The Politics of Palestinian Nationalism*. Berkeley: University of California Press, 1973.

Quandt, William. *Camp David: Peacemaking and Politics*. Washington, D.C.: Brookings Institution, 1986.

Rabinowicz, Harry. *Hasidism and the State of Israel*. Rutherford, N.J.: Fairleigh Dickinson University Press, 1982.

Rackman, E. *Israel's Emerging Constitution, 1948–1951*. New York: Columbia University Press, 1955.

Rafael, Gideon. *Destination Peace: Three Decades of Israeli Foreign Policy: A Personal Memoir*. New York: Stein and Day, 1981.

Ramati, Yohanan. "Strategic Effects of Israel's Campaign in Lebanon." *Midstream* 28:7 (1982): 3–4.

Ranney, Austin. *Pathways to Parliament: Candidate Selection in Britain*. Madison: University of Wisconsin Press, 1965.

Raphaeli, Nimrod. "Military Governments in the Occupied Territories." *Middle East Journal* 23:2 (1969):177–208.

Raphaeli, Nimrod. "The Senior Civil Service in Israel." *Public Administration* 48 (1970): 169–78.

Raphaeli, Nimrod. "The Absorption of Orientals into Israeli Bureaucracy," *Middle Eastern Studies* 8 (1972): 85–92.

Rapoport, Louis. *The Lost Jews: Last of the Ethiopian Falashas*. New York: Stein and Day, 1980.

Ratner, Leonard. "Constitutions, Majoritarianism, and Judicial Review: The Function of a Bill of Rights in Israel and the United States." *American Journal of Comparative Law* 26:3 (1978): 373–97.

Rikhye, Indar. *The Sinai Blunder: Withdrawal of the United Nations Emergency Force Leading to the Six Day War of June, 1967*. Totowa, N.J.: Frank Cass, 1980.

Rivkin, A. "Israel and the Afro-Asian World." *Foreign Affairs* 37:3 (1959): 486–95.

Rivlin, Paul. "The Burden of Israel's Defence." *Survival* 20:4 (1978): 146–54.

Ro'i, Yaacov. *Soviet Decision-Making in Practice, the USSR and Israel, 1947–1954*. New Brunswick: Transaction Press, 1980.

Roshwald, M. "Political Parties and Social Classes in Israel." *Social Research* 23:2 (1956): 199–218.

Rothenberg, Gunther. *The Anatomy of the Israeli Army: The Israeli Defense Force, 1948–1978*. New York: Hippocrene Books, 1979.

Roumani, Maurice, (ed.). "From Immigrant to Citizen: The Contribution of the Army in Israel to National Integration: The Case of Oriental Jews." *Plural Societies* 9:2–3 (1978): 1–145.

Rubin, Morton. *The Walls of Acre: Integroup Relations and Urban Development in Israel.* New York: Holt, Rinehart, and Winston, 1974.

Sachar, Howard. *A History of Israel: From the Rise of Zionism to Our Time.* New York: Alfred A. Knopf, 1981.

Sager, Samuel. "Pre-State Influences on Israel's Parliamentary System." *Parliamentary Affairs* 25 (1972): 29–49.

Sager, Samuel. *The Parliamentary System of Israel.* Syracuse: Syracuse University Press, 1985.

Sahliyeh, Emile. *The Lebanon War: Implications for the PLO.* Boulder, Co.: Westview Press, 1985.

Said, Edward. *The Question of Palestine.* New York: Vintage Books, 1980.

Samuel, E. "A New Civil Service for Israel." *Public Administration* (London) 34:2 (1956): 135–41.

Samuel, E. "Growth of the Israel Civil Service, 1948–1956." *Revue International de Science Administrative* 22:4 (1956): 17–40.

Samuel, E. "Efficiency in the Israeli Civil Service." *Canadian Public Administration* 4:2 (1961): 191–96.

Sankari, Frank. "The Costs and Gains of Israel's Pursuit of Influence in Africa." *Middle Eastern Studies* 15 (1979): 270–79.

Sayegh, Fayez. "The Camp David Agreement and the Palestine Problem." *Journal of Palestine Studies* 8:2 (1979): 3–54.

Schiff, Gary. *Tradition and Politics, The Religious Parties of Israel.* Detroit: Wayne State University Press, 1977.

Schiff, Zeev. *October Earthquake: Yom Kippur, 1973.* Tel Aviv: University Publishing Projects, 1974.

Schnall, David. "Native Anti-Zionism: Ideologies of Radical Dissent in Israel." *Middle East Journal* 31 (1977): 157–74.

Schnall, David. *Radical Dissent in Contemporary Israeli Politics: Cracks in the Wall.* New York: Praeger, 1979.

Schweid, Eliezer. *Israel at the Crossroads.* Translated by Alton Winters. Philadelphia: Jewish Publication Society of America, 1973.

Segev, Tom. *1949: The First Israelis.* New York: Free Press, 1986.

Segre, Dan V. *A Crisis of Identity: Israel and Zionism.* Oxford, Oxford University Press, 1980.

Seliktar, Ofira. *New Zionism and the Foreign Policy System of Israel.* Carbondale, IL: Southern Illinois University Press, 1986.

Shama, Avraham. *Immigration Without Integration: Third World Jews in Israel.* Cambridge: Schenkman Publishing, 1977.

Shamir, Michal, and Arian, Asher. "The Ethnic Vote in Israel's 1981 Elections." *Electoral Studies* 1 (1982): 315–31.

Shangman, Meir. "On the Written Constitution." *Israel Law Review* 9 (1974): 467–76.

Shapira, Y. "Israel's International Cooperation Program with Latin America." *Inter-American Economic Affairs* 30:2 (1976): 3–32.

Shapiro, Danny. "Israel and Religious Orthodoxy." *Jerusalem Post*, June 6, 1988, p. 8.

Sharif, Regina. "The United Nations and Palestinian Rights, 1974–1979." *Journal of Palestine Studies* 9:1 (1979): 21–45.

Sharkansky, Ira. *What Makes Israel Tick? How Domestic Policy-Makers Cope with Constraints*. Chicago: Nelson Hall, 1975.

Sharkansky, Ira. *Whither the State? Politics and Public Enterprise in Three Countries*. Chatham, N.J.: Chatham House, 1979.

Shattan, Joseph. "Israel, the United States, and the United Nations." *World Affairs* 143:4 (1981): 335–45.

Shetreet, Shimon. "Reflection on the Protection of the Rights of Individual: Form and Substance." *Israel Law Review* 12 (1977): 32–67.

Shindler, Colin. *Exit Visa: Detente, Human Rights, and the Jewish Emigration Movement in the USSR*. London: Bachman, Turner, 1978.

Shokeid, Moshe, and Deshen, Shlomo. *Distant Relations: Ethnicity and Politics Among Arabs and North African Jews in Israel*. New York: Praeger, 1982.

Siegel, Judy. "Religion and Politics in Israel." *Jerusalem Post Weekly Edition*, Tuesday, September 9, 1975, p. 8.

Slann, Martin. "Ideology and Ethnicity in Israel's Two Communist Parties." *Studies in Comparative Communism* 7:4 (1974): 359–74.

Slonim, Shlomo. *United States–Israel Relations, 1967–1973*. Jerusalem: Hebrew University Press, 1974.

Smith, Gary, ed. *Zionism: The Dream and the Reality—A Jewish Critique*. New York: David and Charles, 1974.

Smooha, Sammy. "Ethnic Stratification and Allegiance in Israel." *Il Politico* 41:4 (1976): 635–51.

Smooha, Sammy. *Social Research on Arabs in Israel, 1948–1977: Trends and an Annotated Bibliography*. Ramat Gan: Turtledove Publishing, 1978.

Smooha, Sammy. *Israel: Pluralism and Conflict*. Berkeley: University of California Press, 1978.

Snetsinger, John. *Truman, the Jewish Vote, and the Creation of Israel*. Palo Alto, Ca.: Stanford University Press, 1974.

Sobel, Lester, ed. *Peace-Making in the Middle East*. New York: Facts on File, 1980.

Statistical Abstract of Israel. Jerusalem: Central Bureau of Statistics, 1986.

Statistical Abstract of Israel. Jerusalem: Central Bureau of Statistics, 1987.

Stein, Leonard. *The Balfour Declaration*. New York: Simon and Schuster, 1961.

Stetler, Russell, ed. *Palestine: The Arab-Israeli Conflict*. San Francisco: Ramparts Press, 1972.

Stone, Russell. *Social Change in Israel: Attitudes and Events, 1967–1979*. New York: Praeger, 1982.

Sussman, J. "Law and Judicial Practice in Israel." *Journal of Comparative Legislation and International Law* 32 (1950): 30–44.

Syrkin, Marie. *Golda Meir—Israel's Leader*. New York: Putnam's Sons, 1969.

Tamarin, Georges. "Israeli Migratory Processes Today: Does Israel Really Want All Its Immigrants? *Plural Societies* 8:3–4 (1977): 3–32.

Tamarin, Georges. "Three Decades of Ethnic Coexistence in Israel: Recent Developments and Patterns." *Plural Societies* 11:1 (1980): 3–46.

Tessler, Mark A. "Israel's Arabs and the Palestinian Problem." *Middle East Journal* 31:3 (1977): 313–29.

Tiger, Lionel, and Sheper, Joseph. *Women in the Kibbutz*. New York: Harcourt, Brace, Jovanovich, 1975.

Tillman, Seth. "The West Bank Hearings: Israel's Colonization of Occupied Teritory." *Journal of Palestine Studies* 7 (1978): 71–87.

Timmerman, Jacobo. *The Longest War: Israel in Lebanon*. New York: Knopf, 1982.

Torgovnik, Efraim. "Urban Political Integration in Israel: A Comparative Perspective." *Urban Affairs Quarterly* 11:4 (1976): 469–88.

Tsur, Jacob. *Zionism: The Saga of a National Liberation Movement*. New Brunswick, NJ: Transaction Books, 1976.

Tummala, Krishna, ed. *Administrative Systems Abroad*. Washington, D.C.: University Press of America, 1982.

United Nations General Assembly Resolution 181 (II) of November 29, 1947, *Official Records of the Second Session of the General Assembly, Resolutions, September 16–November 29, 1947,* January 8, 1948, p. 135.

United Nations, Special Unit on Palestinian Rights. *The Origins and Evolution of the Palestine Problem*. New York: United Nations Press, 1967.

Weingrod, Alex. "Recent Trends in Israeli Ethnicity." *Ethnic and Racial Studies* 2:1 (1979): 55–65.

Weiss, Shevah. "Women in the Knesset: 1949–1969." *Parliamentary Affairs* 28:1 (1969/70): 31–50.

Weiss, Shevah, and Brichta, Avraham. "Private Members' Bills in Israel's Parliament." *Parliamentary Affairs* 23 (1969): 21–33.

Weizman, Ezer. *The Battle for Peace*. New York: Bantam Books, 1981.

Wilson, Evan. *Decision on Palestine: How the U.S. Came to Recognize Israel*. Stanford: Hoover Institution Press, 1979.

Witkon, Alfred. "Some Reflections on Judicial Law-Making." *Israel Law Review* 2:4 (1967): 475–487.

Witkon, Alfred. "Justiciability." *Israel Law Review* 1 (1966): 40–59.

Wolf, Gary, ed. *Israeli Press Highlights*. New York: Institute of Human Relations, American Jewish Committee, weekly.

Wolf-Phillips, Leslie. "The 'Westminster Model' in Israel?" *Parliamentary Affairs* 26 (1973): 415–39.

Wolffsohn, Michael. *Israel, Polity, Society, and Economy, 1882–1986*. Atlantic Highlands, N.J.: Humanities Press, International, 1987.

Ya'acobi, Gad. *The Government of Israel*. New York: Praeger, 1982.

Yaniv, Avner, and Pascal, Fabian. "Doves, Hawks, and Other Birds of a Feather: The Distribution of Israel Parliamentary Opinion on the Future of the Occupied Territories, 1967–1977." *British Journal of Political Science* 10:3 (1980): 260–66.

Yaniv, Avner, and Yishai, Yael. "Israeli Settlements in the West Bank: The Politics of Intransigence." *Journal of Politics* 43:4 (1981): 1105–28.

Zelnicker, Shimshon, and Kahan, Michael. "Religion and Nascent Cleavages: The Case of Israel's National Religious Party." *Comparative Politics* 9 (1976): 21–48.

Zemach, Yaacov. *Political Questions in the Courts*. Detroit: Wayne State University Press, 1976.

Zenner, Walter. "Sephardic Communal Organizations in Israel." *Middle East Journal* 21:2 (1967): 173–86.

Zidon, Asher. *The Knesset: The Parliament of Israel*. New York: Herzl Press, 1967.

Zionism. Jerusalem: Keter Publishing, 1973.

Zucker, Norman. *The Coming Crisis in Israel: Private Faith and Public Policy*. Cambridge: M.I.T. Press, 1973.

INDEX

Torah Religious Front, 113
Torah, in ideology, 99; and role in
  new constitution, 83
Town Government. *See* Local
  Government
Trade, foreign, 51–52
Transition Law (1949), 82
Transjordan, borders of, 226;
  creation of in 1922, 13. *See also*
  Jordan
Truman, Harry S., 19, 87
Tsomet Party, 112
Turkish influence on Israeli
  parliamentary system, 91
Turkish Law, reflected in current
  legal system, 187

U.S.S.R. *See also* Soviet Union
UNESCO. *See* United Nations
  Educational, Scientific, and
  Cultural Organization
Union. *See* General Federation of
  Workers
United Arab List, 116–17
United Jewish Appeal, 48
United Nations, acceptance of
  Israel, 213; Anti-Suez
  Resolution, 202; Criticism of
  1956 war, 202; Educational,
  Scientific, and Cultural
  Organization, 216; Emergency
  Force, Suez, 202; Israeli cultural
  relations and, 216; Israeli foreign
  policy and, 216; Oil Politics and,
  213; Palestine Liberation
  Organization and, 227, 231;
  Palestine Question and, 227;
  Palestinian Refugees and, 231;
  Partition resolution (1947), 21–
  23, 81; Peacekeeping Forces,
  213; resolution of mandate, 25;
  Security council (1948)
  resolution of armistice, 23;
  Special Committee on Palestine,
  21–23, 200, 227, 236; troops in
  Sinai in final peace treaty, 247

United States, aid to Israel, 214–
  15; diplomatic relations with,
  214; financial aid to Israel, 51;
  foreign policy, 207; guarantor or
  open Suez Canal, 202; Jews in,
  62; military assistance in 1973
  War and, 203–5; Suez War
  and, 202
Universities, 44–45; in West Bank,
  233, 234, 243
UNSCOP. *See* United Nations
  Special Committee on Palestine
Uprising in West Bank. *See* intifada
Urban II (Pope, 1095) and
  Crusades, 4
Urban settings, 46–48

Voting behavior, 142–47; age
  requirement, 129; cross
  pressures and, 143; Jewish
  turnout and, 142; party loyalty,
  in Knesset, 161; results, 1984
  and 1988 elections, 130

Wars: Attrition, 203;
  Independence, 23; legacy of,
  200–7; 1948, 200–1; 1956,
  201–2, 214; 1967, 202–3, 214,
  228; 1973, 203–5, 215; 1982
  (Lebanon), 205–6
Water policy, 185
Weizman, Ezer, military leader,
  119; Yahad Party, 117
Weizmann, Chaim, 12, 86–88
Welfare state, 45–46
West Bank, 226–249; annexation
  by Jordan, 229; demographics
  of, 244; economy and
  commerce, 232; expulsion of
  Arab residents, 234, 243; history
  of, 226–28; "intifada" in, 206,
  233; Israeli claim to, 238; Israeli
  attitudes and policies towards,
  237–44; issue in peace process,
  245; Jordan and, 227–28;
  occupation of, 191, 206; peace
  negotiations and, 238; policy in,

234; population of, 244;
Religious Jews and, 238; West
Bank, 1967 War and, 203, 228
West Germany. *See* Germany
(Federal Republic)
Western Europe, Jews in, 62
Westminster Model of Parliament,
91
White Paper: (1922), 12–13;
(1939), 16
Who is a Jew Question, 68–69;
Citizens' Rights Movement and,
114; Coalition (1988) and, 120;
government policy and, 73
Wilhelm II, Kaiser, 7
Women, Equal Rights for, Law
(1951), 86; in Knesset, 160;
military service and, 73
Woodhead, Sir John, 16
Woodhead Commission, 227; and
Jerusalem, 236; Report, Palestine
Partition Commission (1938), 16
World Zionist Organization, as
interest group, 120; and religious
Zionism, 64
Written constitutions, required by
United Nations, 81

Ya'acobi, Gad, 138–39, 149
Yaad, 115
Yahad Party, 117
Yishuv, 5, 8–9, 25

Yom Kippur War (1973), 48–49,
203–5, 215
Young Guard, of National
Religious Party, 113
Youth Employment Law, 119
Yugoslav influence on Israeli
parliamentary system, 91

Zidon, Asher, 166
Zionism: 61–65; British East
Africa Plan and, 7; classical, 61,
62; compartmentalized, 64;
"cultural", 8, 78; defense policy
and, 210; defensible borders and,
211; development of, 4–5;
development, 25; goals of, 7, 61;
Greater Israel Movement and,
238; growth of, 4–8; ideology,
99; immigration and, 37;
influence on Israeli
parliamentary system, 91; Neo-
Revisionist, 63; new, 64;
"political", 8; religious, 63;
religious parties and, 113;
revisionist, 63; similarity to
Palestinian nationalism, 229;
social class and, 42; socialist, 8,
62; tenets of, 35
Zionist Congress, First (1897),
6–7; Second (1898), 7; Sixth
(1903), 7
Zionist support for Partition, 227

A B C D E F G H I J
9 0 1 2 3 4 5 6 7 8